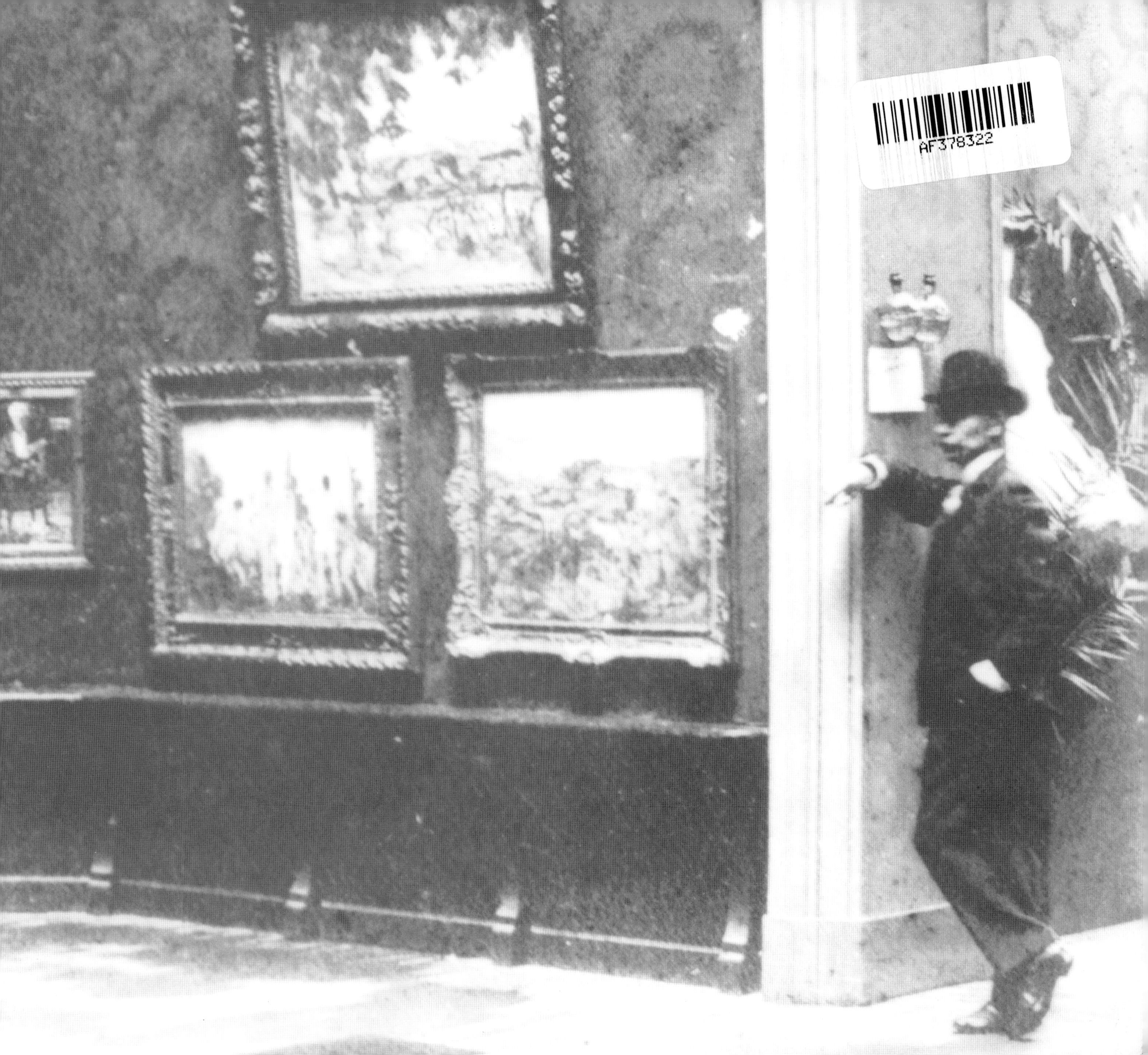
AF378322

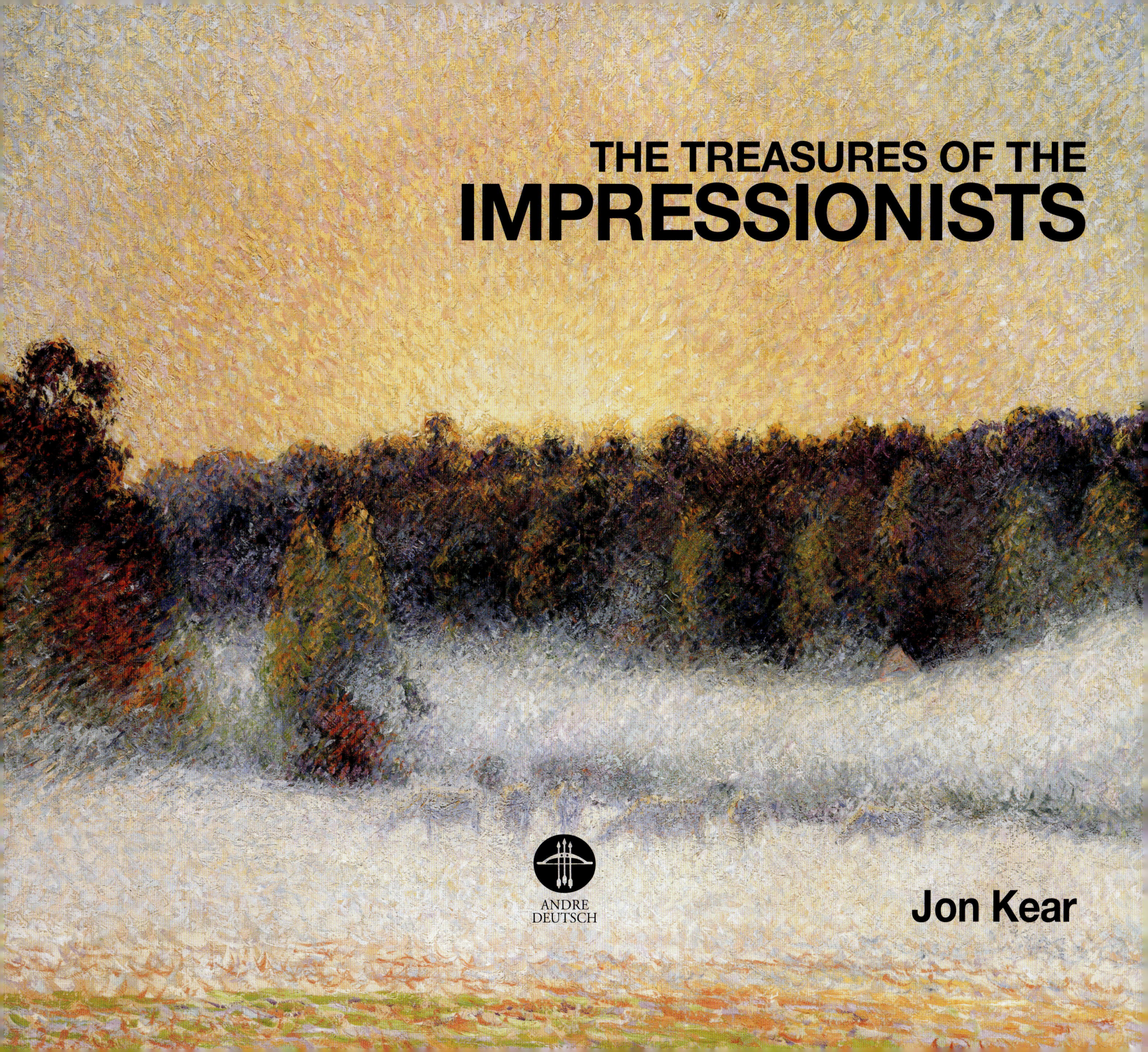

THE TREASURES OF THE
IMPRESSIONISTS
ANDRE
DEUTSCH
Jon Kear

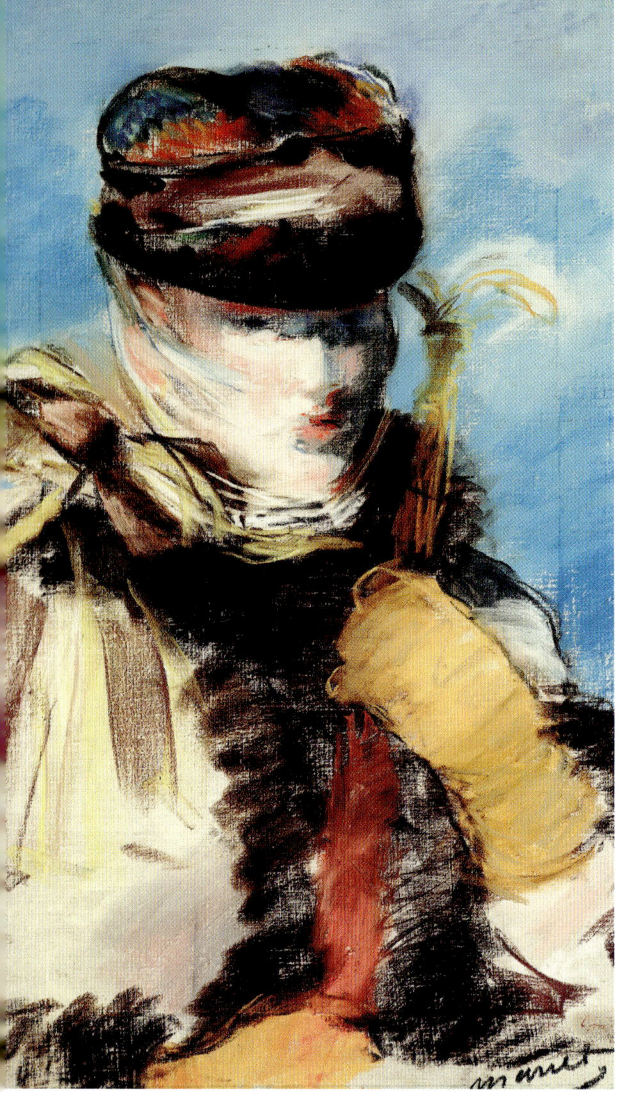

Dedication
For Margaret Kear

Author's Acknowledgments
I would like to thank Monica Turci for her continual support and assistance and my colleagues at the University of Kent. Any book is always a collective venture and the ideas and observations in this text owe much to the work of other academic scholars who have shaped my understanding of Impressionism. I would single out the work of Meyer Schapiro, T J Clark, John House, Paul Smith, Robert Herbert and Richard Thomson, which has continually stimulated my own thoughts and research in this area. I would also like to thank Vanessa Daubney for her help, diligence and scrupulous attention to the text. Her work as editor of this book has been unstinting, her comments always helpful and her work on this project is much appreciated.

Contents

THIS IS AN ANDRÉ DEUTSCH BOOK

Text and Design © André Deutsch Limited 2008, 2014

This edition published in 2014 by André Deutsch
A division of the Carlton Publishing Group
20 Mortimer Street
London
W1T 3JW

An edition of this work was first published in 2008 by André Deutsch.

A CIP catalogue for this book is available from the British Library

ISBN: 978 0 233 00399 3

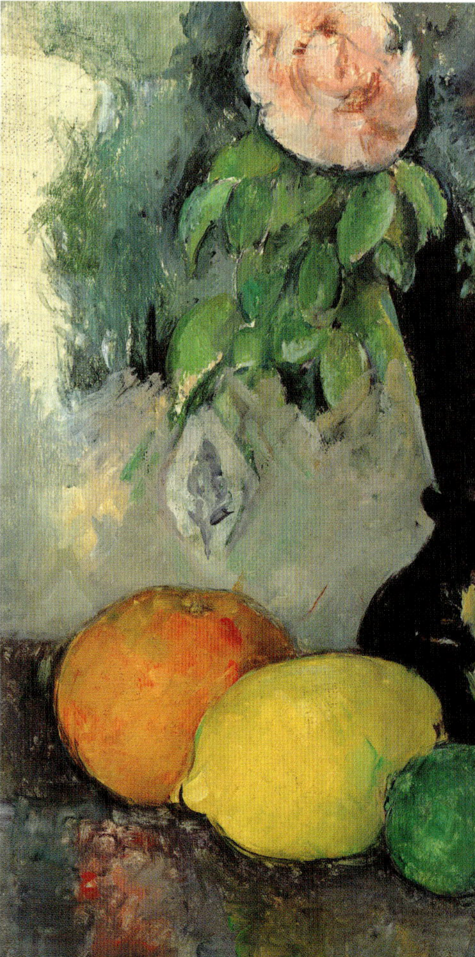

Introduction

Today the Impressionists are among the most popular and admired artists throughout the world. Impressionist pictures are widely reproduced and adorn the walls of major museums. The painters we most readily associate with Impressionism, such as Monet, Renoir, Degas, Pissarro, Sisley, Morisot and Cézanne are regarded as modern masters. Their vibrant paintings are imprinted on our imagination and we see nature reflected through their eyes. The art of the Impressionists evokes the pleasures of a day in the country or the city, of rippling reflections on the surface of a river and the sun-dappled play of light across verdant fields, of fashionable Parisians promenading along boulevards lined with cafés and café concerts. The works of the Impressionists open a window onto this world of the nineteenth century that allows us to imagine those times vividly. For us, the world of the Impressionists seems a familiar one and even one that we take for granted.

In their own lifetime, however, Impressionist painting was a source of contention. The pictures, and the artistic principles on which the works were based, were regarded by many viewers as idiosyncratic and strange, and drew strong criticism from artists and critics who regarded the works as incompatible with the values of the French tradition. The Impressionists challenged the prevailing attitudes about "good composition", "fitting" subject matter and even the broader role of art within society. Breaking with the themes and subject matters favoured by the French Academy, Impressionism embraced motifs within the common realm: everyday scenes that reflected the life, work and leisure of modern France, landscapes of the city, the suburbs and the countryside, portraiture and still lifes. They approached these subjects with a freer, more improvised and informal treatment that emphasized the artist's personal response to his or her motif, and which drew on contemporary research on perception and colour theory. In doing so, the painters developed styles of painting that questioned the ideas on which academic principles of composition were founded.

The history of Impressionism shows a gradual evolution towards these ends. The early careers of the Impressionist painters reveal how their work emerged in response to the influence of precursors such as Manet, Courbet and the artists associated with the Barbizon group, but also in relation to new ideas and experiences. The art of the Impressionists was as much a response to the new economic and cultural conditions of the modern world in which the artists worked and to changing ideas about the role of art itself in modern society, as it was to their artistic forebears. The massive transformations of France during the period in which they lived left its trace on what and how the painters painted. The emphasis on movement, contingency and flux in their paintings reflects the extent to which their art was shaped by the changing world they inhabited. *The Treasures of the Impressionists* examines the evolution of this rich and influential movement and the way the artistic development of the painters was conditioned by the social and artistic debates in which they worked, looking at all aspects of their work and the ideas that informed their technique and choice of subject matters.

The inclusion of facsimile documents, photographs and memorabilia, such as the catalogue of the first Impressionist show, the artists' correspondence and contemporary criticism and reviews, alongside illustrations of the Impressionists' paintings and drawings, creates a vivid context in which to understand their work. These documents bring us intimately into contact with their world.

Jon Kear

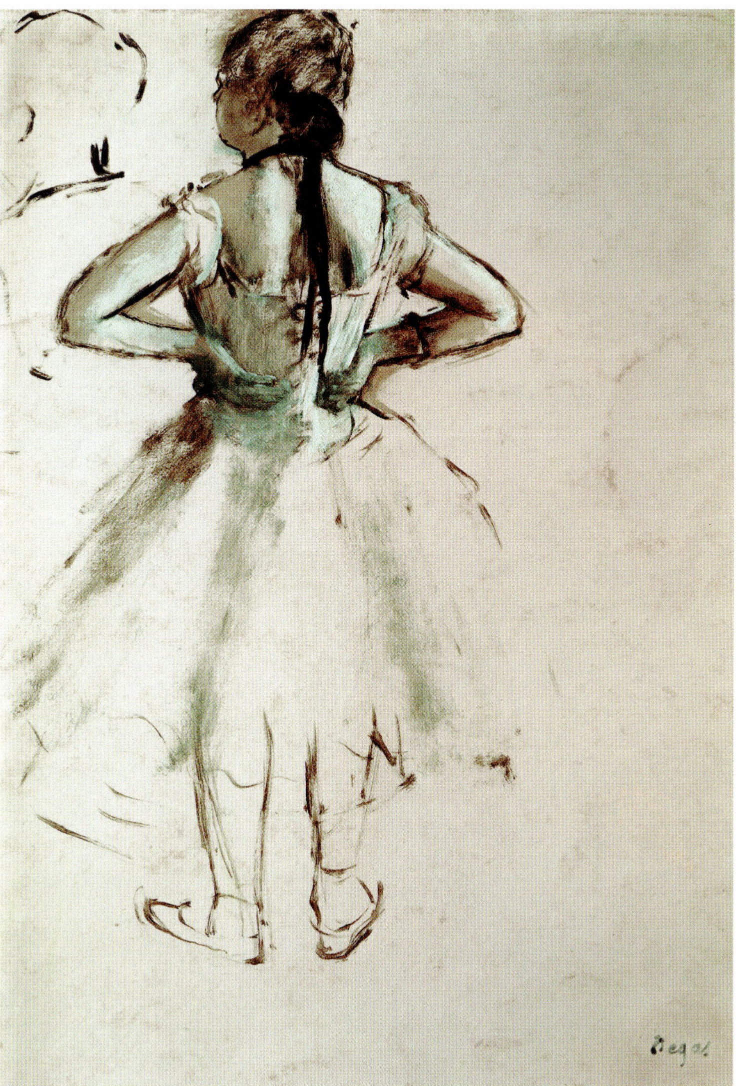

Opposite top *This Manet drawing shows his interest in the fashions of the time, following Baudelaire's call for artists to capture not the eternal beauty of classicism, but the ephemeral beauty of the contemporary world. This sketch also reveals Manet's interest in the revival of pastel as a medium.*

Opposite bottom *While most nineteenth-century painters regarded still life as low subject matter, Cézanne continued to see it as an important genre for artistic expression throughout his career. His slow manner of working made still life an ideal subject for him, and pictures like these were seen by his contemporaries as best exemplifying his method of painting, with its strong colour accents and painterly brushwork.*

Above *Degas's many drawings of ballerinas reveal his fascination with the subject of the rehearsal of the ballet. That fascination reflected his recognition of a parallel between his own art as a draftsman, needing to practise continually and repeat the act of drawing his subjects in order to refine the form of his drawing and master his metier, and that of the ballerina, who needed to repeat continually the movements of the dance to master her craft.*

The Impressionists in Context

Today we live in a world indelibly marked by the art of the Impressionists. The images of their world impress themselves on our own. We see the world through their eyes and Impressionists such as Monet, Renoir, Degas and Cézanne are among the most revered artists of all time. It is hard to imagine when it was otherwise, but in their own time Impressionist painting was controversial and an art that challenged the values of the French artistic tradition.

The art world in which the Impressionists grew up was dominated by the Academy, formed by royal decree in 1648. Members of the Academy, alongside government officials, sat on the jury of the Salon, the annual official exhibition of contemporary art. The Academy also controlled the Ecole des beaux-arts, the most prestigious school of artistic training. At the Ecole, students endured a wearying programme of copying from plaster casts after the antique and, after graduating to the life class, encountered the model posed in classical fashion. This training was designed to produce artists with the mastery of the figure required for large-scale, didactic, History paintings, whose themes were taken from classical mythology or the Bible. Academic art was structured by a hierarchy of genres that placed narrative subjects of this

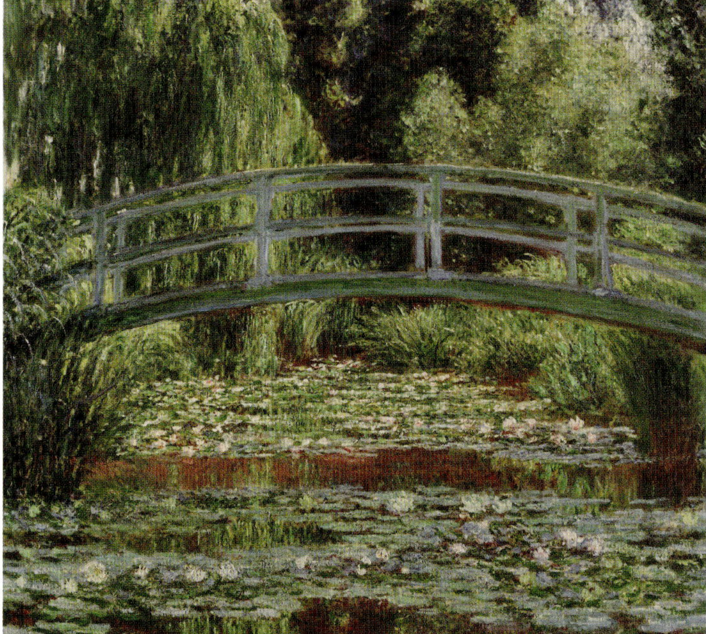

Left *Claude Monet's* The Water Lily Pond *(1899) represents the culmination of his work as an Impressionist with its vivid, yet liquid brushstrokes and vibrant colour work. Visitors to Monet's house in Giverny can still recognize this scene today, although the original bridge was replaced during renovations in the 1960s.*

Bottom left *Pierre-Auguste Renoir's* Luncheon of the Boating Party *(1880–81) shows a typical modern-life scene of the time. The Impressionists determined to paint contemporary subject matter as opposed to following the tradition of producing scenes from classical mythology and the Bible. Such scenes caught the spontaneity of the moment and showed life in Paris and its environs as never before.*

Opposite right *Phryné before the Jury (1861) by Jean-Léon Gérome is a typical example of the neo-classical tradition of art that was taught in art schools and which ran counter to the Impressionists.*

kind at its apex and non-figurative subjects like landscape and still-life painting at the bottom. The art world was centred on an official system of rewards and State commissions. Artists competed for these lucrative, public commissions that entailed depicting morally elevated subjects to decorate civic buildings, churches and monuments.

The leading artists of the first half of the nineteenth century were generally drawn from the Academy's ranks, many emerging from the studio of the neo-classicist Jacques-Louis David. David's most brilliant pupil, Jean-Auguste-Dominique Ingres, was widely recognized as the greatest draughtsman and painter of his generation and the heir to the French classical tradition of Nicolas Poussin. For Ingres, the artist was a public educator, transmitting universal and timeless artistic values, and the mission of art was to perpetuate and extend the example of the old masters. Yet, these values began to be challenged: first, by the Romanticism of Eugène Delacroix and his followers, which emphasized a subjective, freer, more original approach to painting, and second, by a school of realism that sought "truth to nature" and chose modern life subjects. The example of both these movements was to influence the direction of Impressionist painting.

As young artists painting informal subjects in an untraditional style, many of the Impressionists struggled to gain success at the Salon and suffered rejections by the jury. However, gradually the tide was to turn. During the course of their careers, the Impressionists witnessed the decline of the authority of the Academy and the emergence of a market

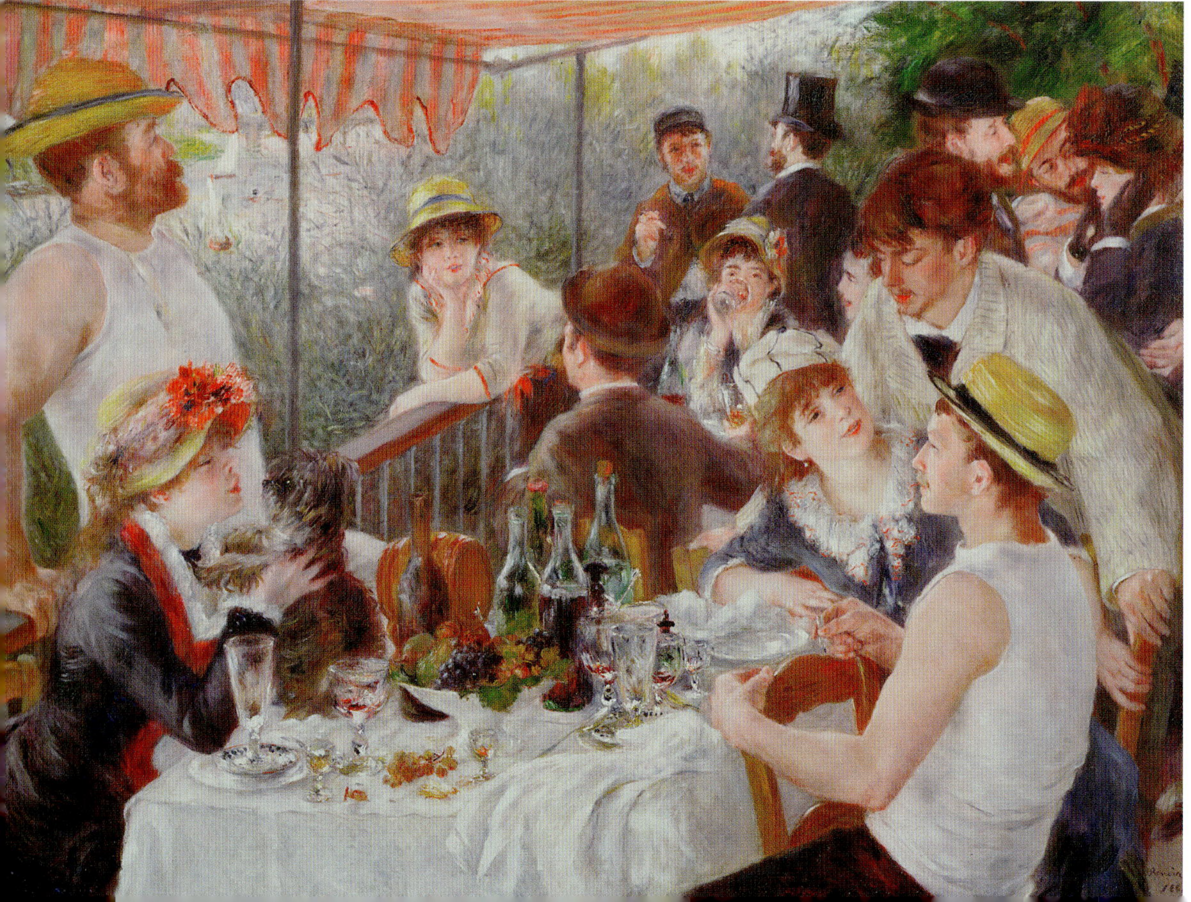

economy of the arts, where artistic success was no longer determined from above. Changes in public taste and government art policy, along with reforms to the Academy and the Ecole des beaux-arts, paved the way for the Impressionists' success. By the mid-1850s discontent with the status quo was becoming widespread. The Salon jury's hard-line policy led to public demonstrations from artists and proposed reforms.

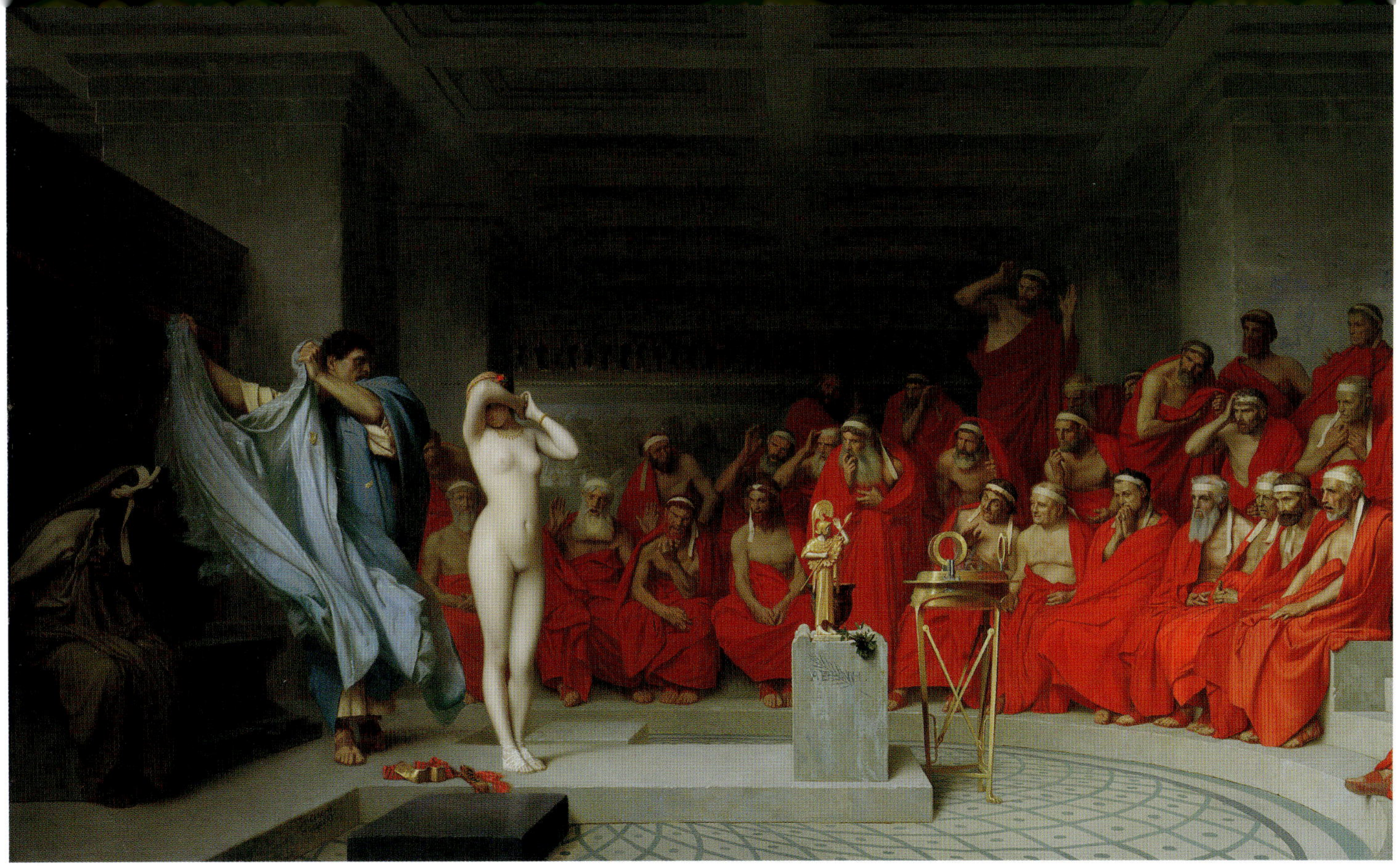

In 1863, the emperor, Napoleon III, in a liberalizing gesture, intervened to allow a *Salon des Refusés*. In the same year, the Ecole was reformed and more liberal teaching practices put in place. By the late 1860s, many of the greatest French Academicians had died and the death of Ingres in 1867 represented a watershed moment, signalling the passing of the old established order. The French art world was changing. By the end of their careers the Impressionists had become the leading artists of their time and were recognized as having made an important contribution to the development of modern art.

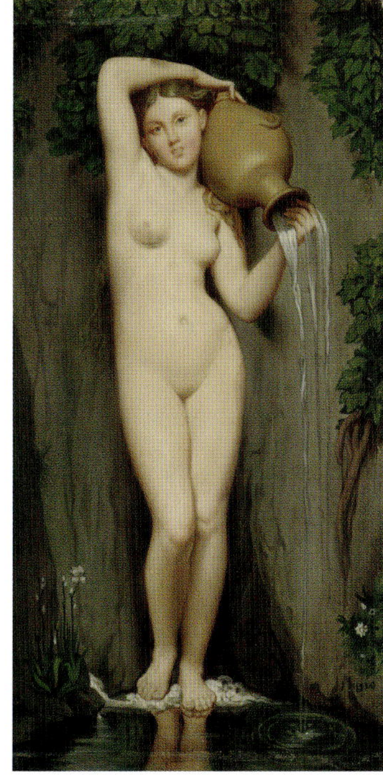

Above *The pose of the water carrier in Jean-Auguste-Dominique Ingres's The Source is a fine example of figurative painting that would have resulted from the student first drawing figures based on statuary and then life classes in which the model would have posed in a traditional style.*

Below far left *Eugène Delacroix was a huge influence on the Impressionists. Influenced himself by Rubens, he created this painting, Death of Sardanapalus (1827–28), based on a poem by Byron, in the style of the Flemish master, adding a verve and energy to it that was uncommon among many of his contemporaries. His dramatic use of colour deeply impressed Monet, Cézanne and Renoir.*

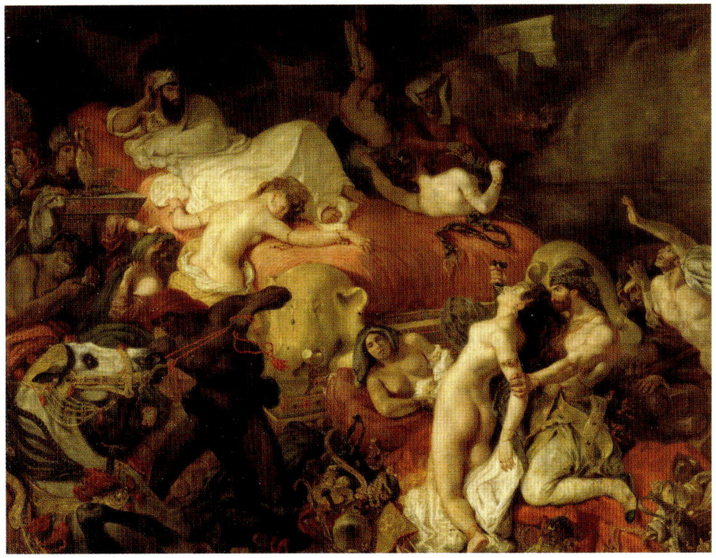

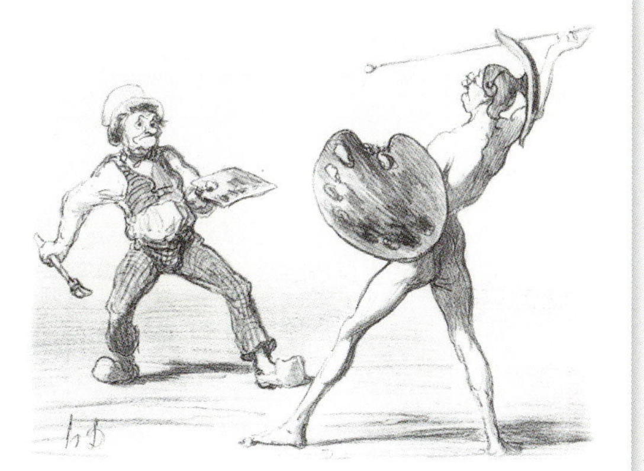

Classical Idealism versus Realism

This cartoon by Honoré Daumier, which appeared in the review *Le Charivari* in 1855, satirizes the divisions between the "school of the antique" and the "moderns". Daumier, a caricaturist and painter, was himself connected with realism, coining the slogan *"Il faut être de son temps"* (one must be of one's time). Realism was a broad, diverse movement that had many tendencies, including some associated with Academic painting, but artists shared the belief that art should be renewed through contact with nature and not rely on inherited artistic rules and conventions. While Classicists chose subjects set in the antique, realists generally favoured modern subjects that took the life around them as their starting point.

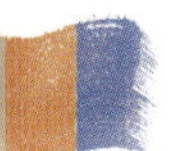

Impressionism: Origins and Precursors

The origins of Impressionism lie in the debates about realism and landscape painting that emerged in the 1830s and '40s. The term "Impression" itself was not new and had been used in philosophical investigations into the nature of perception, specifically in relation to whether our knowledge is determined by sensory impressions of the material world or if our ideas condition the sensory impressions we have of the world. It was also a term which had currency in the art world: an impression was a type of loose oil sketch – an *esquisse* – that appealed to art collectors who valued the sketch as a more direct vehicle of artistic expression than a finished work. While the term "impressionism" was not new, its application to public exhibition pictures was, and in the 1870s it began to be used widely to represent a new tendency in painting represented by the work of Edouard Manet, Claude Monet, Berthe Morisot, Camille Pissarro, Pierre-Auguste Renoir, Alfred Sisley, Paul Cézanne, Armand Guillaumin, Gustave Caillebotte and Edgar Degas and his followers. Their work was seen as an outgrowth of the realist and naturalist tendencies of the 1840s and '50s and part of a new demand within French art for contemporary subject matter and a renewal of the French tradition.

A key influence on the development of Impressionism, at least on the landscapists of the group, was the work of the Barbizon painters, who painted in the forest of Fontainbleau, a centre for artists since the eighteenth century, and achieved recognition in the 1830s as having

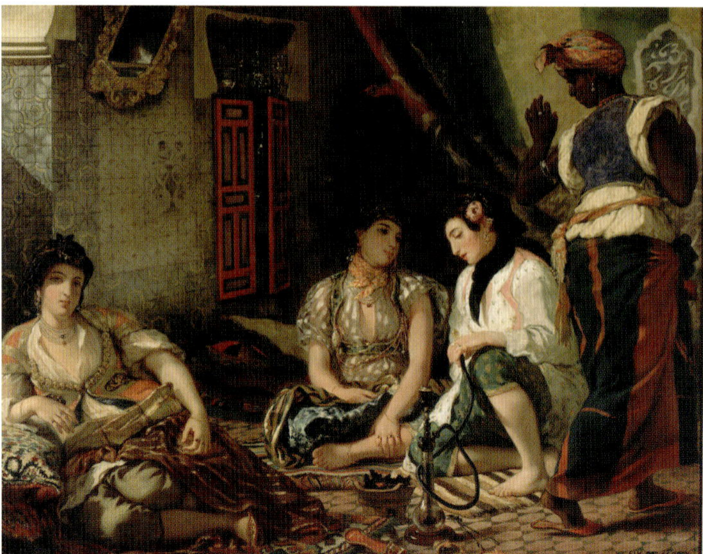

introduced a new, more naturalistic tradition of landscape painting into France. Drawing on Dutch and English models of landscape, most notably J M W Turner and John Constable, its principal members were Théodore Rousseau, Charles-François Daubigny, Constant Troyon, Narcisse Diaz, Jean-François Millet and Camille Corot. Their paintings expressed a strong feeling for light, mood and atmosphere and eschewed

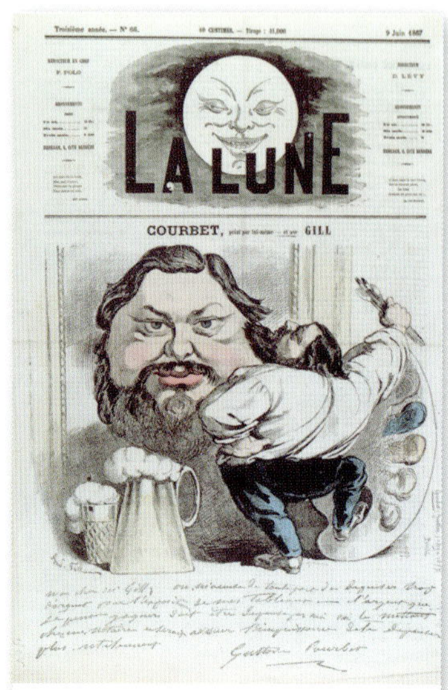

Gustave Courbet
1819–77

Courbet was a radical in art and a revolutionary in politics. His painting was committed to the depiction of his native region of Ornans in the Franche-Comté and his imagery often provided a critical vision of the idealized and sentimentalized images of his contemporary's portrayals of the countryside. Courbet's portrayal of himself as a "visionary" realist combined with his larger-than-life persona galvanized the public and critics alike. His feeling for his native landscape and innovative untraditional techniques made him an essential source for the Impressionist painters, especially for Cézanne, Pissarro, Sisley and Renoir, despite his keen rivalry with Manet.

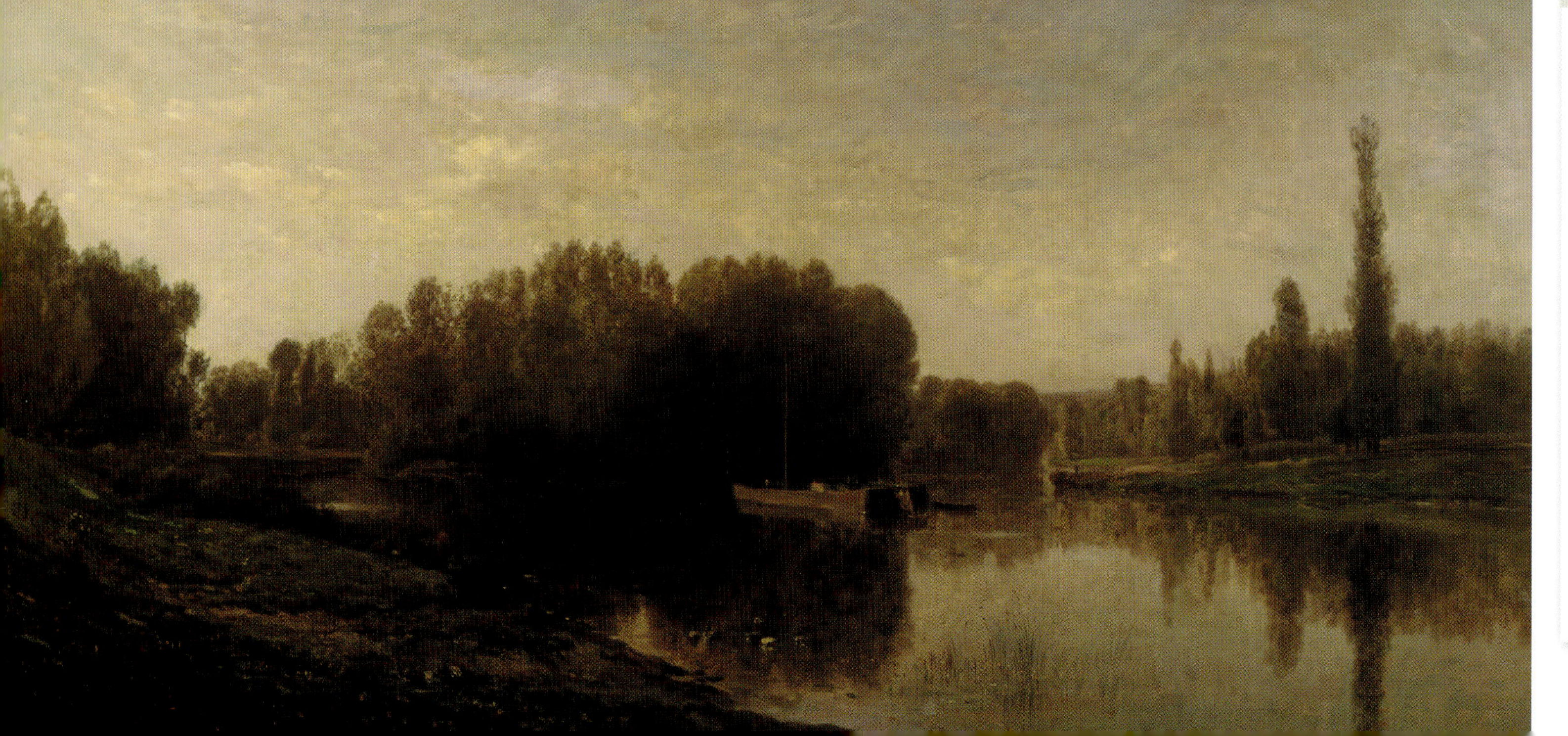

the traditional criteria for landscape motifs in favour of more discreet and incidental motifs that reflected the artist's temperament and personal response to nature. The Barbizon painters were committed to sketching *en plein air*, out of doors and before nature, in order to retain a fresh and strong impression of their motifs and exploited the new artists' pigments in tubes and portable easels that had become available.

Alongside the Barbizon painters, to whom he was closely connected, Gustave Courbet exercised a powerful influence over early Impressionism. In the late 1840s, Courbet became recognized as one of the leaders of the realist tendency that was gaining ascendance in France. Like Millet, his painting took the peasantry and everyday rural life as its principal subjects. Courbet's bold technique, applying thick impastoed paint often with a palette knife, exerted a particularly powerful and enduring influence on Paul Cézanne. His choice of "democratic", contemporary and untraditional subjects that eschewed religious symbolism and patriotic propaganda combined with his status as an embattled rebel against the artistic and political status quo helped establish the climate in which Impressionism could emerge.

The Romantic painter Eugene Delacroix, whom the poet Charles Baudelaire considered the greatest French artist of his age, also exerted a profound and decisive influence on the development of Impressionism. While Impressionists reacted against the onus on imagination and literary subject matters associated with Romanticism, nevertheless they valued Delacroix's vibrant and uninhibited tonality, his understanding of colour theory, vigorous brushwork and constant technical exploration.

But although these painters represent the most immediate contemporary reference points for Impressionism, the influence of the Dutch, Venetian and Spanish schools of the sixteenth and seventeenth centuries and the French eighteenth-century rococo tradition on the Impressionists indicate that their work also evolved out of an engagement with other long-standing artistic tendencies.

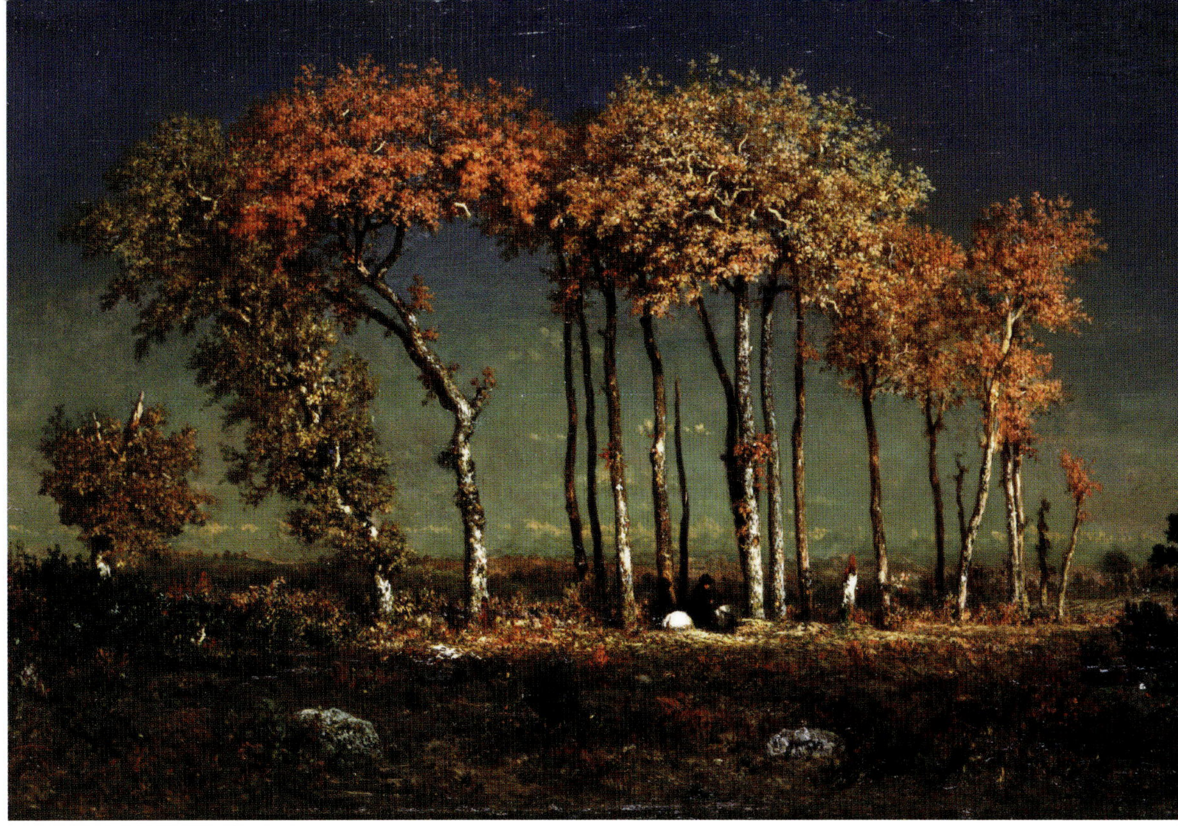

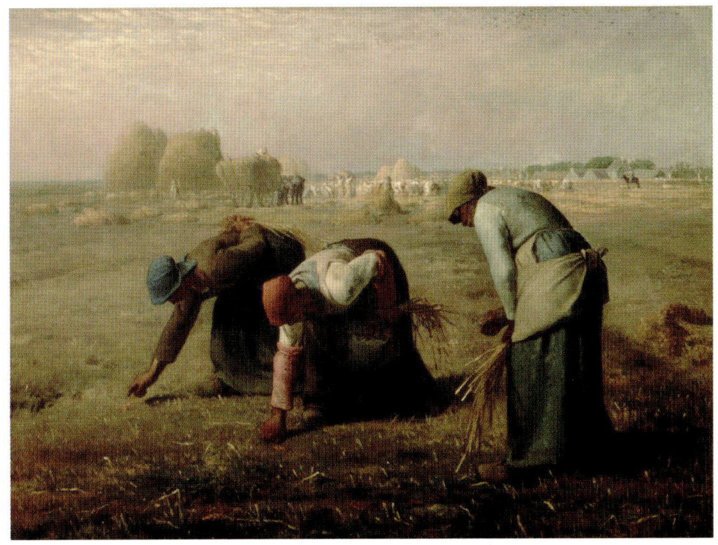

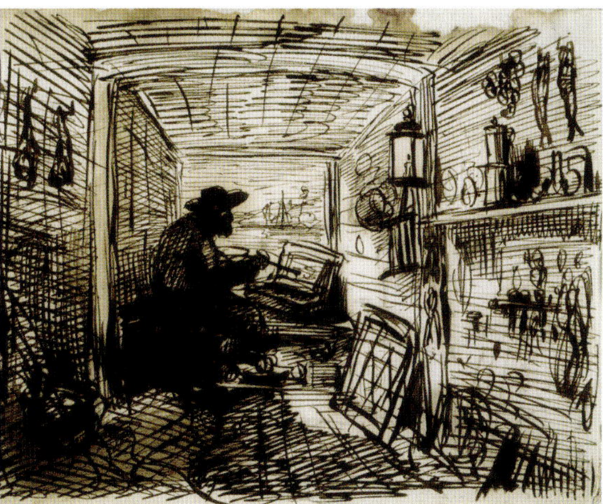

Opposite below *The landscapes of Daubigny and other members of the Barbizon group were highly influential, and by the 1850s Daubigny was recognized as one of the leading artists of his time. Their rustic scenes proved popular for an urban audience and the Salon was increasingly full of similar landscapes. The Impressionists, however, saw in Daubigny's "impressionistic" technique and discreet choice of motifs a radical departure from the classical tradition of landscape painting.*

Above *Like Daubigny, Rousseau was a leading member of the Barbizon group. His moody evocative landscapes demonstrate his ability to capture spectacular climatic and lighting effects. Based in the Barbizon forest, near Fontainbleau, a site made famous by Jean Jacques Rousseau's reveries on nature, his landscapes often exude a quiet poetry and melancholic mood and take the solitary immersion in nature as their central theme.*

Left *Jean-François Millet was Camille Pissarro's favourite painter and an abiding influence on his choice of subject and way of painting. The Gleaners (1857) is now recognized as one of his masterpieces, but was controversial in its own time as it pointed to huge disparities of wealth and poverty in the countryside.*

Charles-François Daubigny
1817–78

Daubigny was the most influential of the Barbizon painters on the Impressionists. He studied in the studio of the academic painter Paul Delaroche but turned to landscape painting, gaining his first success at the 1848 Salon. Influenced by Dutch landscapists and by John Constable, his increasingly bold and free brushwork and his choice of incidental motifs, particularly river scenes, made him popular among the younger generation of painters and the general public. In the late 1860s, he gained official recognition and sat on the Salon jury. This etching shows him painting a river scene in his *botin*, on which Monet based his own *"floating studio"*.

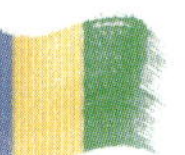

The Example of Manet

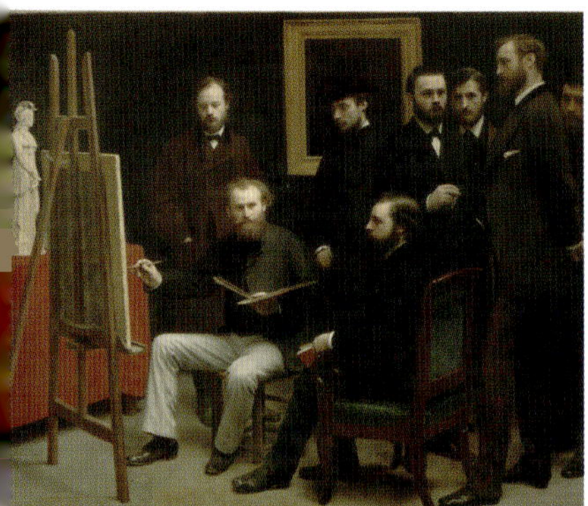

Edouard Manet occupies a prime position in the history of Impressionism as one of its most important guiding spirits, a fact already acknowledged in Fantin-Latour's *A Studio in the Batignolles* (1870), which shows Manet painting, surrounded by his admirers, who include Bazille, Renoir, Monet and the influential realist authors Zola and Champfleury. Manet was not only a formative influence on the Impressionists, but under the reciprocal influence of Monet and Morisot, became one of its greatest exponents, adapting his painterly touch and subject matter in response to the painting of the younger artists. Although he never exhibited at the Impressionist group shows, believing the Salon or one-man exhibitions to be the most appropriate context for his work, he was widely regarded as their leader. The poet Stéphane Mallarmé acknowledged this in an article published in 1874, stressing the importance of Manet's wish to unlearn received artistic rules and thereby to see nature afresh, rendering the visual aspect of the motif without preconceptions. Recounting the painter's theories he wrote, "Each work should be a new creation of the mind… the eye should forget all else it has seen and learn anew from the lesson before it… as for the first time."

In 1863, Manet painted two pictures that were to bring him public attention and galvanize the younger generation of artists who would later become the Impressionists: *Le Déjeuner sur l'Herbe* (*Luncheon on the Grass*), then known as *Le bain* (*The Bath*), and *Olympia*. Often taken as the starting point of modern painting, the two much emulated pictures, like so many of his paintings of this period, made clear references to traditional sources. The frontal figure grouping of *Le Déjeuner sur l'Herbe* is taken from the seated river gods on the right-hand side of Raimondi's engraving after Raphael's lost painting of the *Judgment of Paris* (1529), though it also refers to Titian's *Concert Champêtre* (1508). *Olympia* is based on Titian's *Venus of Urbino* (1538). In each case, Manet, under the influence of the poet Charles Baudelaire, updated these sources, translating them into the context of the modern France. In transforming Raphael's river gods into Parisian picnickers, *Le Déjeuner sur l'Herbe* combined the nude with figures in contemporary dress. Rejected by the notoriously severe jury at the 1863 Salon, the work was shown at the Salon des Refusés where, despite its mixed reviews, it attracted the attention and support of younger artists. However, it was the exhibition of Manet's *Olympia* at the 1865 Salon that propelled him into the limelight. The strange combination of the signs of high and low prostitution and the translation of Titian's iconic *Venus*, the model for which was herself a representation of a contemporary courtesan, into the

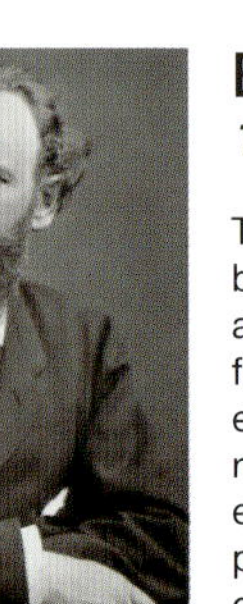

Edouard Manet
1832–83

The son of a magistrate, Edouard Manet was born in Paris. Nadar's portrait captures the artist's refined *haute bourgeois* tastes and fashionable status as a man about town. Well-educated, urbane and witty, Manet's pictures reflect his knowledge of tradition and his eye for humour and irony. Despite his radical painting and left-wing republicanism he craved official recognition and when he finally received the Legion d'honneur, the highest award the State could bestow on an artist, he complained that it had come too late to make up for 20 years of artistic failure. By the time he died in 1883, he was recognized as one of France's most important contemporary artists.

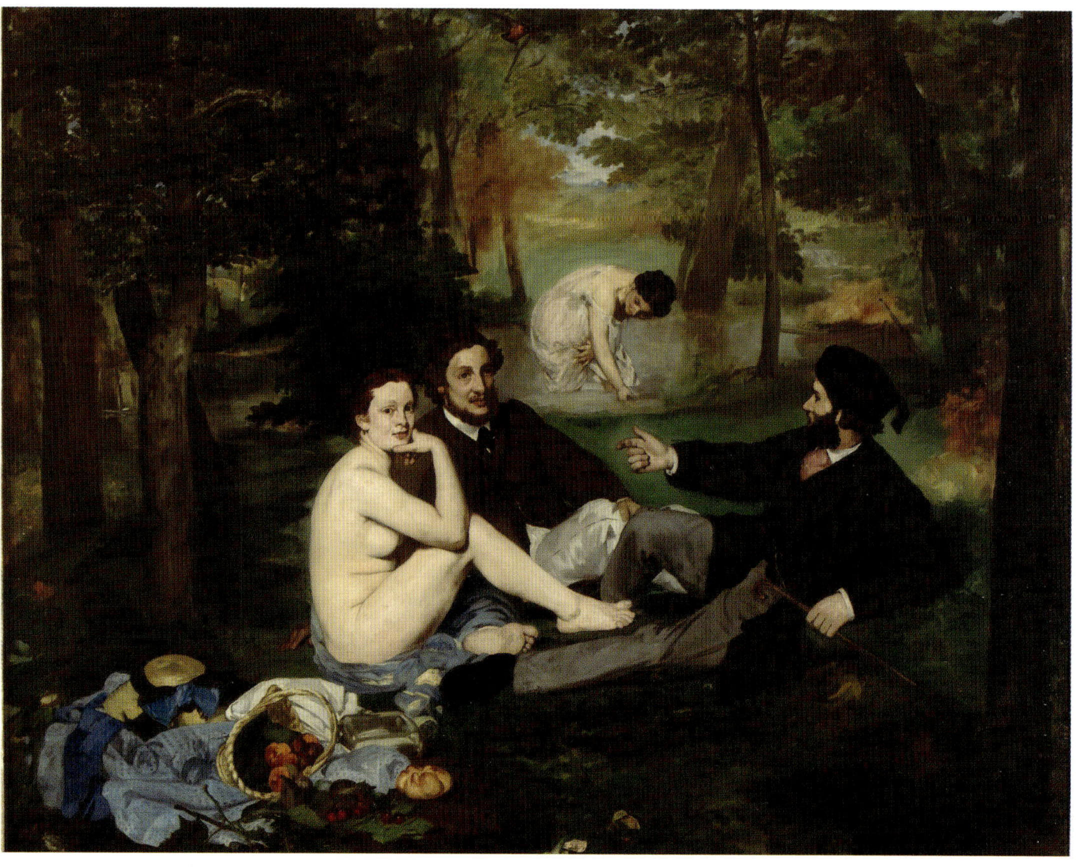

Left Fantin-Latour's A Studio in the Batignolles *(1870) is an homage to Manet from a painter within his inner circle. The picture testifies to his importance for the younger generation of Impressionists who watch him painting a portrait of the writer Zacharie Astruc. Other figures included in the composition are the German painter Otto Scholderer, Pierre-Auguste Renoir, who is framed by the picture on the back wall, the critic Emile Zola, Edmond Maitre, Frédéric Bazille and Claude Monet.*

Below Manet's Le Déjeuner sur l'Herbe *(1862–63), was a key reference point for the Impressionists. Cézanne, Renoir and Monet painted numerous variations on its theme. In updating a classical theme into a contemporary setting, Manet seemed to point the way to a renewal of the nude within modern painting, but it was as much the freshness and improvised nature of Manet's technique that influenced his admirers.*

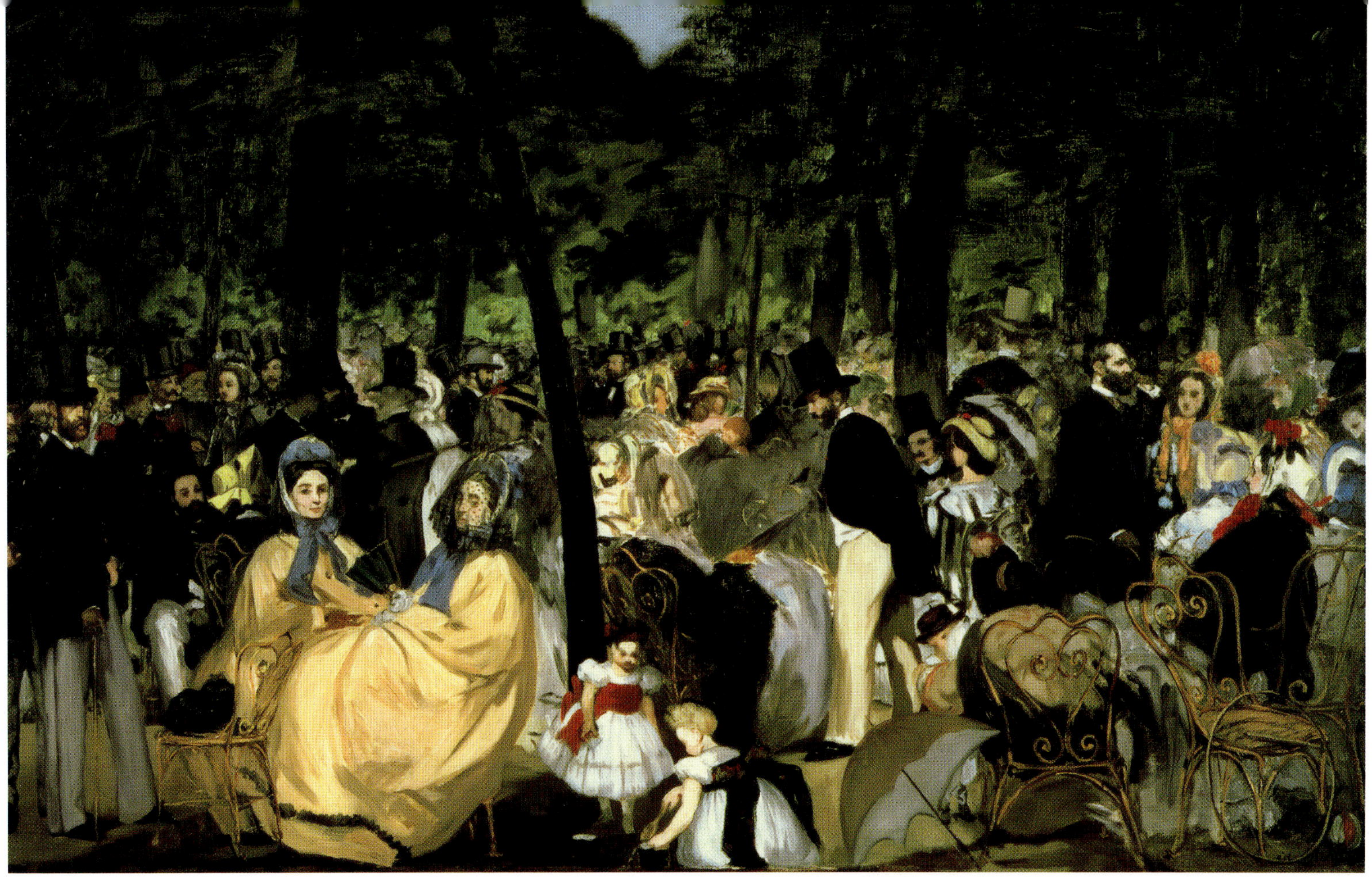

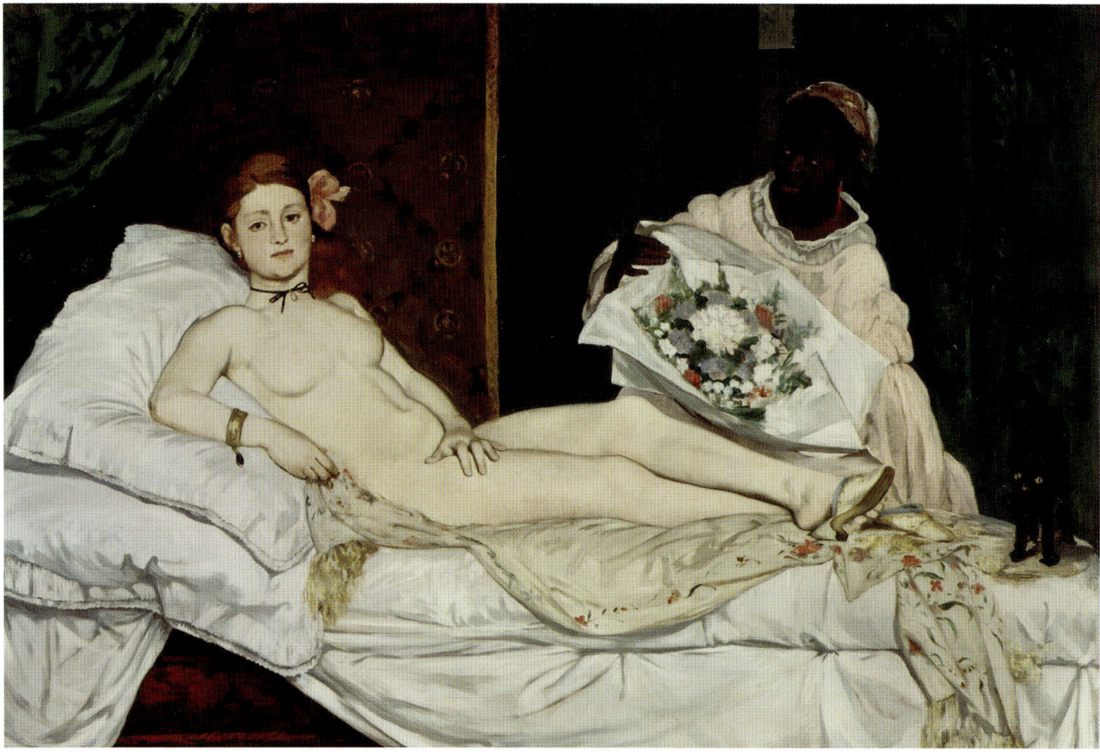

world of Parisian prostitution left critics perplexed and scandalized. *Olympia* became notorious, a picture around which the critical debates about modern painting were articulated. The harsh critical reception Manet's picture received served only to consolidate his reputation for younger generations of artists. To them, Manet was the leading modern painter of his generation and an example to be emulated.

It was not only Manet's adaptation of traditional sources that made his work controversial, but his technique, which radically departed from academic norms. His broad modelling, avoiding the academic practice of using demi-tints to create subtle transitions from one tone to another, lush painterly brushwork and concentration on the general effect to the exclusion of detail, created fresh and vigorous impressions. Zola made much of the individuality of Manet's manner of painting in his essay on the painter published in 1867, arguing that it was his technique rather than his subjects which most fully expressed the painter's sensibility. Zola's article anticipated the shift in attention that would characterize the Impressionist response to Manet. For, by the mid-1870s, it was less his reworking of traditional subjects in modern form than the impressionistic technique of Manet's style that preoccupied the painters.

Impressions of Paris

Early impressionist painting was pre-eminently the painting of metropolitan imagery, the landscape of the city and its periphery. The Paris depicted by the Impressionists was undergoing substantial transformation. During the 1850s, the Second Empire embarked on an ambitious project of urban renewal that would continue for much of the next two decades. The rebuilding of Paris, under the supervision of Baron Haussmann, created *une ville éclairé*, a more sanitary and less polluted city. The old Paris with its narrow winding streets and slums was swept away and replaced by wide, straight boulevards lined with imposing apartment blocks. Centralized zones of commerce were established, flanked by cafés and department stores, while streets were adorned with trees and new parks were built to allow the city to breathe. The modernizing of the city also had political motives. The Second Empire followed in the wake of a second revolution in France in 1848. The new Paris was designed to be effectively monitored and policed and to prevent further uprisings.

Charles Baudelaire
1821–67

Charles Baudelaire is regarded as one of the defining writers of the tradition of modern art. By the early 1860s he had established a name for himself as a poet, translator and critic, championing the romanticism of Eugène Delacroix. The publication of *Les Fleurs du Mal (The Flowers of Evil)*, in 1857, confirmed him as one of the most important poets of the Second Empire period, but led to his prosecution for immorality. His essay "The Painter of Modern Life", written in 1859 but not published until 1863, was a continual touchstone for the Impressionists in justifying their artistic aims. He died prematurely four years later depleted by alcohol and drugs.

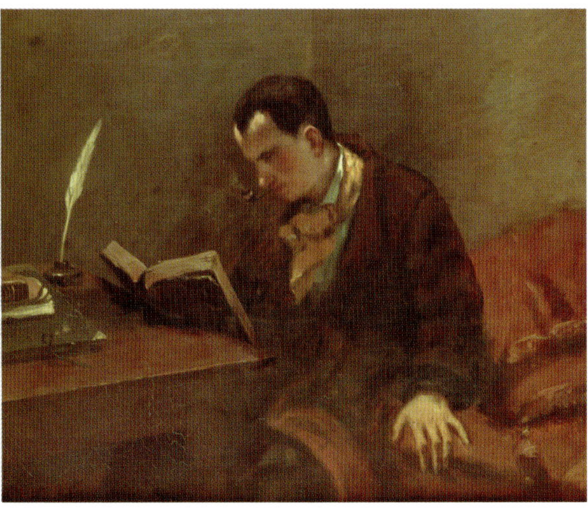

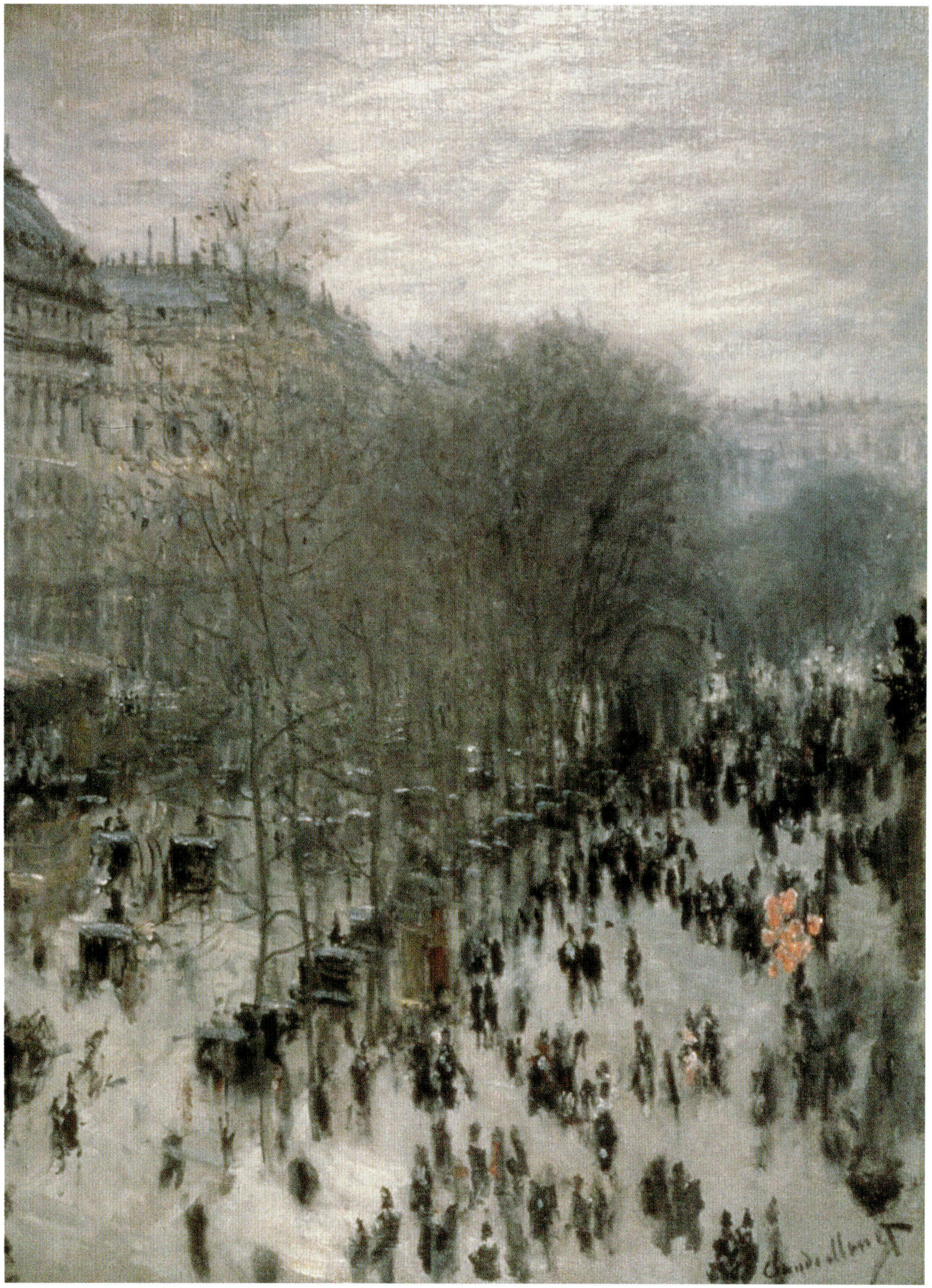

Left *Courbet's portrait of Baudelaire is a study of solitude, showing the poet utterly absorbed in the act of reading. This was one of a number of oil sketches he made of him and which he later used for his masterpiece* The Painter's Studio *(1955).*

Above *In one of the key works of his early career, Monet represents one of the fashionable new boulevards of Haussman's rebuilt Paris. In choosing a high aerial vantage point, looking down onto the street from a balcony, he exploits the spectacular new viewpoints the apartment blocks provided. Monet's rapid, notational brushwork captures the animated quality of a busy street almost instantaneously.*

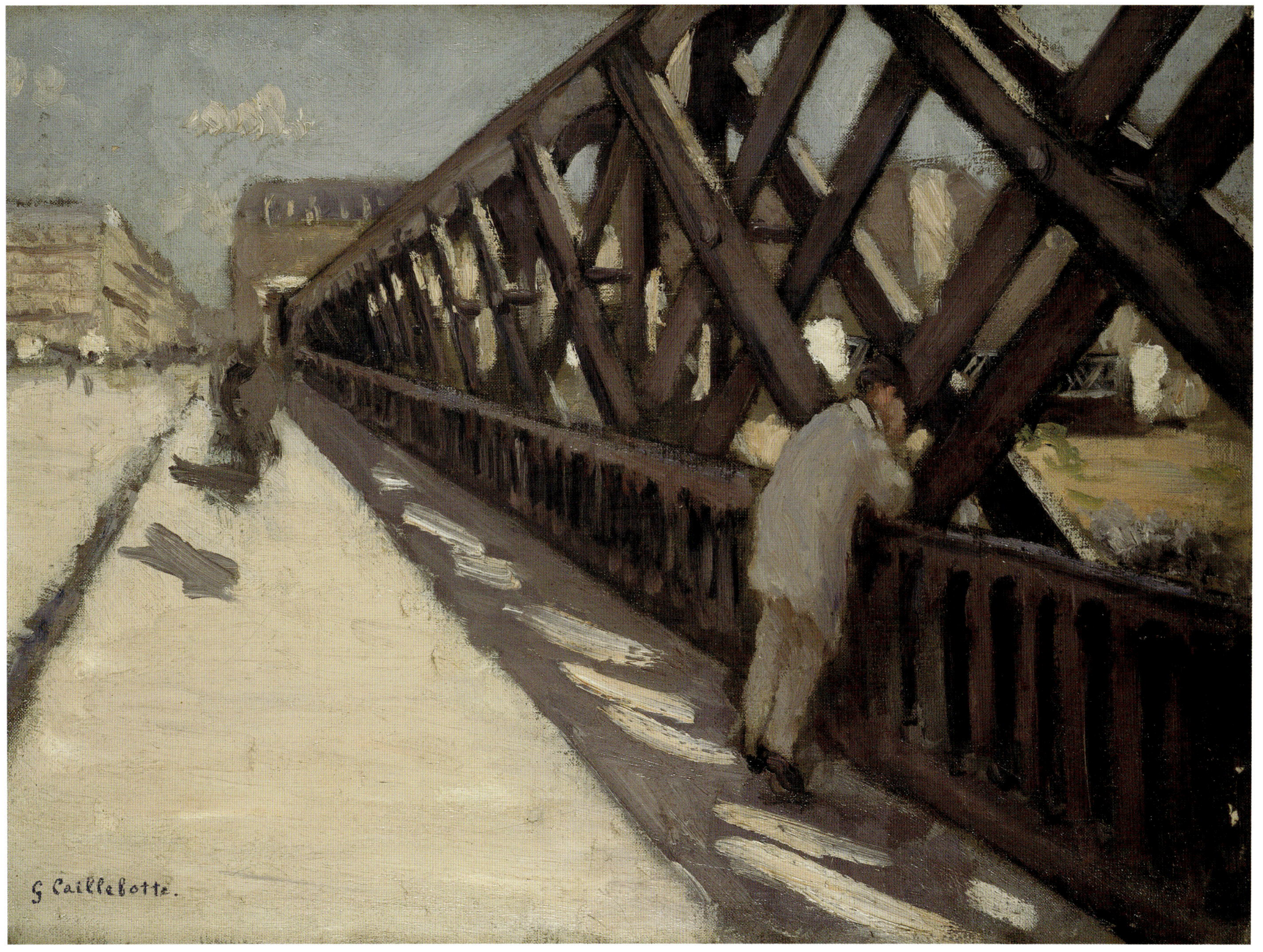

G Caillebotte.

Impressionist images of the city are diverse and wide-ranging, charting various aspects of the labour and leisure of Parisian life, its social types and classes, and typically focus on its newer quarters. Monet painted the spectacular topographies of Paris's parks and fashionable boulevards, which he depicted from elevated viewpoints that emphasize the dramatic, expansive quality of the city. The *Boulevard des Capucines* (1873–74), is one of several pictures he painted of the scene from the second-floor apartment of the photographer Nadar's studio, on the corner of the rue Daunou and the Boulevard des Capucines. The picture's modernity, as Jules Castagnary noted, consisted not only in Monet's painterly technique but the way it makes use of the novel points of view afforded by the new apartment buildings.

Like Monet, Caillebotte concentrated on the breathtaking perspectives offered by the *grands boulevards*, but other Impressionists,

Above Le Pont de l'Europe *by Gustave Caillebotte shows the wide expanse of the new streets and bridges that were built in Paris under the aegis of Baron Haussmann, while the heavy iron struts of the bridge acknowledge the rapid industrialization of the country and the burgeoning infrastructure of the country's railways.*

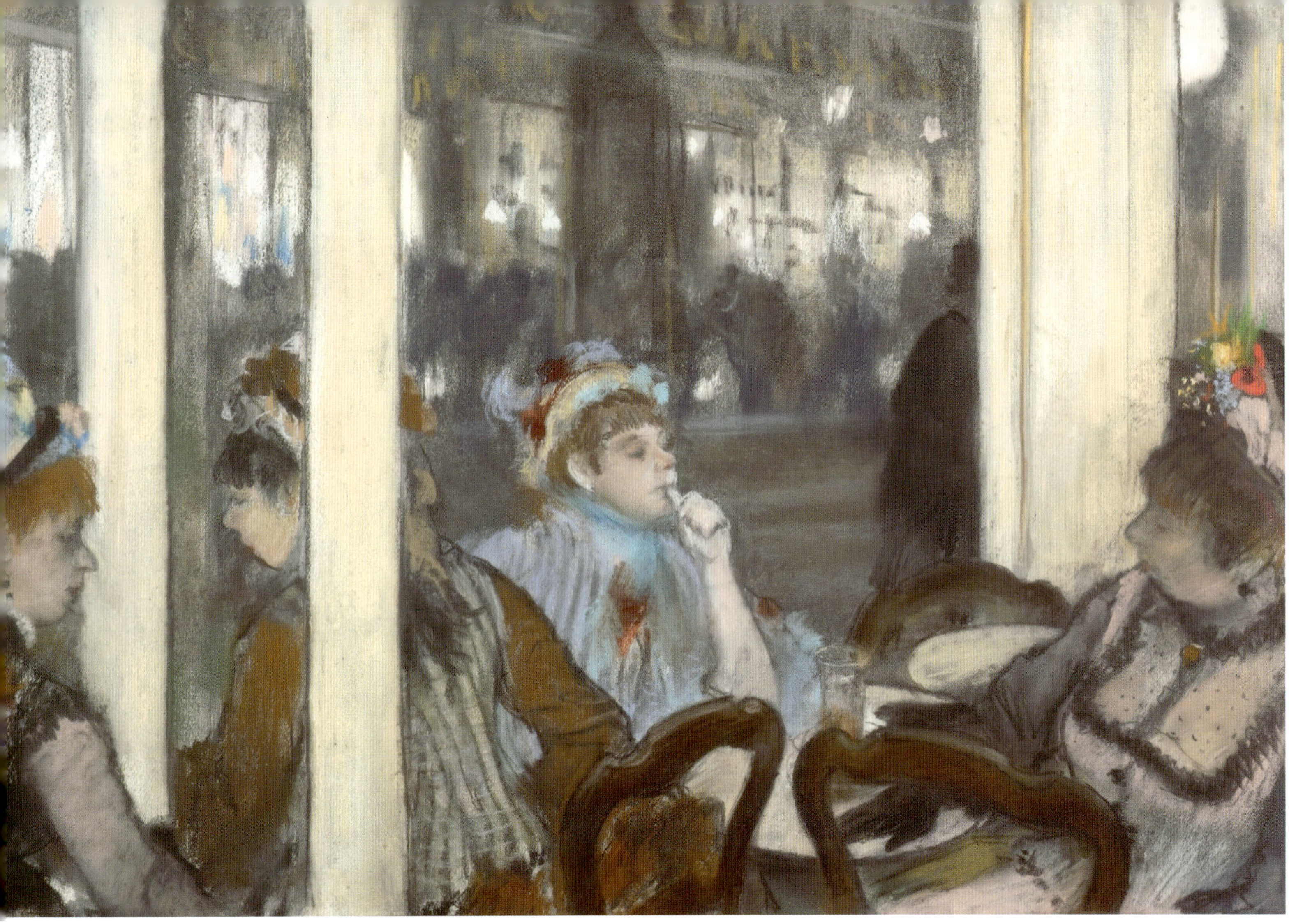

such as Degas, Manet and Renoir, turned their attention to the city's entertainments: the opera, the ballet and the innumerable cafés and café-concerts. Their images capture the hedonism of the times, but also, more ambivalently, the experience of alienation and isolation. Often these pictures suggest a snapshot effect, as though a fleeting and arbitrarily chosen moment had been snatched from the flow of life. In this, they followed the poet Charles Baudelaire, whose essay "The Painter of Modern Life", published at the end of 1863, urged the artist to seek out the discreet, poetic correspondences that constitute the essence of contemporary life and to give form to "that indefinable something we may be allowed to call modernity… the transient, the fleeting and the contingent". In these respects, Impressionist paintings communicate a strong sense of immediacy and immersion in the world of Paris, qualities enhanced by the way, as in Degas's *Women on a Café Terrace* (1877), that their compositions are often cropped at the borders, implying continuity between the representational space of the picture and the life outside it. These

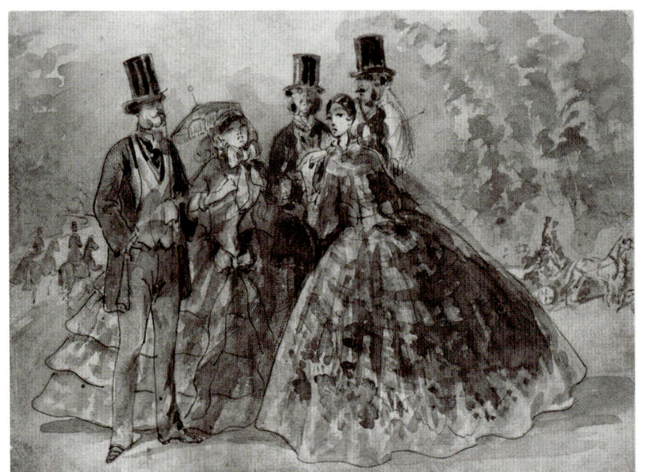

Constantin Guys
1805–92

Baudelaire's "The Painter of Modern Life" describes the work of Constantin Guys (referred to anonymously as M. G.), a popular illustrator and friend of the poet who worked as a journalist for the *Illustrated London News* covering the Crimean War, but who is best known for his drawings of the life of Paris, executed with a quick, impressionistic stroke of pencil, pen or brush washed with watercolour. These include many images of the lifestyle of the *haute bourgeoisie*. He had a particular interest in the latest fashions and the fashionable women and men of his time, but also explored the low-life imagery of Paris.

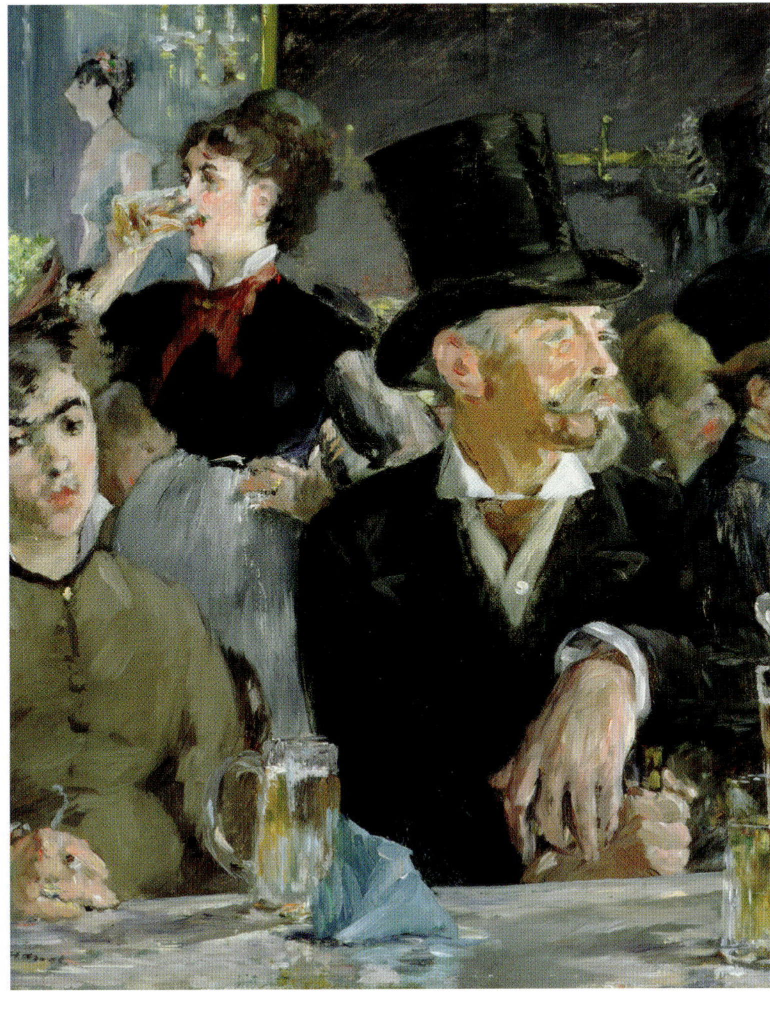

novel features of Impressionism, particularly the lack of any clear
significance to what is represented, were constantly criticized. In *Le
Pont de l'Europe* (1876), Caillebotte appears to leave to the viewer the
role of interpreting the relationships between the figures in the picture.
Similarly, Degas leaves open to interpretation the gesture of the central
woman in *Women on a Café Terrace*. Such ambiguities suggest that the
painters were giving full force to the visual aspect of the life around
them, avoiding the taste for anecdotalism and narrative painting of many
of their contemporaries. The impression of a "slice of life" snatched
from reality was seen by the movement's defenders as an indication
of Impressionism's honesty and truth to appearances. George Rivière
described *Women on a Café Terrace* as "an extraordinary page of history".

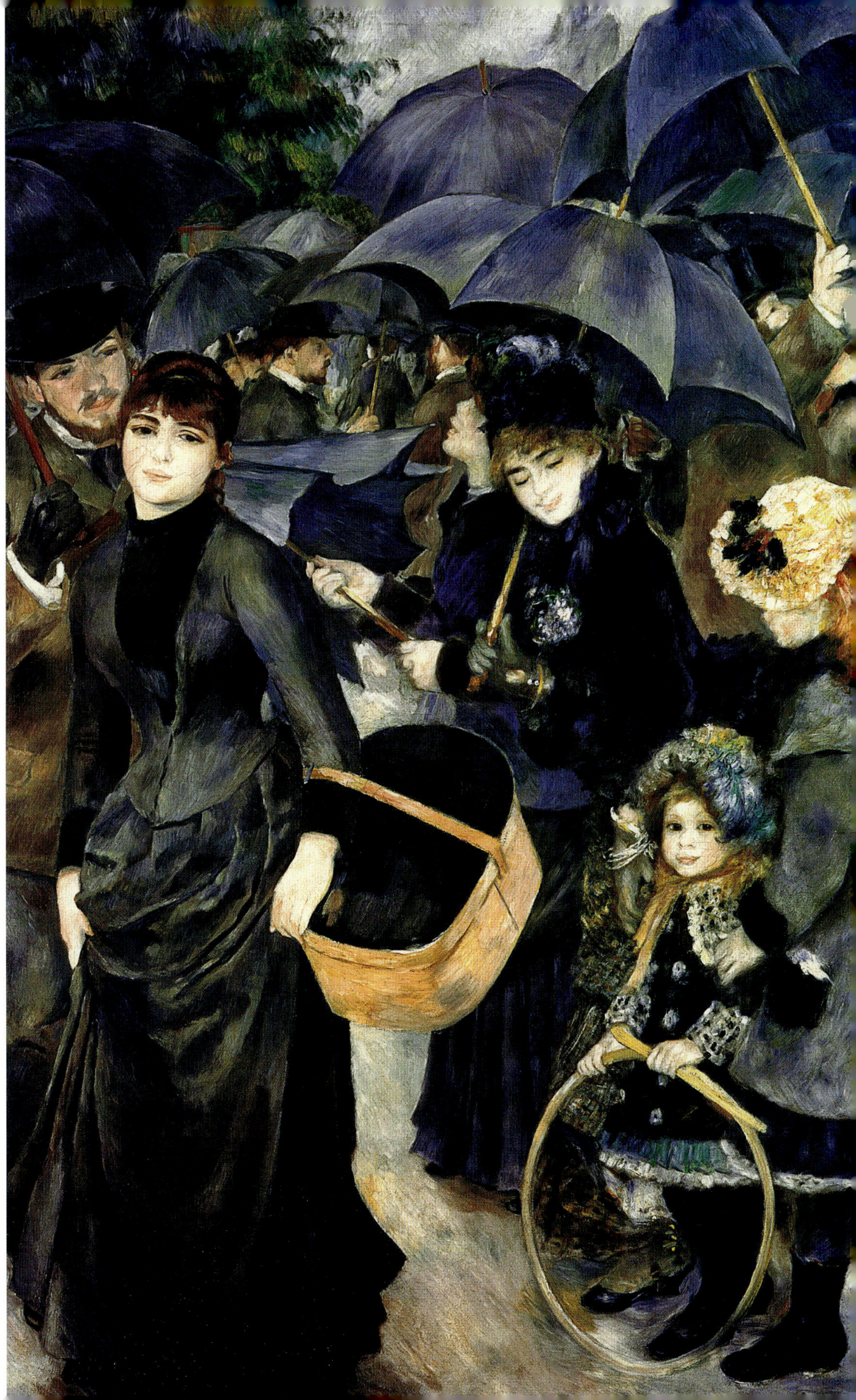

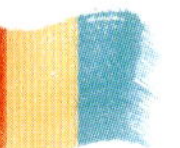

aesthetic spectacle, painted with an eye for the atmospheric and transient qualities of nature. Pictures like *Jetty and Wharf at Trouville* (1863) set an important precedent for Monet, who began to adopt Boudin's subject matter after meeting him in Le Havre in the late 1850s and who would later pay tribute to the formative influence of Boudin in encouraging him to paint in the open air. Likewise, though not a *plein-airiste*, the incidental seascapes of Jongkind, the ex-patriot Dutch landscapist with whom Monet established a lasting friendship, were important in encouraging Impressionism's embrace of coastal and harbour scenes, as Morisot's *Seascape* (1869) of the harbour at Lorient shows.

Far left *With its international flags blowing in the wind and its array of figures conversing and promenading, Monet's picture economically captures the glamorous, fashionable and cosmopolitan life of seaside hotels. The Hôtel des Roches Noires was a favourite resort of American tourists and an American flag can be seen in the distance.*

Below left *The Terrace at Sainte-Adresse (1867) is one of Monet's most important early marine paintings, illustrating his use of elevated viewpoints and primary colours in vibrant combinations. Monet here combines his longstanding interest in seascapes with that of depicting fashionable bourgeoisie in garden settings, a more ephemeral aspect of his career. The painting reveals his awareness of the marines of Manet, Courbet and Whistler, but also of Japanese prints, such as Hokusai's* The Sazaido of the Gohyaku Rakanji Temple *(right) with which it bears many constitutional affinities.*

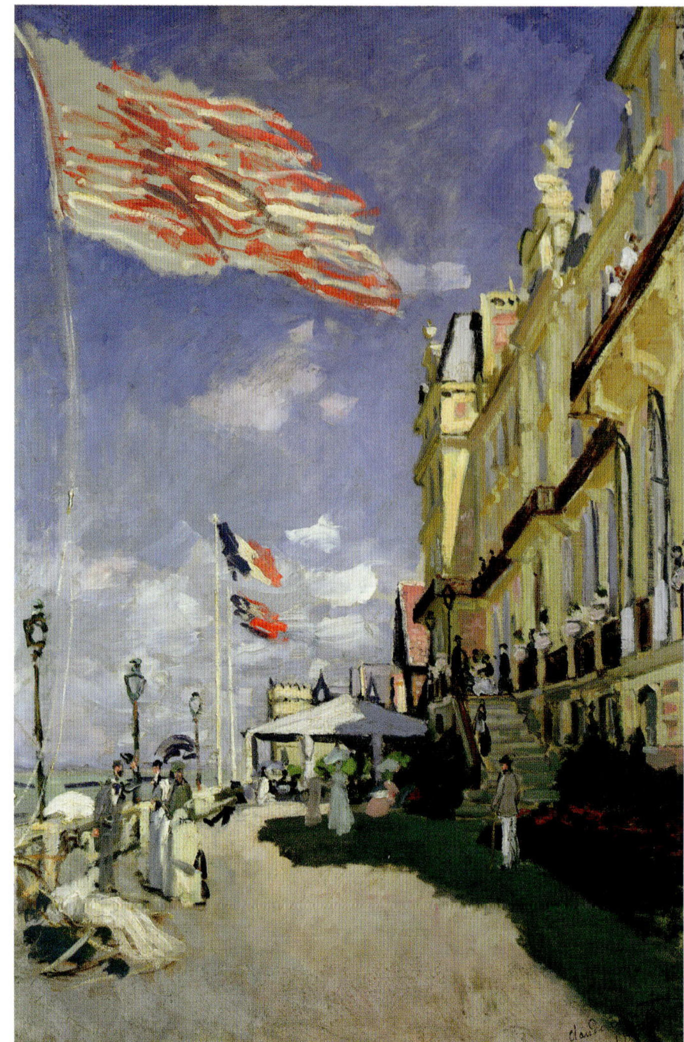

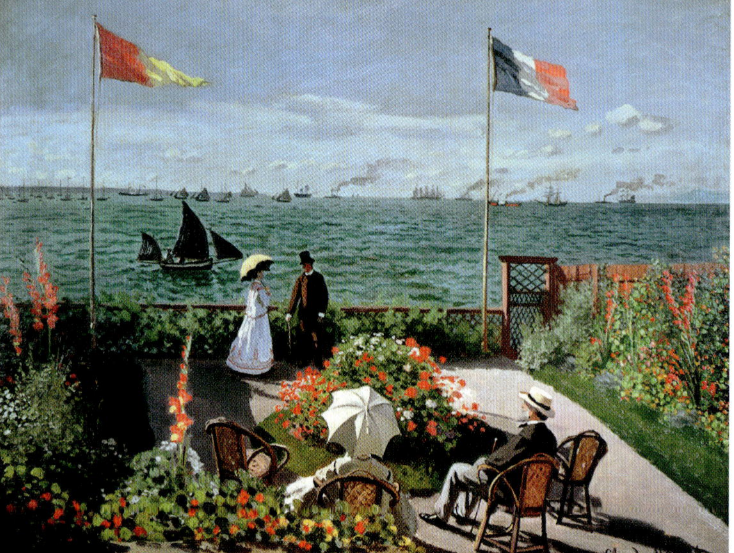

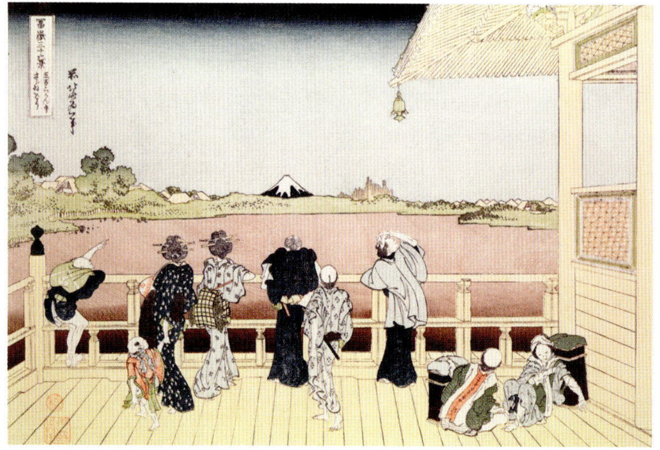

During the 1860s and 1870s, Impressionist painting began to extend beyond the city to take in France's coastline. Pictures of France's harbours, and most especially the life around its shores, featured strongly in the work of Manet and Morisot in the 1870s and were an enduring aspect of Monet's imagery. By mid century marine painting had long been in decline and was kept alive only in the storm-tossed visions of romantic painters like Eugène Isabey and Paul Huet. In the 1860s, however, a new kind of picture of the coast was pioneered, centring on the new vogue for holidays by the sea and the transformation of villages into seaside resorts catering for vacations and tourism. Eugène Boudin's beach scenes at Trouville, a fishing village on the Normandy coastline, focus on precisely these new forms of social leisure and the pleasures of the coast as an

Japanese Prints

Japanese prints were a major influence on many Impressionist painters, providing them with novel, decorative, compositional devices that departed from western artistic conventions of pictorial containment and harmoniously balanced composition. The radical compositional cropping at the margins and pictorial asymmetry, which we often see in Impressionist painting, derives from Japanese art, and references to oriental prints abound in the work of Manet, Degas and Monet. The latter had a large collection of such prints and his pictures of the terrace at Saint-Adresse, and later of the Japanese bridge he had built in his garden at Giverny in the 1890s, testify to their enduring influence on him.

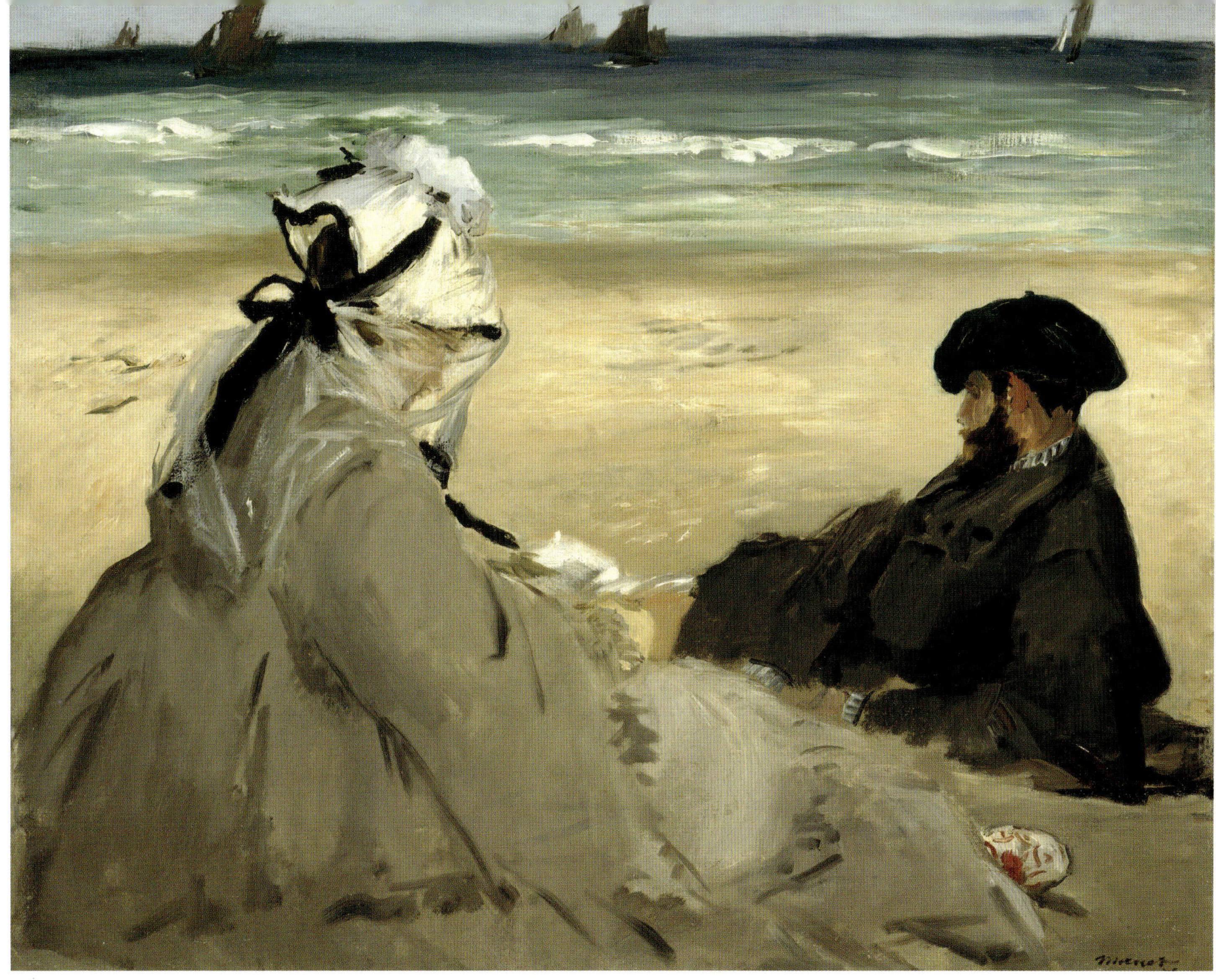

The Beach at Trouville

This picture was painted around late June 1870, during Monet's honeymoon at Trouville with his wife Camille Doncieux, the painting's principal figure, and their son Jean (born in 1867), whose presence is discreetly implied by a child's brown beach shoe on the foreground chair. The other figure may be Boudin's wife, Marie-Anne, as the couples spent time together at Trouville that summer. The presence of grains of sand in the paint layers indicates that it was painted in the open air and reflects the breezy conditions depicted. The painting, with its fluid, notational brushstrokes and modern life subject, is typical of Monet's work of the time.

Portrayals of Normandy and other emerging seaside villages made by writers and artists played a significant role in spurring on the interest in and popularity of these coastlines for Parisians, and by the 1870s, many had become major resorts with fashionable hotels and restaurants catering to a predominantly foreign or urban clientele. The influx of visitors changed these regions rapidly and dramatically, blurring the boundaries between the forms of city and country life. Trouville became known as the "Boulevard des Italiens of the Normandy beaches", an allusion to one of the fashionable new boulevards of Paris. Monet's *The Hotel Roches Noires, Trouville* (1869) captures the new commercialized world of the Normandy coast to striking effect, picturing one of its newest and most luxurious hotels, whose façade and terrace dominated the seafront at Trouville. His free handling of paint, rapid, fluent and varied in tone and texture, conveys the improvised and spontaneous pleasures of the scene he shows, but does so dispassionately, broadly picturing the social byplay of the hotel's wealthy clientele from the position of an outsider watching from afar rather than as someone on intimate terms with those he depicts.

Representations of the coastlines continued to be an important aspect of Impressionist imagery well into the 1890s, but their later depictions reflect broad changes in the choice of motifs that they favoured. Monet's views of the Normandy coastline at Fécamp, Pourville and Etretat in the 1880s turn away from the hotels, holidaymaking and promenading that had previously been the focus of his attention and concentrate exclusively on elemental aspects of the coastline, the cliffs, the spectacular rock formations and the ebb and flow of the sea itself, all viewed in isolation and presented under different climatic conditions. Although Renoir continued to depict fashionable holidaymakers on the beaches, he paid no attention to the transformations of the coastline, reaching back instead to the idyllic, Arcadian imagery of the past. Only Caillebotte continued to represent those modern aspects of the region that Impressionism had preoccupied itself with in the 1860s.

Monet and Renoir at La Grenouillère

La Grenouillère (The Froggery) was a fashionable bathing and boating resort along the Seine, located on the island of Croissy, near Bougival in the western suburbs of Paris and within easy reach via the railway line from the Gare Saint-Lazare to Chatou. In addition to its reputation for bathing, boating and canoe hire, Grenouillère boasted a floating restaurant with riverside tables for eating and drinking and a dancehall where the latest cancans were performed. It was also a popular place for fishing, picnics and promenading along the bankside and drew large crowds of day-trippers from the city, including the Emperor and his wife, Princess Eugènie.

During the late summer of 1869, Monet and Renoir painted several views of Grenouillère while Monet was living in a village close by. Both painters were embracing landscape motifs that represented the modernity of the contemporary world and were attracted to those very

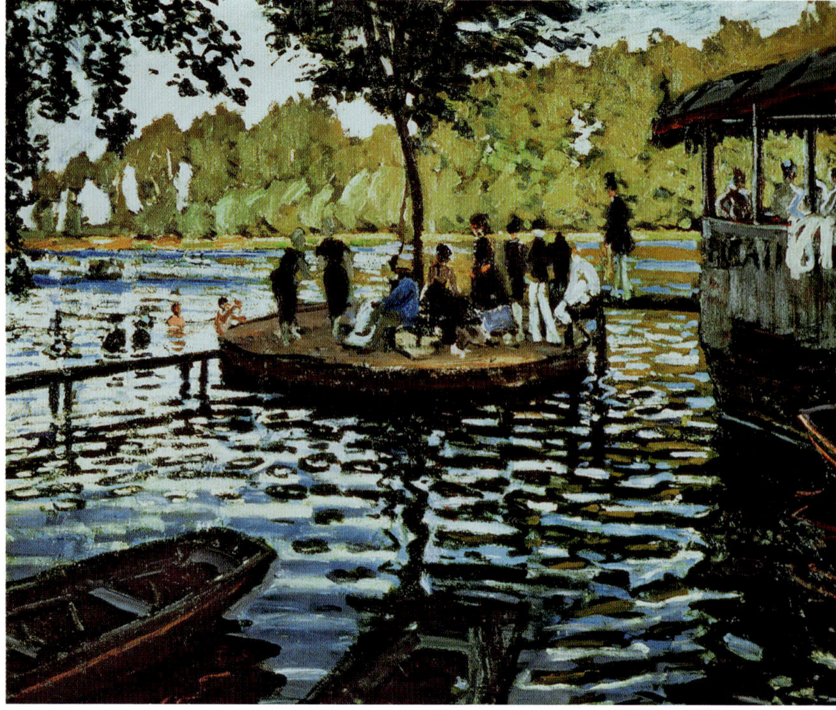

Right *Monet produced three oil sketches of La Grenouillère while he and Renoir were living close by at Saint-Michel. Monet probably intended these works to be sketches for an ambitious treatment of the subject, but if so, it was never realized.*

Below Painting alongside Monet, Renoir also produced three paintings of Grenouillère. Here the view is similar to that of Monet's but Renoir adopts a closer viewpoint, giving more emphasis to the figures. Comparison between the two pictures shows how, despite similarities, each painter treated the scene differently, Renoir using a more varied and piquant palette and softer brushwork in his treatment of the motif.

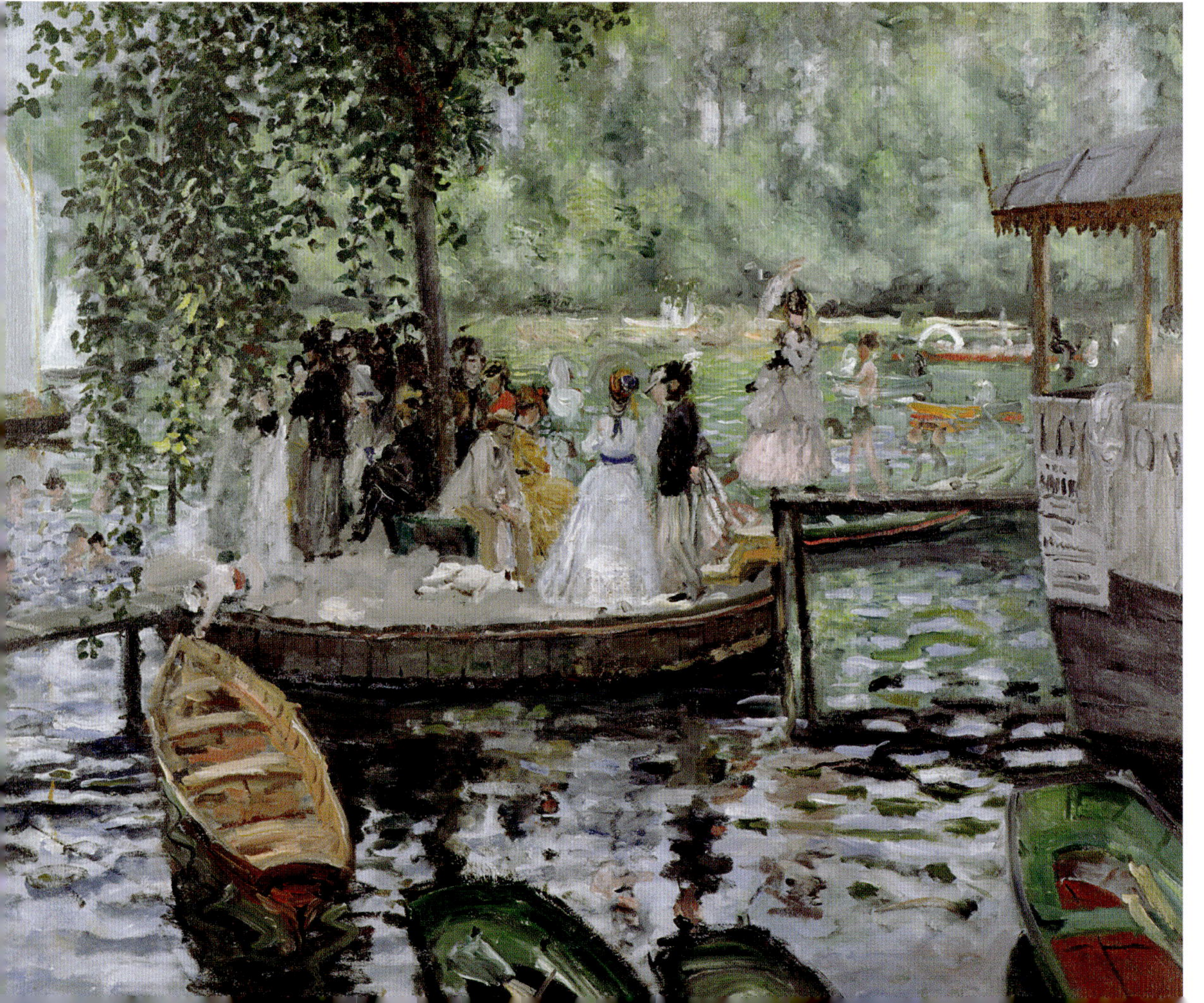

qualities that made Grenouillère modern, popular and fashionable. The pictures they made of it were mostly painted in front of the motif and show the painters exploring the possibility of presenting the same motif from different points of view. The Renoir in Moscow was painted from the bankside looking down the river, while others, like the Monet in the Metropolitan, are painted from further back to the right, looking across the pontoon and floating island to the opposite bank of the river.

While representations of bathers were a common subject in French art, painters generally set their pictures in timeless and universal settings, often with allusions to classical mythology. Few painters chose to depict the new bathing resorts, as such subjects were regarded as incompatible with tradition, though the subject was frequently treated by popular illustrators, whose images were not constrained by Academic principles. A rare exception was Ferdinand Heilbuth's *By the Waterside* (1869–70), depicted from a position similar to that of Renoir and Monet's own images of La Grenouillère. A comparison between Heilbuth's painting and their works highlights the artistic differences between the latter's conventional realism, with its more traditional compositional values and eye for anecdotal detail and Monet and Renoir's freer, more spontaneous and improvised composition. Their pictures emphasize the painter's individualized style and subjective response to the subject, placing more accent upon the sensory qualities of nature, the dappled play of light on the surface of the river and the vibrant impression of the momentary visual effect, rendered in a vivid range of brightly coloured tones. While Heilbuth's picture defined the figures more distinctly than the natural surroundings of the setting, in the more rapidly executed versions of Monet and Renoir, every element is given equal accent and the figures, rendered with broad, blurred touches of pure pigment, almost seem to dissolve into landscape. The modernity of Monet and Renoir's painting rests as much on the innovative qualities of their technique with its broken and summary brushwork, as on the treatment of such a modern subject.

These paintings from La Grenouillère anticipate many of the qualities of later Impressionism with its concern for capturing the fugitive and atmospheric quality of the motif, but are by no means typical of the artists' pictures of the time. On 25 September 1869, Monet wrote to Frédéric Bazille from La Grenouillère: "I have a dream of executing a picture of bathing at La Grenouillère, for which I've made some bad sketches, but it is a dream. Renoir who has been spending two months here also wants to do this picture."

The small scale and broad treatment of these pictures suggests they were preparatory sketches for a large-scale work on the subject for the Salon that was never realized. Nevertheless, the significance of these pictures for Monet grew over time and in 1876 he showed one of them at the second Impressionist exhibition.

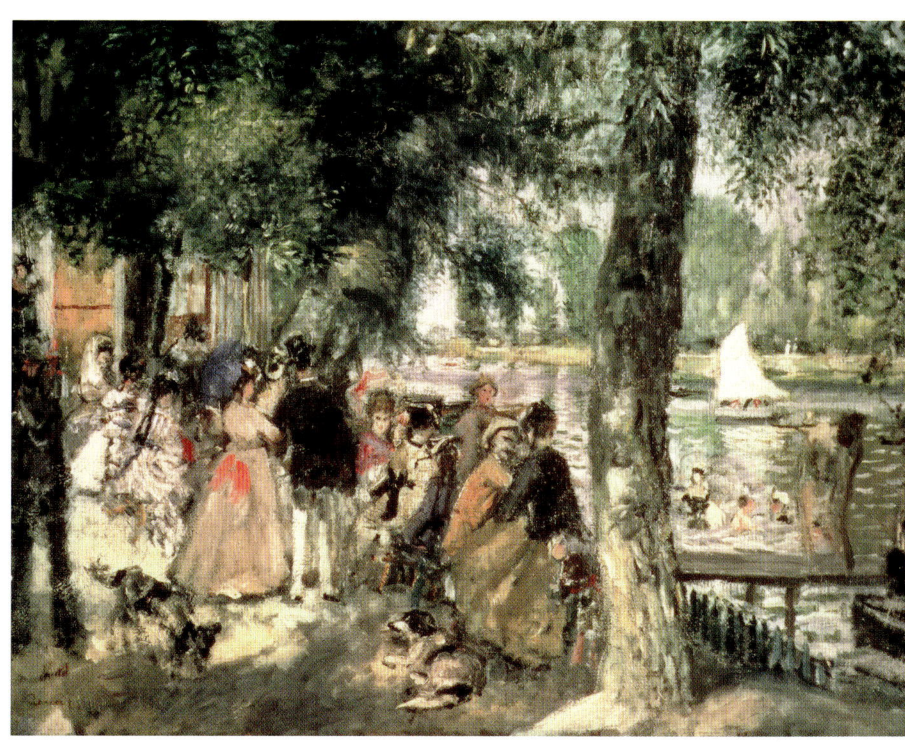

Right *Renoir's pictures reveal his eye for the social customs and manners of his time. His attentiveness to the modern fashions and forms of leisure of the middle classes is evident here in his depiction of a crowd enjoying the pleasures of La Grenouillère. The informal brushwork and improvised composition serve to convey the spontaneity of the scene.*

Below *Despite the similarities between Monet and Renoir's pictures at Grenouillère, there are subtle differences of emphasis. Monet pays more attention to the natural landscape, while Renoir's pictures are more attentive to the social ambience of such bathing resorts. Monet chose a viewpoint that allowed him to place the figures in the far middle ground, thereby giving more breadth to the landscape. By contrast, Renoir included more figures and positioned the crowd closer to the foreground.*

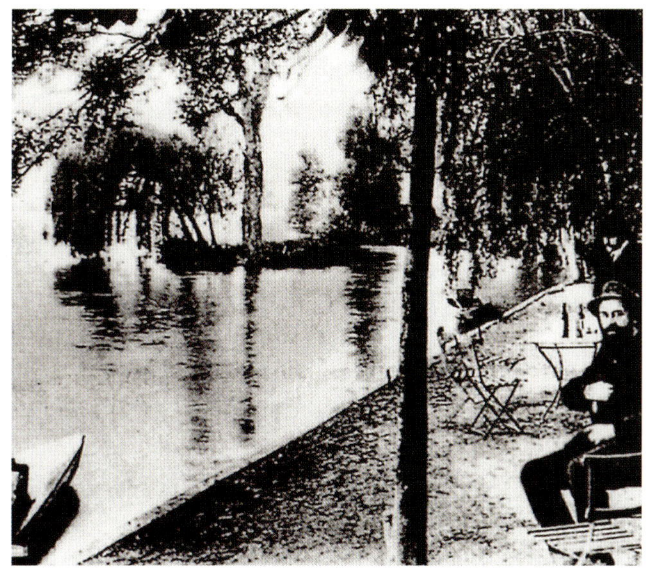

Monet and Renoir

Claude Oscar Monet (1840–1926) and Pierre-Auguste Renoir (1841–1919) were quickly recognized as leading figures of the emerging Impressionist movement. By the mid-1870s, their work was grouped together as representing one major strand of Impressionism, despite the recognition of different artistic aims within their work. While Monet eventually devoted himself exclusively to landscape, Renoir remained preoccupied with the figure. The artists shared a long, close friendship and admiration of each other's work and painted together on a number of occasions, including several painting excursions at Argenteuil. In the late 1880s, both painters enjoyed huge critical success and public popularity.

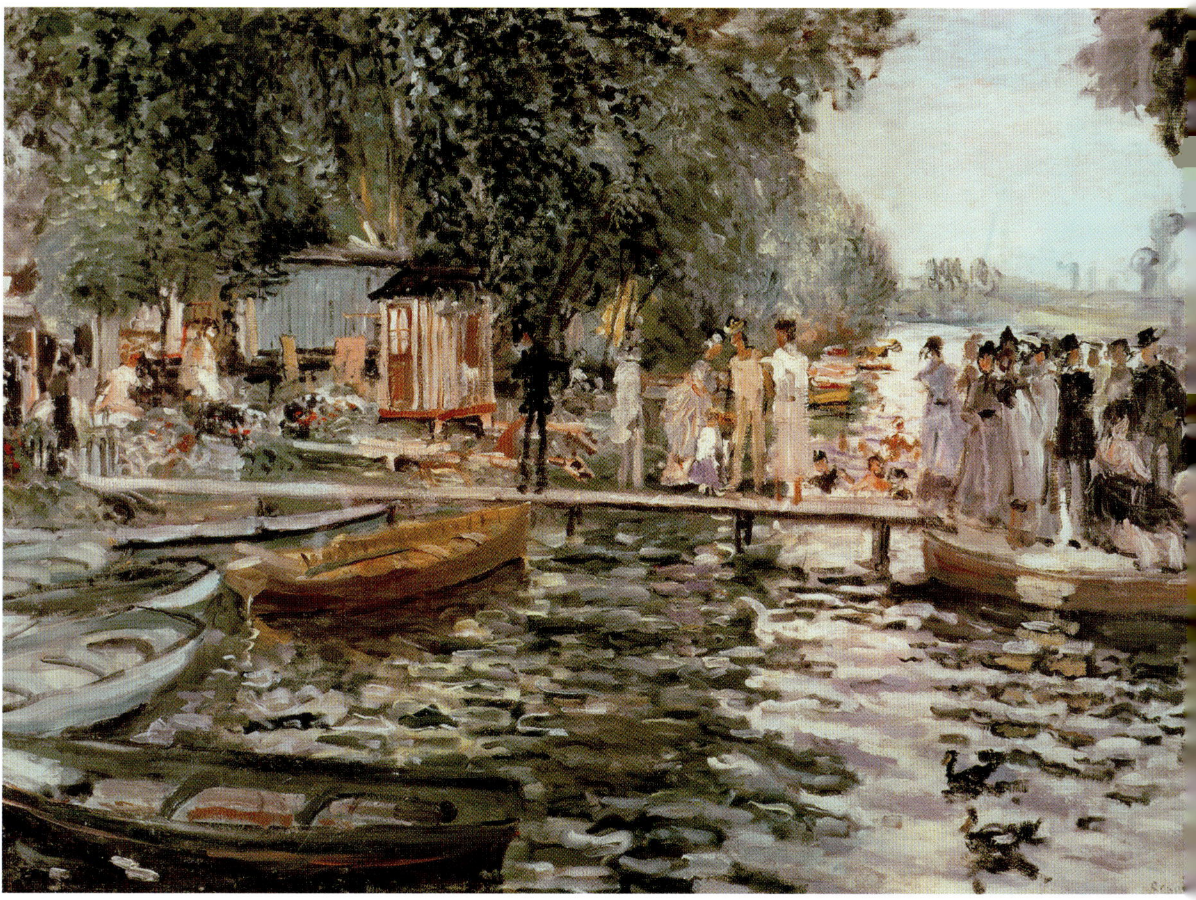

A Day in the Country

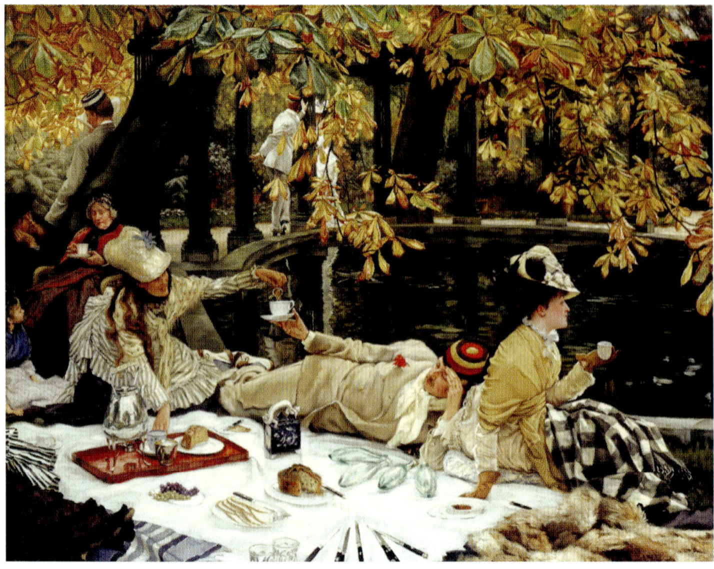

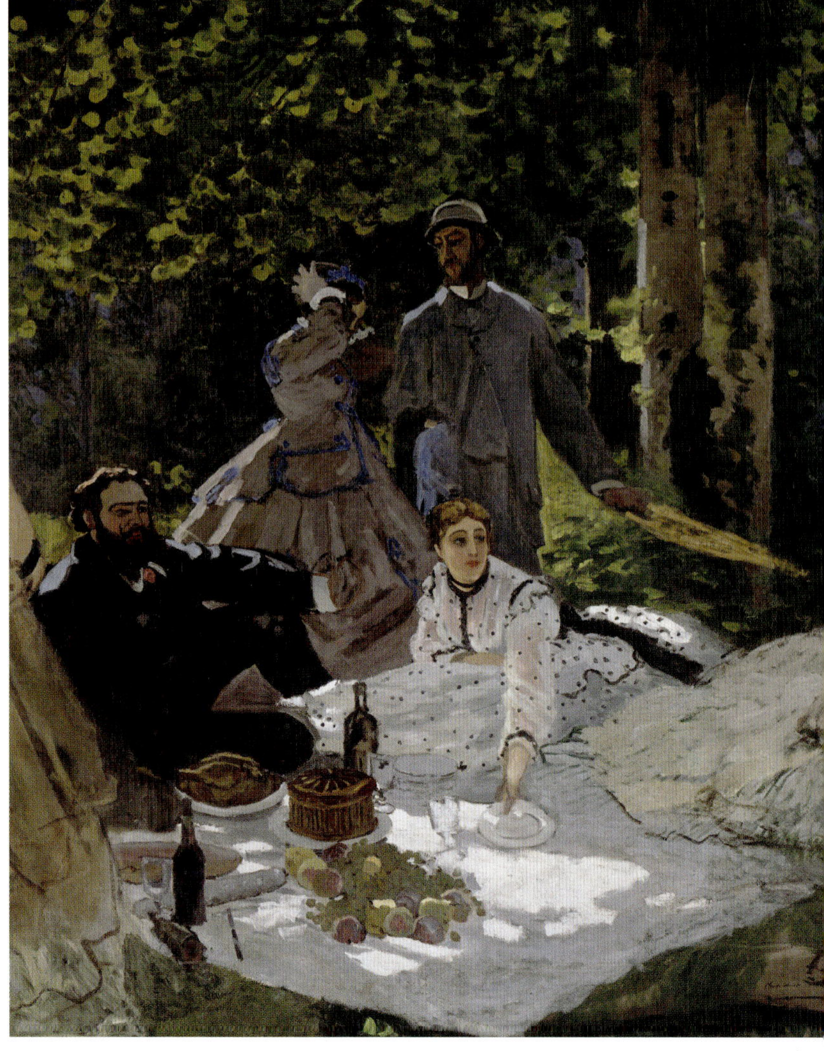

Pictures of picnics in the woods are one of the most enduring images of Impressionism, though the subject was mainly confined to the Impressionists' early pictures. Manet, Monet, Renoir and Cézanne all treated the theme in the 1860s and '70s and their pictures point to the different ways that the subject could be construed. Monet's *Le Déjeuner sur l'Herbe (Luncheon on the Grass)* (1865–66) was his most ambitious picture to date, executed on a life-size scale that he had not worked on before, and was intended to be the centrepiece of his submission to the Salon in 1866. The title, compositional arrangement of the figures and the loose, painterly treatment of the picture all alluded to Manet's treatment of the theme exhibited at the Salon des Refusés two years before, although Monet's picture was almost five times larger and studiously avoided the most controversial feature of Manet's picture, the inclusion of a naked woman sitting beside the two male students. Instead, Monet represents the idyllic pleasures of an outing to the countryside.

The picture shows a group of well dressed Parisians on a day trip to the forest of Fontainbleau, the site of the artistic colony of the Barbizon painters, made famous by Jean Jacques Rousseau's *Revelations of a Solitary Walker*. Unlike the wooded landscapes of the Barbizon artists, populated by indigenous shepherds and woodcutters, Monet depicts the new forms of leisure that the region was attracting. The area was a popular place for excursions and in the process of being turned into a large park with transport, drink and food services. The new railway network in France put such places within easy reach and encouraged the vogue for day trips to the country, a relatively new aspect of

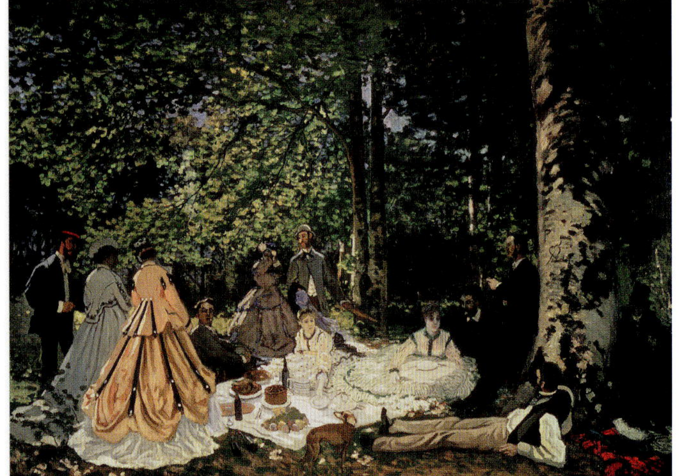

Le Déjeuner sur l'Herbe

Monet's *Le Déjeuner sur l'Herbe* is one of the great aborted masterpieces of early Impressionist painting. Unable to afford models, Monet had his friend Bazille and his future wife Camille Doncieux pose for the picture; the lanky Bazille, appears four times in the surviving oil sketch. Monet's failure successfully to realize his *Le Déjeuner sur l'Herbe* points to the initial difficulties the Impressionists had in translating the intimacy and spontaneity of their sketch-like technique onto a mural scale. Frustrated by his inability to make sufficient progress on the painting, he eventually divided it into panels, of which only two fragments survive.

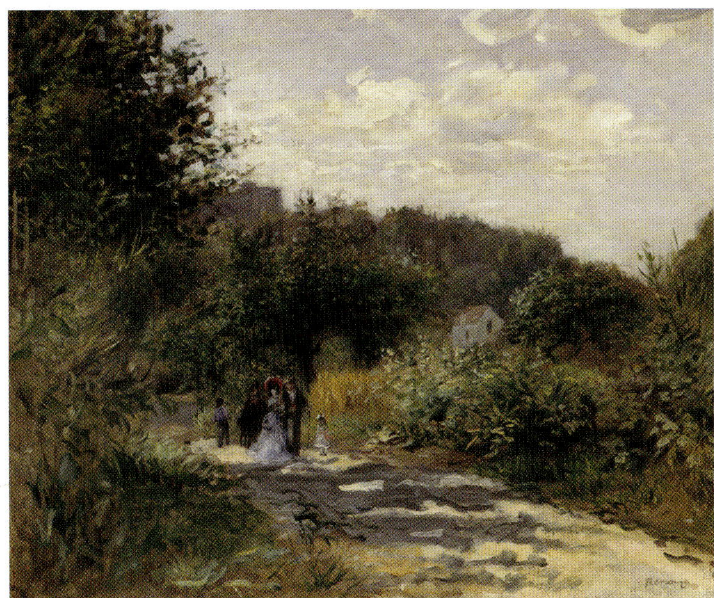

middle-class patterns of leisure. Working on such a large scale – the picture measures nearly 6 metres (19.5 feet) wide – posed considerable technical problems for Monet and he eventually abandoned the picture.

The discreet detail of a heart and arrow inscribed onto the silvery bark of the foreground tree along with the initial "P", alludes to the imagery of amorous rendezvous commonly associated with the representations of the forest and the woods. This was a subject that other Impressionists treated more overtly in this period. Renoir frequently chose the association of the forest with love and desire as his theme. Pictures like *Outing in a Rowboat* (1866) or *The Promenade* (1870) alluded to the secluded islands or isolated spots where groups of revellers or courting couples ventured in search of solitude. The imagery of amorous excursions in the woods evoked the traditional imagery of the *fêtes gallantes* and "isle of love", immortalized in the work of eighteenth-century rococo painters and given its modern counterpart in contemporary literature.

Cézanne treated the theme on a number of occasions in the 1870s, also making clear reference to Manet's seminal picture, though interpreting it in quite different ways. Unlike Monet's idyllic imagery, these paintings present a more brooding, darker treatment. In *Pastoral* (1870), as in his *A Modern Olympia* executed a few years later, Cézanne includes himself as a protagonist, depicted deep in contemplation by the riverbank. The three Rubensesque nudes beside him are figments of his imagination, external manifestations of his inner thoughts and the turbulent landscape takes on a visionary aspect that seems to allude to the deep seated conflicts within the artist's psyche. The landscape beyond the river is made over into a reflection of the glass and bottle of alcohol that rests beside him, suggesting the theme of intoxicated or hallucinatory visions that preoccupied Cézanne at the time.

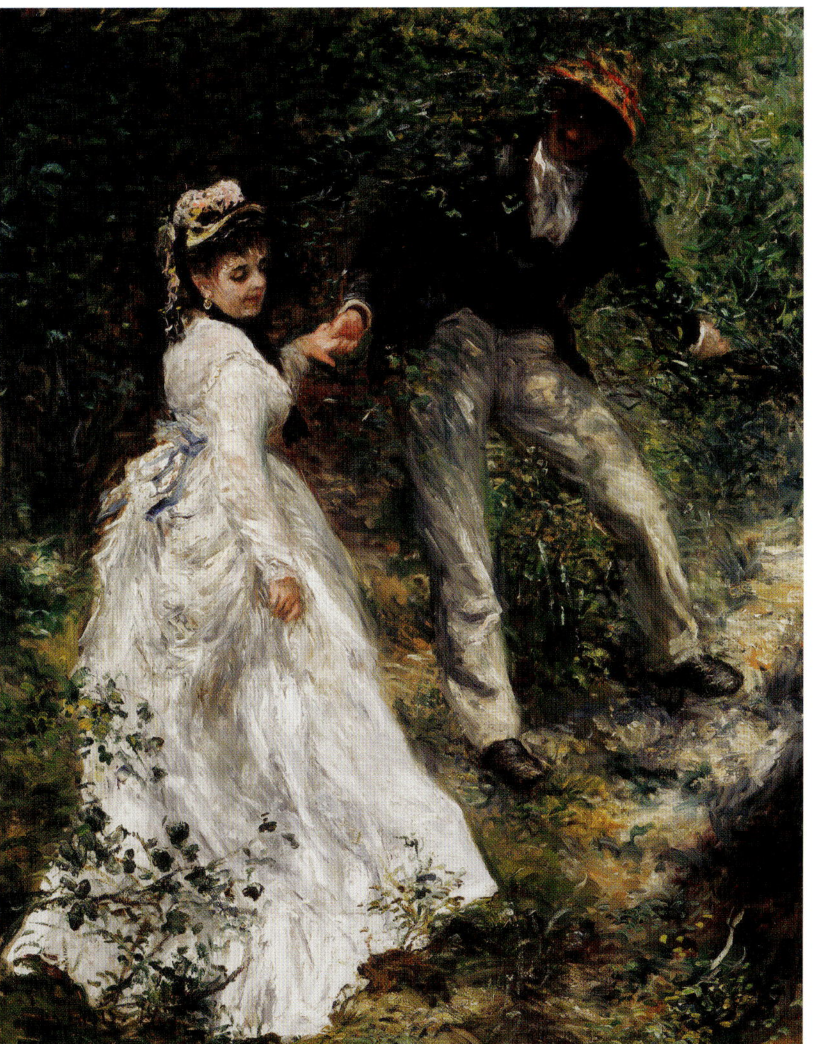

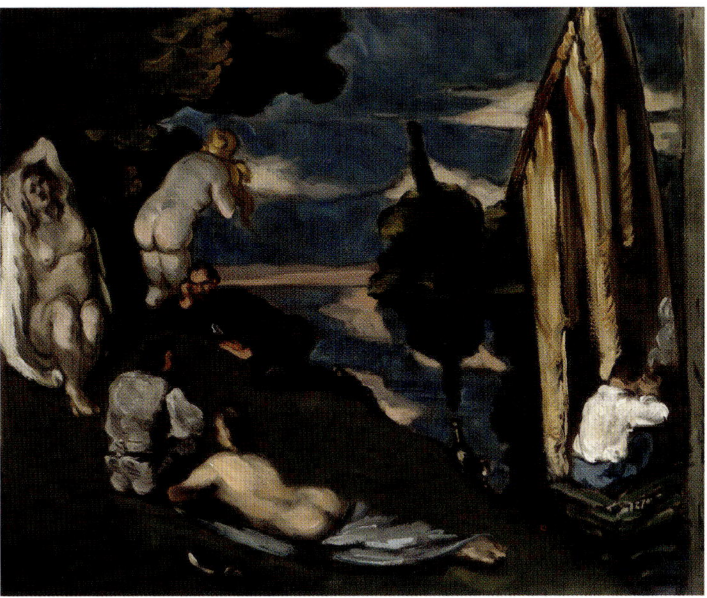

Left *Cézanne's* Pastoral *(1870–72) is one of a series of pictures that features the artist as the protagonist. He depicts himself brooding at the bankside in a strange dream-like landscape setting. The picture owes much to Manet's* Le Déjeuner sur l'Herbe, *on which Cézanne made several variations in the 1870s. But it also owes something to Fantin-Latour's* Tannhäuser, *which was shown at the Salon of 1864. Both artists were great admirers of Wagner.*

The Franco–Prussian War

On 18 July 1870, Napoleon III declared war with Prussia in a fateful decision that was to have major consequences for France. Anticipating a swift victory, the French army was humiliatingly defeated in a matter of months. Paris was besieged and occupied, and Napoleon III sent into exile in London. The reaction in Paris against the newly founded Republic's surrender to Prussia led to the Commune, whose bloody suppression resulted in casualties on the scale of the first French revolution. The reverberations of these catastrophic events were to continue well into the twentieth century.

The war dispersed the Batignolles group of Manet and his followers. On 10 August 1870, Bazille enlisted in the Zouaves regiment and was tragically killed in action four months later. Renoir joined the cavalry and was stationed in Tarbes. Manet was a staff officer in the National Guard. As the Prussian army advanced on Paris, Monet, Pissarro and Sisley, who was born in Paris but of English parents, fled France and took refuge in London, where Daubigny, Fantin-Latour and Bonvin also sought shelter. It was in London that the Impressionists first came into contact with the dealer Paul Durand-Ruel, who had also fled to the capital and established a gallery on New Bond Street. Afterwards, he was to become an enthusiastic dealer in Impressionist paintings, showing their work in Paris, London and later America. While in London, Monet painted a number of views of the Thames looking across to the Houses of Parliament. Pissarro produced a number of landscapes of Norwood in south-west London where he had settled. Both painters were deeply impressed by the landscapes

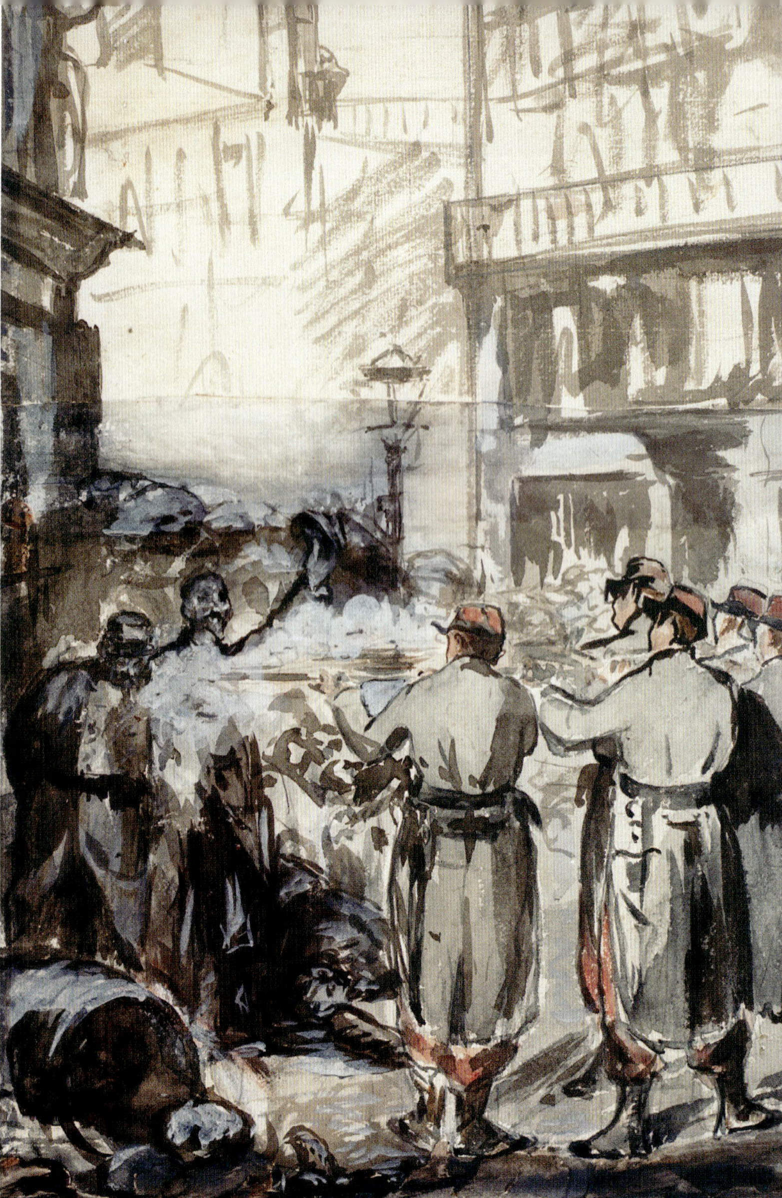

of Turner and Constable that they encountered during their brief stay.

The time they spent in London left a lasting impression on them and all three painters were to make subsequent visits to the capital. Monet made three or four visits to London during 1899–1904, staying at the Savoy Hotel. While there, he revisited his motifs along the Thames river in a series of evocative paintings that picture the Houses of Parliament shrouded in fog. Pissarro also returned to London during this period, painting a number of scenic views of Charing Cross Bridge, Kensington Gardens, Hyde Park and Hampton Court, a favoured motif of Sisley who had painted a series of views of it in 1874. Sisley, whose family fortune was ruined by the war and who was dogged by poverty afterwards, returned to Britain on several occasions, spending several months in Wales in 1897 and working on the Isle of Wight, a favoured resort of Berthe Morisot and her family, in 1881.

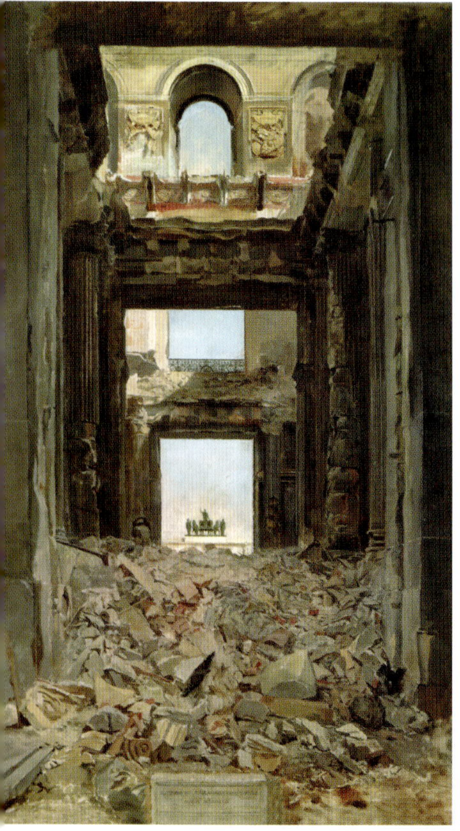

Above *Ernest Meissonier's* The Ruins of the Tuileries Palace *(1871) depicts the devastation to the Salle des Maréchaux during the Commune. The inscription in the central foreground refers to Napoleon Bonaparte's famous victories at the battles of Marengo and Austerlitz, while in the far background the quadriga of the Arc de Triomphe du Carrousel can be seen. It rises above the ruins as a potent symbol of regeneration.*

Top right *Manet's watercolour and gouache sketch,* The Barricade *(1871) depicts summary executions of Communards by the French artillery of the National Guard. The conception of the picture looks back to Goya's* Third of May 1808 *(1814), which Manet had already used as a source for his* Execution of Maximilian *(1867).*

Opposite bottom left *During the Franco–Prussian war, Cézanne went into hiding at L'Estaque in his native Provence. It was while he was there that landscape began to emerge as an important feature of his painting. This tumultuous, stormy landscape perhaps alludes to the dark times France was experiencing.*

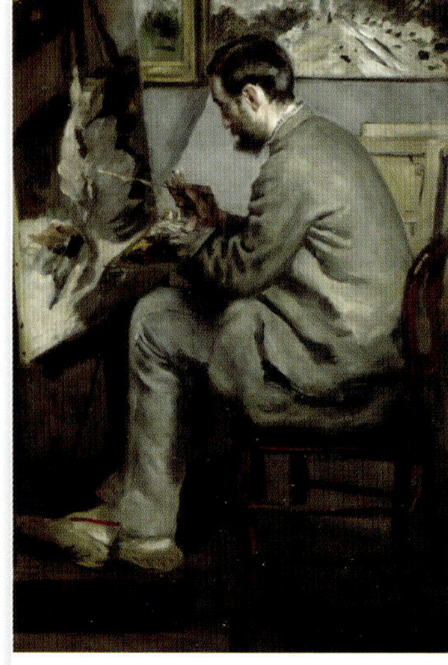

Frédéric Bazille
(1841–70)

Bazille was one of the leading figures of early Impressionism but was killed during the Franco–Prussian War in a skirmish at Beaune-la-Ronde on 18 November 1870. Bazille originally came to Paris to study medicine but joined the studio of Charles Gleyre where he met Renoir and Monet. He went on several painting trips with Monet to Chailly and Honfleur and shared a studio with him between 1865 and 1866. The following year, he rented a studio in the rue Visconti, near the Ecole des beaux-arts with Renoir, who shared his enthusiasm for Delacroix and Wagner.

Although Cézanne was conscripted, his father bought a substitute enabling him to avoid fighting in the war. He spent the war in L'Estaque, where, separated from his colleagues and denied the opportunity to study at the Louvre, he began to paint a series of landscapes. Initially, these show his early penchant for dramatic scenes. *Snow at L'Estaque* (1870) pictures a landscape that seems perched on the edge of dissolution, an intimation perhaps of impending disaster. However, his subsequent views of L'Estaque, painted *en plein air*, reveal the more patient and responsive attitude to nature found in the landscapes of the second half of the decade.

The immediate years following the Franco–Prussian war led to a reactionary backlash. France was required to cede Alsace and Lorraine to the Prussians and pay a huge indemnity that resulted in a climate of severe economic and cultural constraint. In the arts, the Third Republic fostered a return to traditional values and a reaction against the landscape subjects favoured by the Impressionists, only later liberalizing its stance at the end of the decade.

Right *During his exile, Pissarro settled in Norwood, then a relatively undeveloped suburb of south London. His pictures of the town are reminiscent of his portrayals of his family home in Pontoise, Pissarro choosing motifs that emphasize the quiet everyday life of the town.*

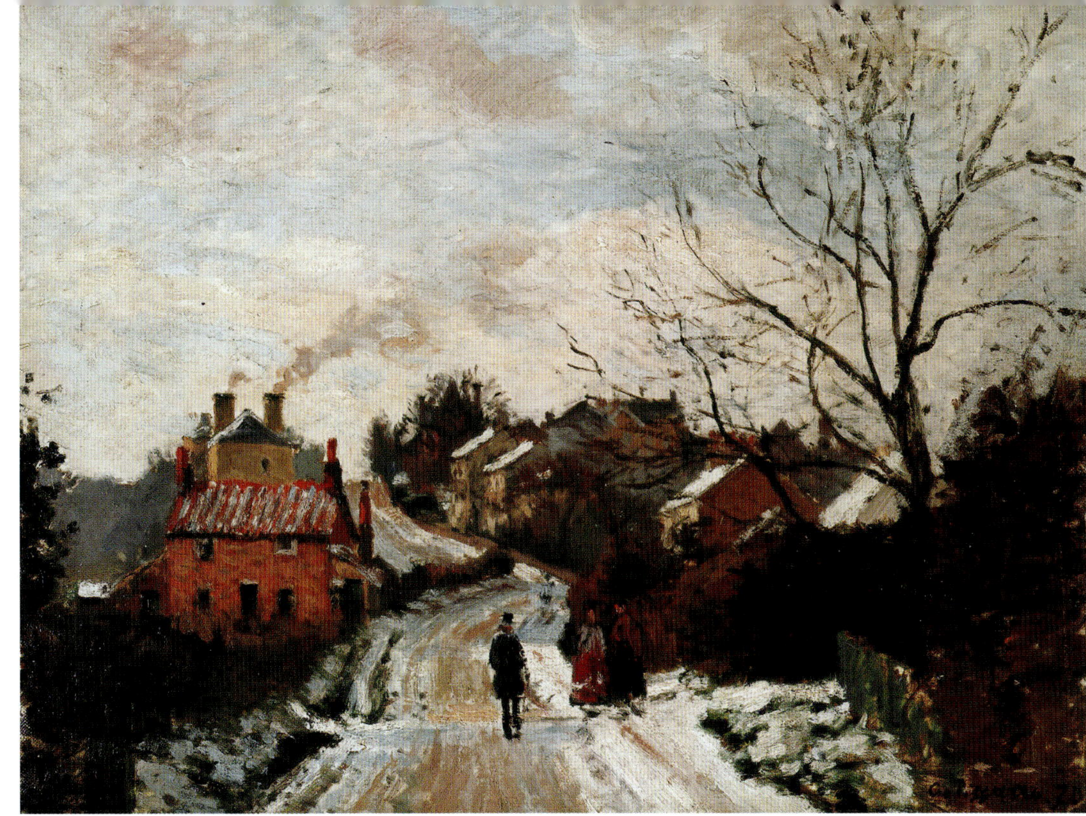

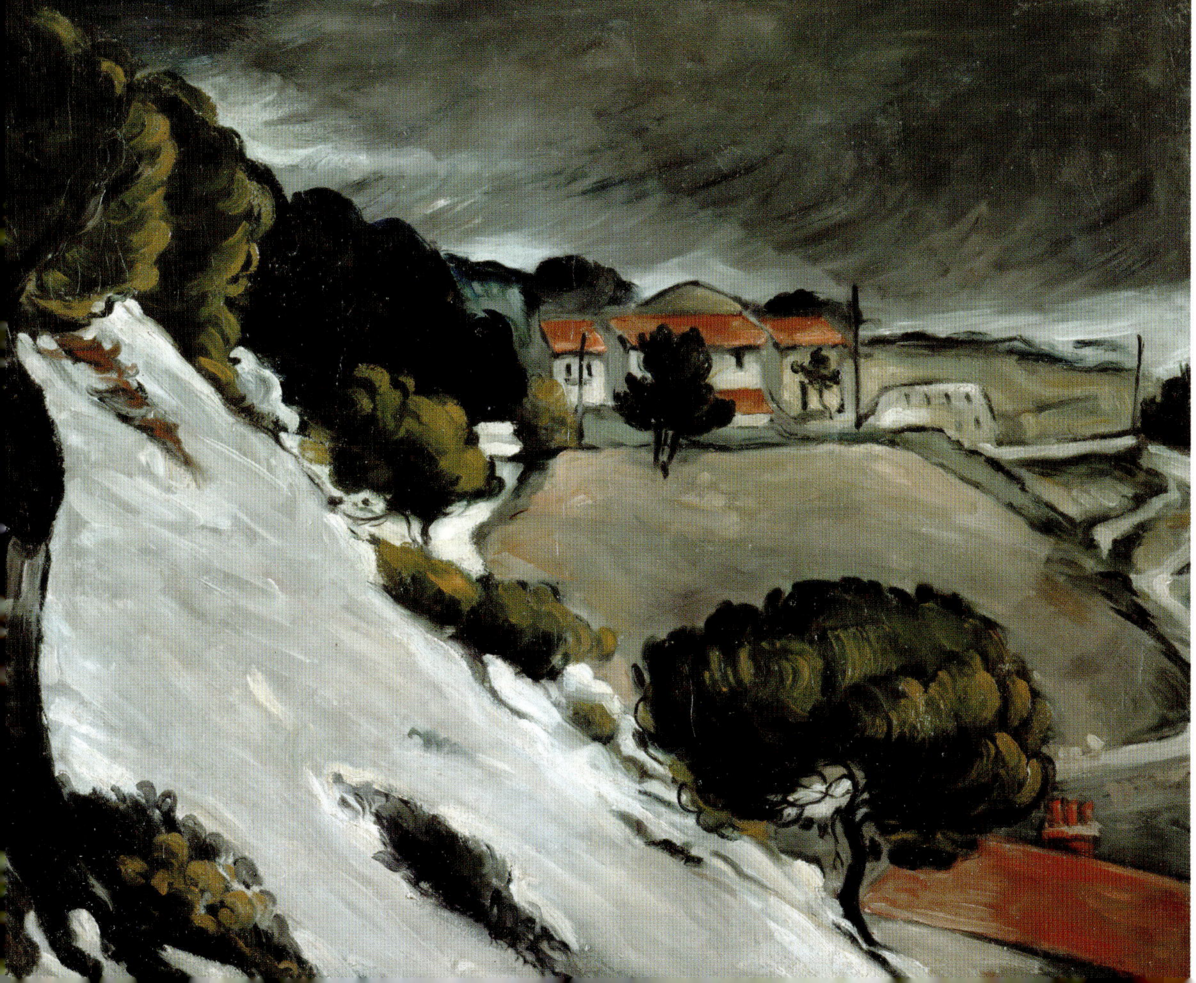

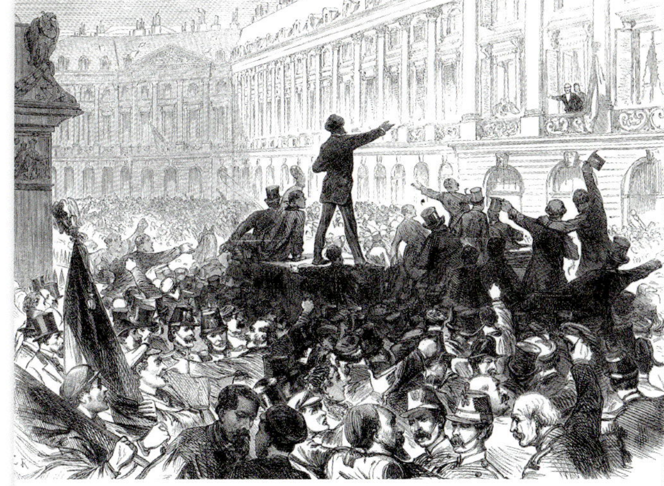

The Commune

On 18 March 1871, a popular revolution in Paris against the military measures imposed by the new republican government led to the Commune. The revolutionary artist Gustave Courbet was elected as a representative of the people and president of the General Assembly of Artists. The bloody suppression of the short-lived Commune by French troops a few months later drenched the capital in blood, leaving a lingering wound in the French national psyche. Paris remained under martial law for the next five years. The association of Courbet with the destruction of the Vendôme column resulted in his imprisonment. He was forced personally to pay for its restoration and afterwards made his way to Switzerland where he died in 1877.

The French Landscape in the 1870s

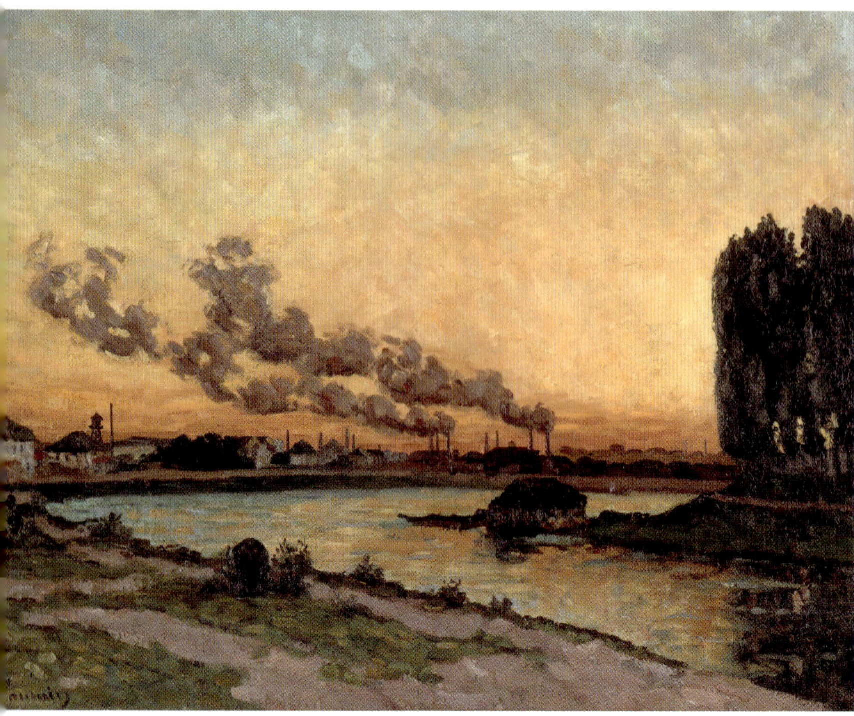

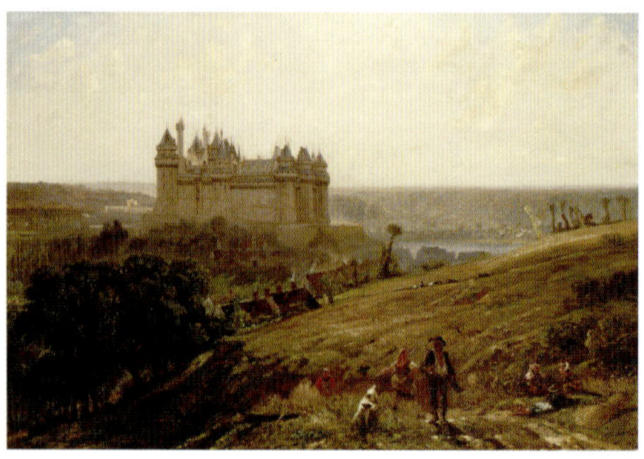

Left *Armand Guillaumin made an important contribution to the development of Impressionism. His uncompromising adoption of heavily industrialized motifs, as in* Setting Sun at Ivry *(c. 1869), pioneered landscape subjects that were to be central to Impressionism in the 1870s, but which were controversial at the time.*

Above *Paul Huet's* The Château of Pierrefonds Restored *(1866) conforms to traditional notions of the well chosen motif, structuring his landscape around a building of historical interest. Huet's traditional technique creates clear transitions from foreground to background and marshals the use of blonde light to convey the majestic monumentality of the Château and its setting.*

Right *Though Pissarro mostly focused on the traditional aspects of the countryside, his paintings sometimes uncompromisingly represented the changes to the landscape wrought by modernization. In* Factory near Pontoise *(1873), which is compositionally unusual for Pissarro in its frontal viewpoint, he has somewhat harmonized the disjunction between the man-made and natural aspects of the landscape. The factory chimneys are echoed in the forms of the adjacent trees on the right hand side, while the smoke ushering from them is integrated into the vigorously painted clouds. In order to achieve this effect, Pissarro altered the scale and position of the trees and factory roofs and sheds.*

the subjective response of the painter's way of painting them. Daubigny's choice of subjects radically challenged conventional ideas of what was a legitimate motif. This aspect of his painting, combined with his unorthodox, sketchy technique led Louis Lagrange to characterize him as the leader of the "school of the impression" at the Salon of 1865. The example of Daubigny was crucial to the development of Impressionist landscape painting in the 1860s and '70s, although the painters avoided the strong suggestion of mood in his landscapes and extended these motifs to ultra-modern subjects that dealt with the interface of city and country. Armand

At the beginning of the nineteenth century, landscape held a low position in French painting. However, by the end of the century, it was regarded as one of the most vital aspects of the nation's art. The French tradition of landscape painting was dominated by the Italianate pictures of Poussin and Claude Lorrain and, despite the onset of realism and naturalism, contemporary painters were judged against this standard. Academic landscape paintings presented clearly ordered and detailed landscape motifs, with topographical or architectural points of interest that offered the viewer the illusion of imaginatively being transported into a rural space, appealing to common conventions of visual representation shared by artists and their audience. Their compositions closely corresponded to traditional criteria of what constituted a well chosen and harmoniously balanced motif, focusing on those aspects of the landscape that their audience would regard as of historical interest or poetic significance.

By the 1830s, an alternative paradigm of landscape painting had emerged in the work of the Barbizon painters, whose choice of motif and way of treating them differed considerably from traditional models. During the 1860s, Daubigny rejected the conventions of the classical model of landscape as well as the more naturalistic alternative of the Dutch tradition, in favour of painting discreet fragments of nature, that are attentive to representing light and atmosphere and call attention to

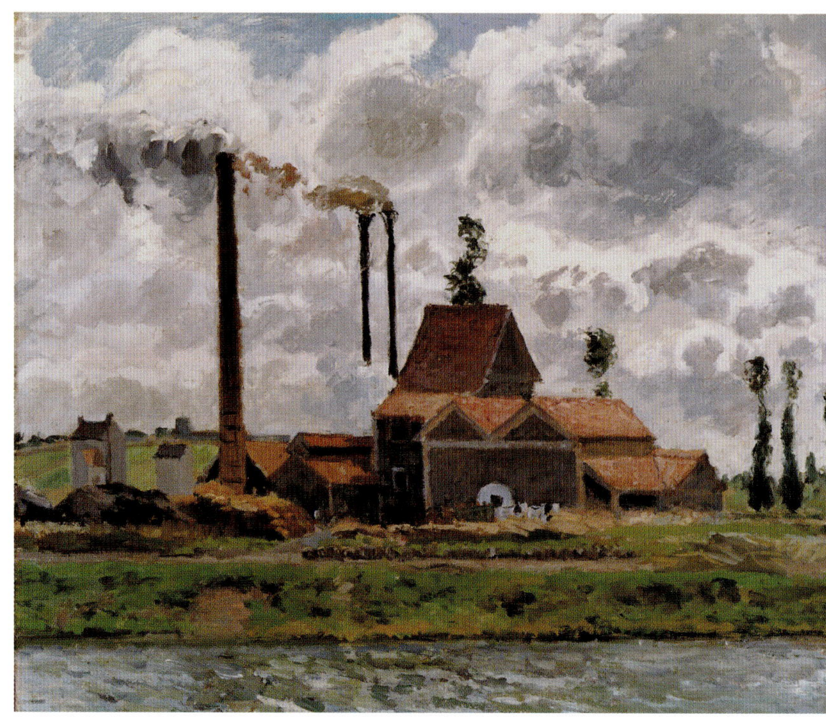

Guillaumin's *Setting Sun at Ivry* (c. 1869) and Camille Pissarro's *Factories, Saint-Ouen l'Aumône* (1873) show industrial landscape motifs in an uncompromising fashion, selecting precisely the kind of "unprepossessing" subjects that were regarded as entirely devoid of poetic content. Similar motifs were also favoured by Monet, who often referred to the new railway network that gave painters the opportunity to travel to and paint the diverse landscape regions of France.

Though the informality of Impressionist landscape painting gained increasing legitimacy as the century wore on, the painters continued to draw criticism from conservative critics who saw the abandonment of poetic themes and historically redolent motifs as symptoms of a decline of traditional values. This was particularly so in the early 1870s when the Republic vainly sought to foster a return to traditional values in painting. The "undiscerning" and "indiscriminate" presentation of nature of Impressionist motifs opened their work to the charge of having misrepresented the truth of nature and failing to grasp the raison d'être of landscape painting. The empirical basis of Impressionism with its emphasis on visual appearances implicitly critiqued the idealist notions that underpinned the notion of *la belle nature*. Similarly, the technical means of Impressionism undermined the basis of Academic principles of composition. Monet's radiant *Autumn Effect at Argenteuil* (1873), painted from the vantage point of the studio boat he had built in the 1870s, gives full force to the ambiguities of perception, in the way the shadows and the light reflecting off the surface of the river occlude any clear distinction between shoreline and river. While such paintings remained true to visual effects found in nature, they were criticized as lacking the clarity, perspective and orderly presentation of nature demanded from academic critics.

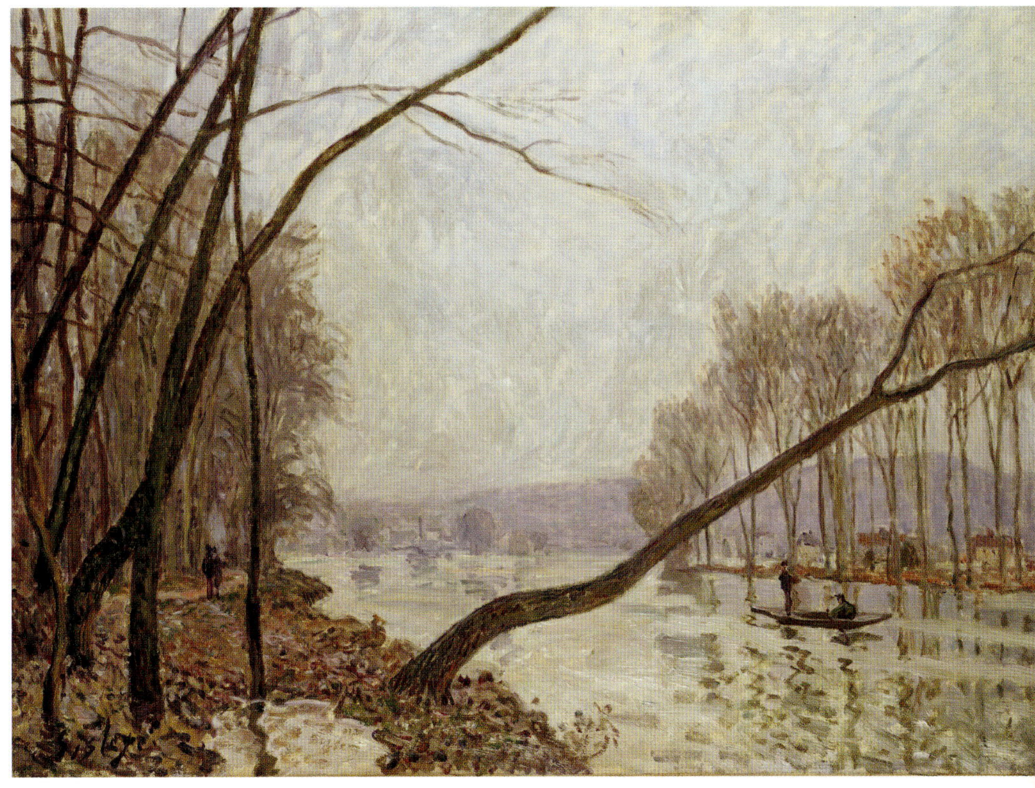

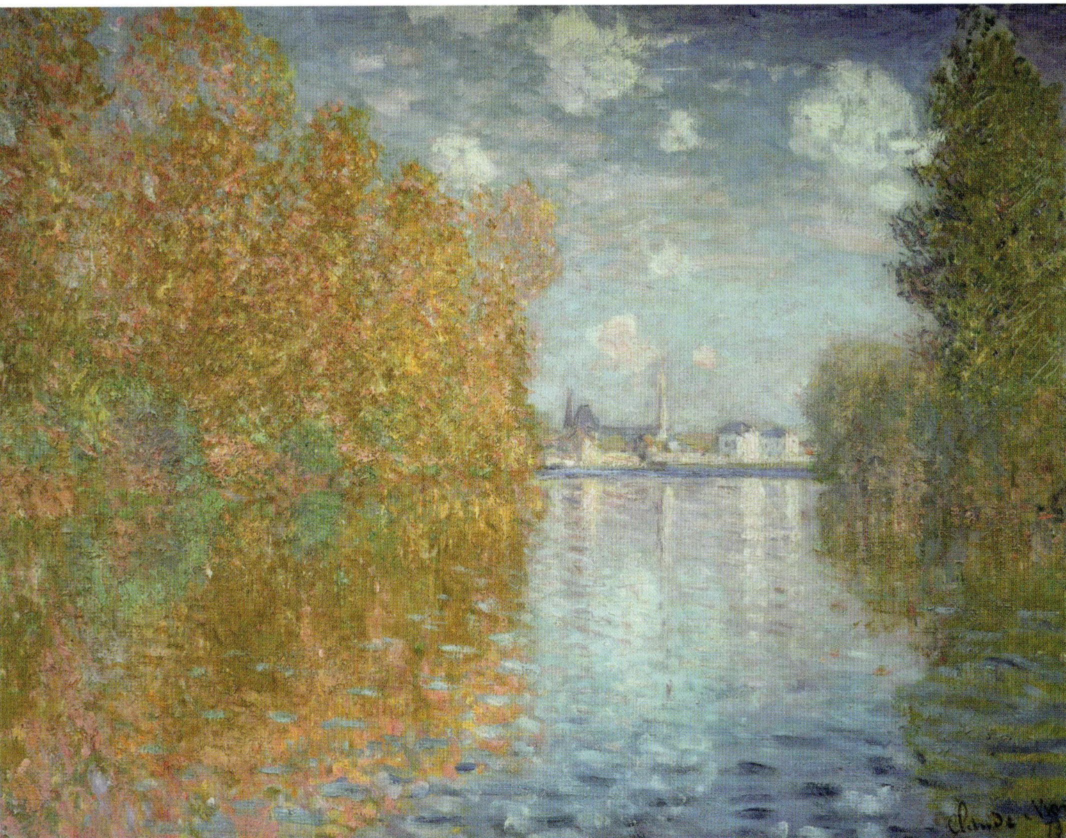

Above The Banks of the Seine in Autumn *(1876)* shows Sisley's eye for the expressive possibilities of quiet, understated motifs. His picture economically captures the misty atmosphere of an autumn day and the rippling reflections of light on the river. It also shows the Impressionist's fascination with the linear patterns of trees in their compositions.

Left *Monet's* Autumn Effect at Argenteuil *(1873) shows Monet intensifying the primary colour schemes of his palette and using his broken brushwork to suggest the radiant effect of light on the landscape and rippling reflections of the surface of the river. Monet painted the picture from his studio boat.*

Armand Guillaumin
1841–1927

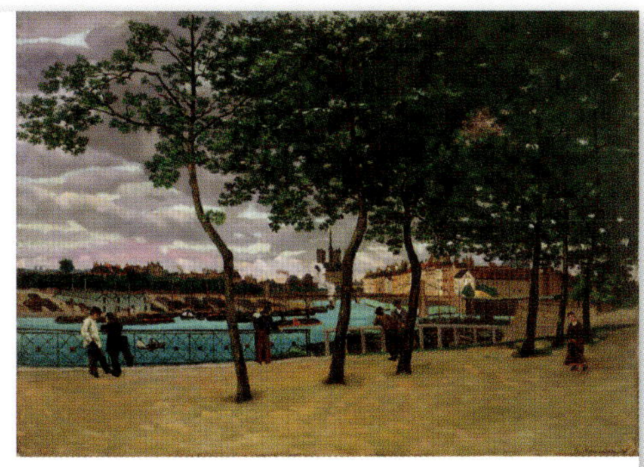

Guillaumin is one of the most underrated and overlooked of the Impressionists. He met Pissarro and Cézanne at the Académie Suisse in 1861 and painted with them at Pontoise and Auvers-sur-Oise. Cézanne was much impressed by Guillaumin's vigorous brushwork and strong colour, which subsequently influenced Matisse and the Fauves. He copied his *Seine at Paris* (1871), which he also included in the background of a self-portrait he painted in 1875 and his *Seine at Bercy* (1876–78). Guillaumin exhibited at most of the Impressionist exhibitions and befriended Vincent van Gogh whose work shows affinities with his own later style.

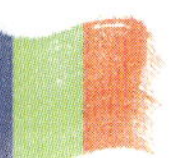

The Imagery of the Suburbs

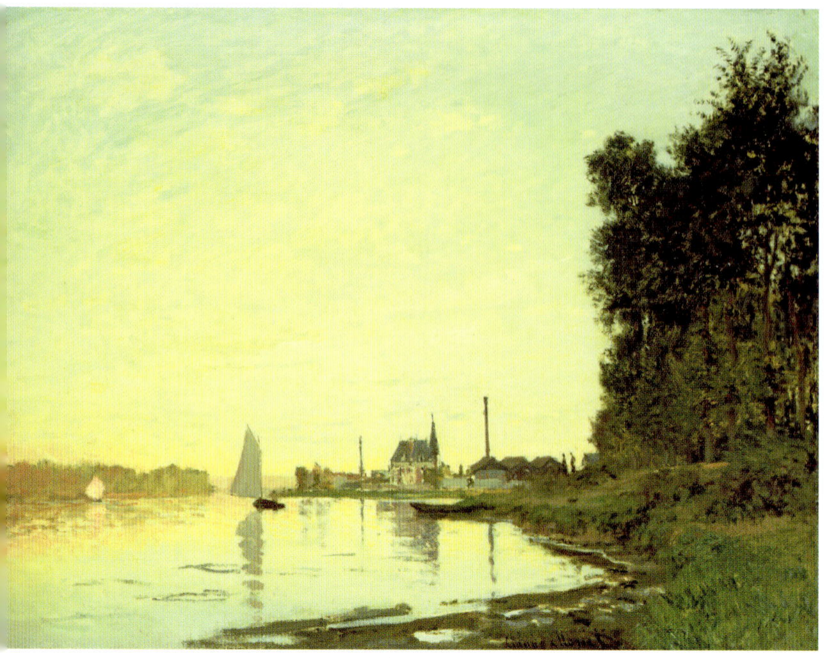

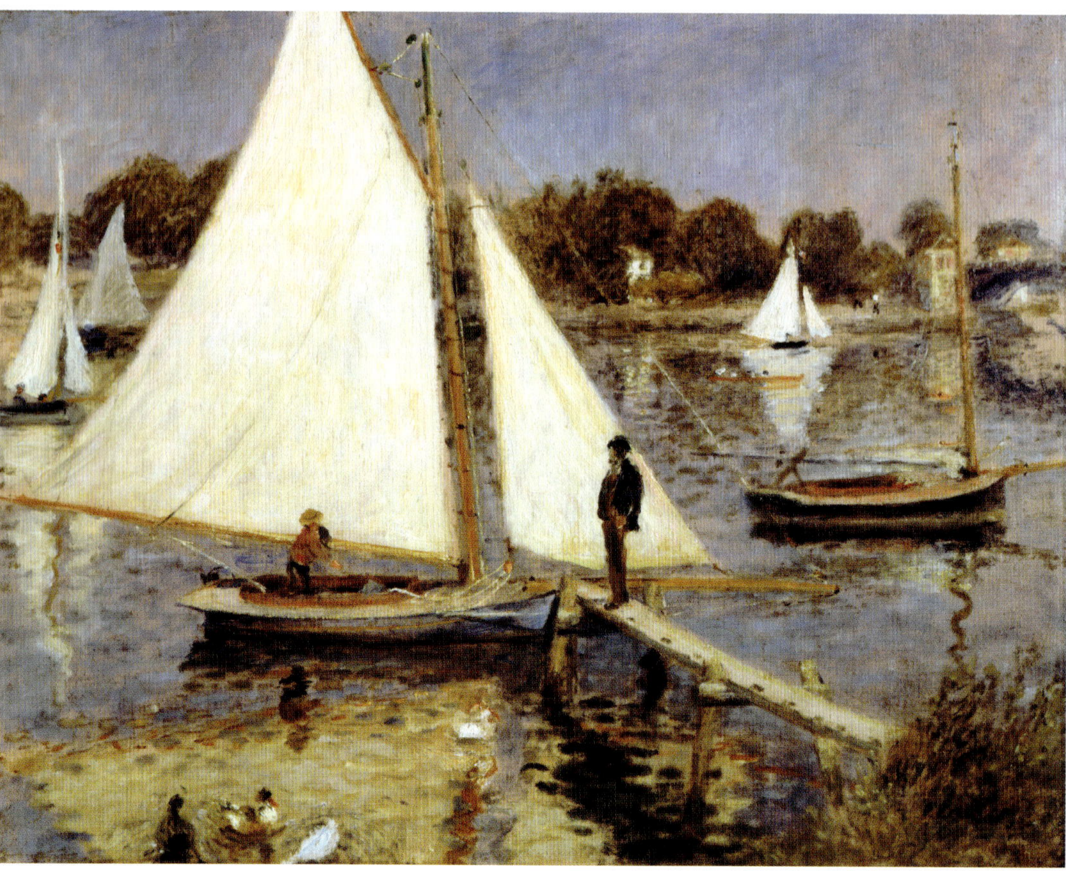

One of the key sites of Impressionist landscape painting in the 1870s was the Parisian suburbs. These were places undergoing enormous change in a short period of time as the process of modernization spread from Paris to the countryside. As the borders of new Paris began to swell, places like Asnières, Bougival, Chatou and Argenteuil saw large influxes of new inhabitants and commercial enterprise. Some of these places were little more than wastelands dominated by the heavy industry lured out to the city's edges by cheap rents; others became scenic resorts, made accessible for day tripping by the expansion of the railway network. Most, like Argenteuil, were a mixture of the two, places where aspects of the traditional rural life and urban modernity co-existed.

Located some 30 minutes by train from the Gare Saint Lazare, Argenteuil was a case in point. Positioned where the mouth of the Seine widens, it was an ideal location for pleasure-boating and amateur canoeists, or for simply promenading along the waterside at the weekend. By the 1870s, the once small village had become one of the most popular and attractive recreational landmarks for Parisians, with an array of flamboyant entertainments – fêtes, regattas, restaurants and cafés. Argenteuil was a popular motif for Impressionists, one that expressed their commitment to most modern landscape subjects. Monet made some 150 views of it during the seven years he lived there from 1871 to 1878. He was often joined by Renoir who made several paintings of the boating at Argenteuil and portrayed Monet and his family in their garden. Sisley and Manet were also among its visitors.

Day-trips from Paris

Day-tripping to the countryside in the immediate vicinity of Paris was a favourite subject of satirists and cartoonists who parodied the "false nature" of the surburbs and its visitors' "pretensions". The fiction was that Paris was far away, yet places like Argenteuil were replete with the signs of Paris: smoking factory chimneys, restaurants, fêtes, railway lines, steamboats and industrial refuse. For the cartoonist, the most overt sign of Paris was the visitors themselves, whose presence stimulated the burgeoning commercial industry of regattas, cafés and restaurants that catered to such tourism and its urban forms of social entertainment.

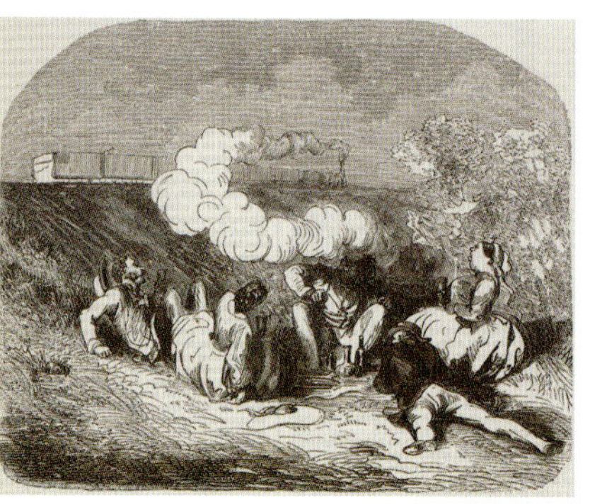

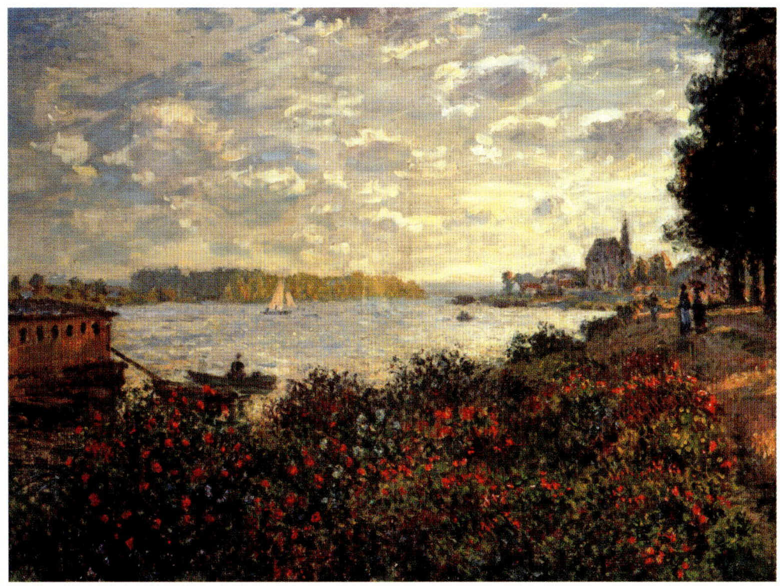

The pictures dating from the first three years of his time at Argenteuil show Monet vitally alive to the many subjects its landscape offered him. In a series of boldly experimental works, he painted the pleasures of Argenteuil, with its yachts, canoes, boathouses and villas for rent, and its promenading couples and families picnicking. Monet dominantly painted Argenteuil as a place in which modernity and nature co-existed harmoniously. Many of his earliest pictures are bold portrayals of the most modern features of the locality – its new railway bridge, the factory chimneys and the yachts and steamboats traversing the river, but the majority of his paintings depict the boat basin flanking the highway bridge and the area close to the Ile Marante, and provide a selective view of the modernization of Argenteuil, minimizing the signs of industrialization.

After 1875, Monet's ambivalence about modernization became evident and he restricted his imagery to views of his garden, the village streets and nearby fields and the boats on the river, only occasionally acknowledging the presence of industry in some unresolved pictures towards the end of his stay. Most of his views of the river are from the north bank looking away from the industrialized quarter in order to emphasize the painter's visual pleasure in viewing nature. Where figures appear, they are kept at a distance, in order to reduce the social meanings of the landscape. By contrast, Manet's *The Boaters, Argenteuil* (1876) focuses on the visitors rather than the landscape. The tone of the picture is subdued and a mood of uncertainty prevails, as if the painter were questioning the pleasures such places provided their visitors with. The blank expression of Manet's figures, combined with the mood of hesitancy provoked the critic Chaumelin to complain that Manet had "chosen the grossest types – an amorous marine – and a trollop seated by his side, decked out in horrible finery and looking horribly sullen". Underlying Manet's painting and Chaumelin's commentary is the issue of the aspirations of the lower middle classes to the pleasures that were once the sole preserve of the upper classes. The contrast of Monet's and Manet's paintings of Argenteuil reflects the difference between the critical vision of modern society in the paintings of Manet, Degas and Pissarro and the visual pleasure and the aestheticism of the landscape of Monet.

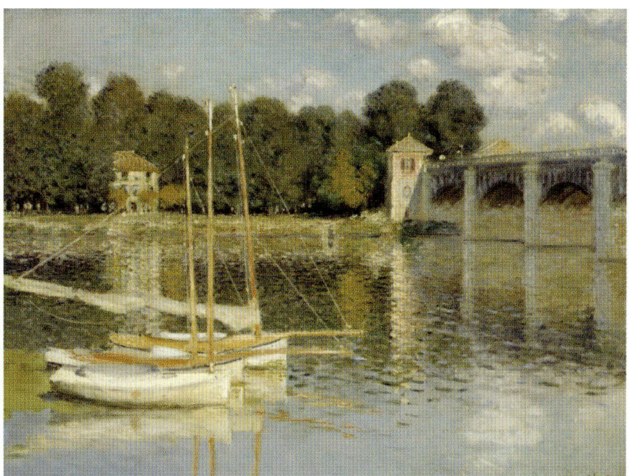

Argenteuil

The railway bridge at Argenteuil features in a number of Monet's early pictures of the region. Sometimes these show trains arriving, conveying travellers to the locality. The imagery of the train was a symbol of ultra modernity and progress; Monet's depictions of trains crossing the railway bridge are among his boldest works and unusual motifs for landscapists of the time. As a painter who attempted to chart the different regions of France, Monet realized that the railway network was integral to his artistic enterprise, but his attitude towards modernity was an increasingly ambivalent one and he eventually abandoned such imagery.

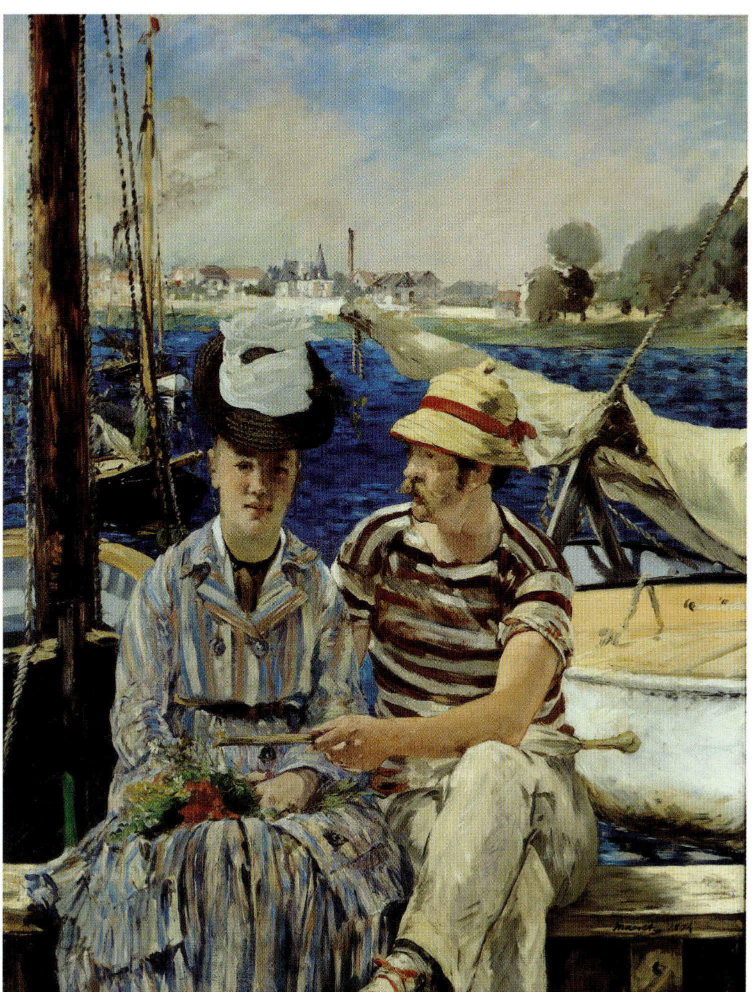

Top left *Possibly Monet's final picture of Argenteuil, Flower-bank at Argenteuil (1877) is one of several pictures boldly divided into two planes, contrasting the natural and cultural aspects of the landscape. The foreground shows wild flowers flourishing on the bankside, seen from very close-up. In the misty amber background we see a melange of factory chimneys, a turreted house, a steamboat, some boaters and promenaders.*

Left *During the 1870s, Manet began to take up many of the subjects favoured by his young admirers and to use similar colour schemes. Like Renoir and Monet, he depicted the leisure pursuits and pleasures of places like Argenteuil, yet his paintings seem to suggest a more ambivalent response to the subject matter, far removed from the spontaneity and ease of the depictions of his younger admirers.*

Pissarro and Cézanne at Pontoise

While other Impressionists focused on suburban motifs in the mid-1870s, Pissarro and Cézanne concentrated their attention on the countryside of Pontoise and Auvers-sur-Oise. In the autumn and winter of 1872, Cézanne, disenchanted with his painting of the previous decade, began working with Pissarro in Pontoise and moved to neighbouring Auvers the following year to continue working with him on a daily basis. This collaboration went on for several years and even as late as 1882, Cézanne made visits to Pontoise to work with Pissarro. Their collaboration resulted in important new developments for both painters, as each later acknowledged.

Under the example of Pissarro, the most theoretically minded of the Impressionists and the elder statesman of the group, Cézanne placed a greater accent on studying and painting nature *en plein air*. He later stated to Emile Bernard that it was "when I was with the indefatigable Pissarro that I first developed the taste for the work to come". His pictures from Pontoise reveal the more patient submission to the motif that was to characterize his later painting. Cézanne started to work with

Below left *Pissarro's* Gleaners *(1889) revisits one of Millet's most famous subjects. Yet, while Millet's picture spoke of the class disparities in the countryside, Pissarro's version focuses on the co-operation of the workers in gathering in the harvest. Pissarro's anarchism committed him to a utopian rural vision of syndicalism in which workers would unite and share the spoils of their labour, living in collective harmony with nature.*

Below right Hoarfrost *(1873) reflects the influence of Millet's painting on Pissarro in his choice of rugged agrarian subject matter. Here a peasant gathering firewood is shown walking across the frosty earth of the fields that shimmer in silver and golden tones. Octave Mirbeau wrote that in Pissarro's representations of the peasantry, "man is always in perspective in a vast telluric harmony".*

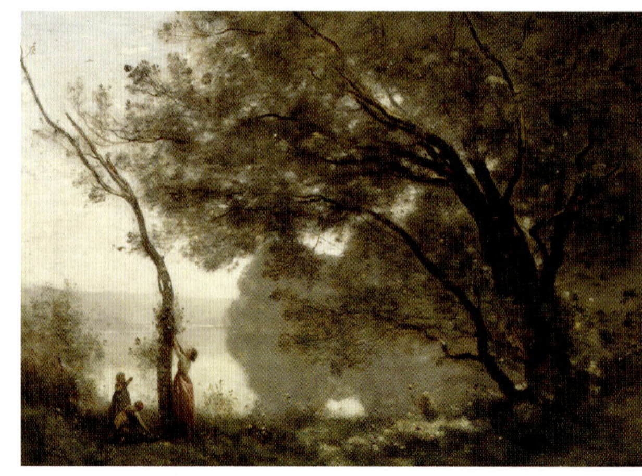

Camille Corot
1796–1875

Alongside Daubigny, Corot exerted a powerful influence on the Impressionists and expressed a genuine interest in their work, offering counsel and advice to Pissarro, Morisot and others. His lyrical landscapes from Fontainebleau, the banks of the Seine and the Channel coast prefigure the choice of motifs and the acute study of light that would characterize the work of the Impressionists. While drawing on the landscape tradition of Poussin and Claude Lorrain, he revised their work in line with the more naturalistic preoccupations of his own age. Pissarro paid tribute to Corot's influence when he exhibited two pictures at the Salon of 1864 as his pupil.

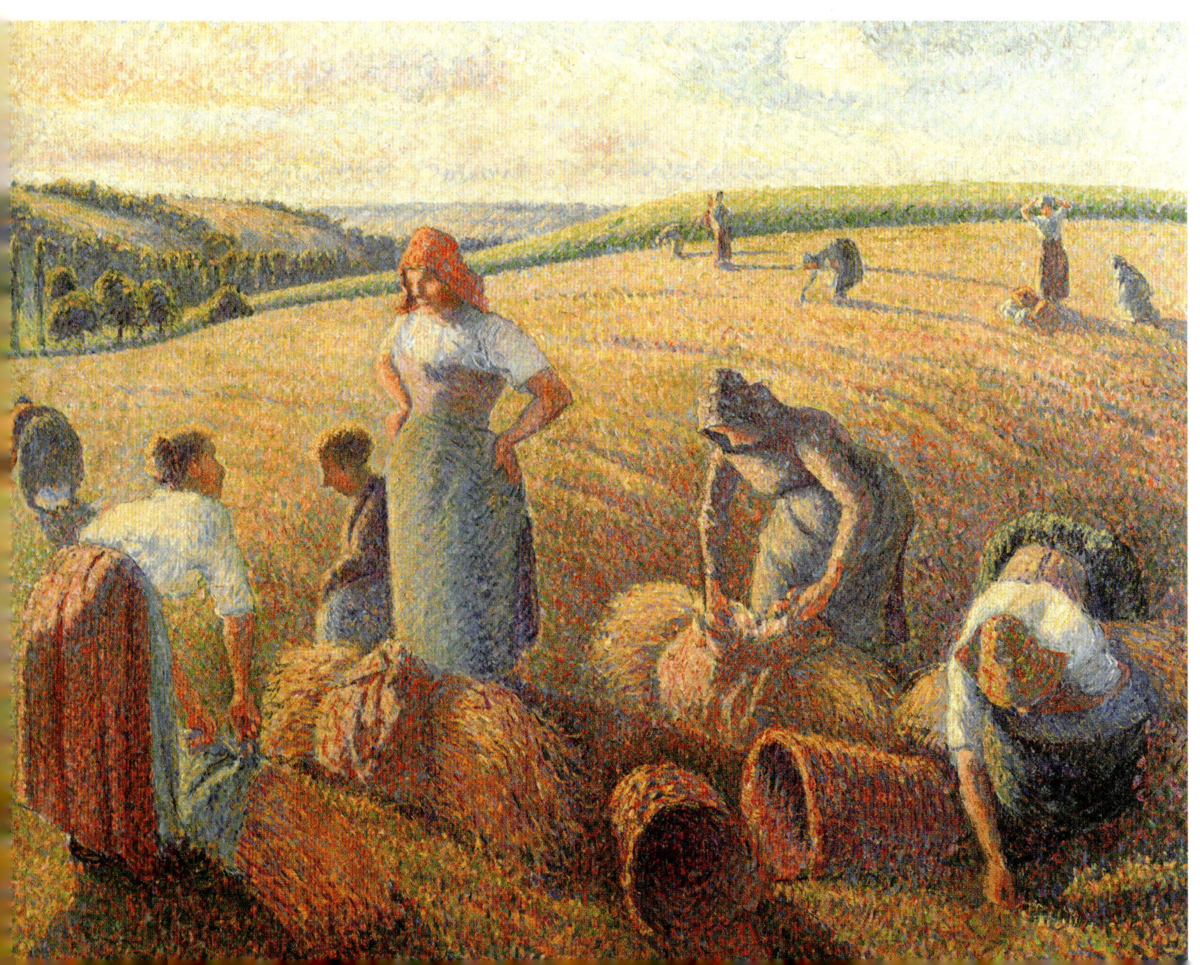

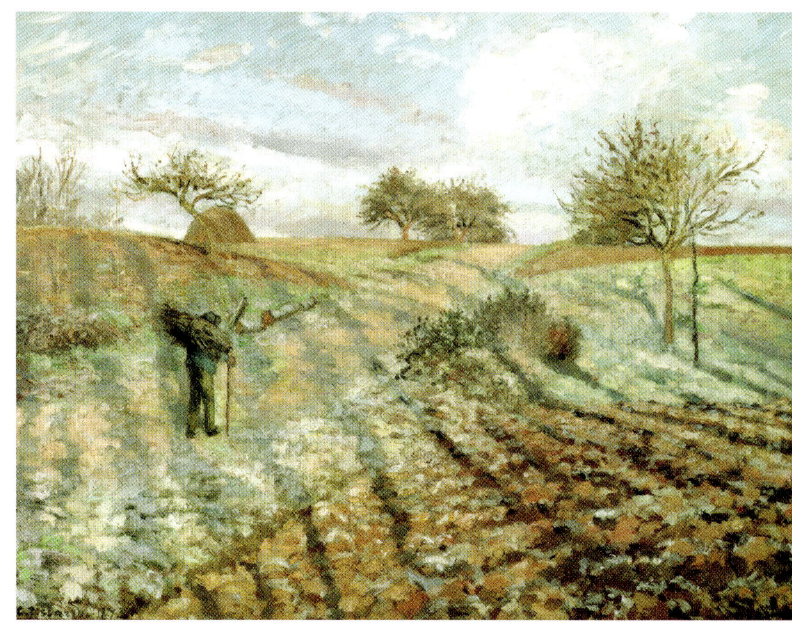

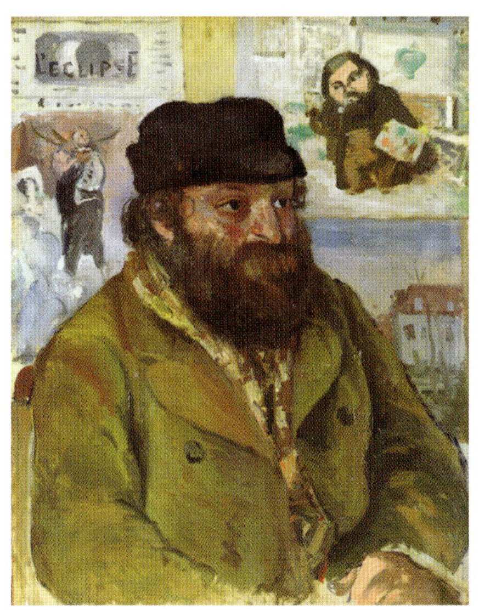

greater deliberation, employing a thinner paint application and a wider register of tones in order to achieve more varied pictorial effects. These differences in his art are evident in *House at Auvers-sur-Oise* (c. 1873) (later to become known as *The House of the Hanged Man*, a title Cézanne would not have favoured), shown at the Impressionist exhibition of 1874. In turn, Pissarro acknowledged the reciprocal influence of Cézanne, while maintaining that each painter retained his own sensation of nature.

Their choice of motifs in Pontoise focused on, by contemporary standards, incidental subjects that were influenced by the discreet landscape subjects pioneered by Daubigny in the 1860s. Both Pissarro and Cézanne preferred motifs that lacked any strongly suggestive point of reference or mood. They chose viewpoints that largely avoided salient points of interest in the landscape, relegated topographical detail to a secondary consideration and which instead emphasized the artist's "individualized" manner of seeing and handling.

The choice of discreet fragments of nature is most apparent in paintings such as *Forest at Osny, Près de Pontoise* (1877), one of the series of "screen of trees" motifs (works which feature a line of trees arranged across the foreground plane) that owed much to the example of Camille Corot. Following Pissarro's lead, Cézanne favoured such motifs, which provided a visual counterpoint to his views of the town. By adopting this compositional format attention was placed on viewing the motif as a field of pure perception.

Pictures like these suggest the artist's solitary immersion in nature. Frequently, the choice of vantage point suggested a secluded view from within the woods that provided one-to-one communion with nature. Despite the similarities one finds in their work of this period, the painters' choice of subjects also reveals differences. Cézanne largely avoided figures in his landscapes, while Pissarro, who admired above all the peasant painter Jean-François Millet, often included references to the local peasantry toiling and harvesting, sometimes even representing the commercial transactions at market. For Pissarro, nature had a moral value, and the countryside offered an alternative way of life to the modernity of the metropolis and capitalism. The city was associated with progress and modernity, but also with alienation and rootlessness. By contrast, the countryside for Pissarro was a place in which man and nature still lived in an intelligible relation to each other.

A Long Friendship

Pissarro and Cézanne first met at the Atelier Suisse in 1861, an independent studio where a number of the Impressionists studied in the 1860s, and established a long-standing friendship. Their artistic collaboration in the 1870s was based not only on their artistic affiliations but their shared attitudes about nature and politics. Pissarro's affectionate portrait of Cézanne (1874), presents him as the heir to the radical Courbet. While working at Pontoise and Auvers-sur-Oise, they were often joined by other painters, such as Armand Guillaumin and Dr Gachet (the physician who would later treat van Gogh and who was an amateur painter and enthusiast of Dutch landscape painting).

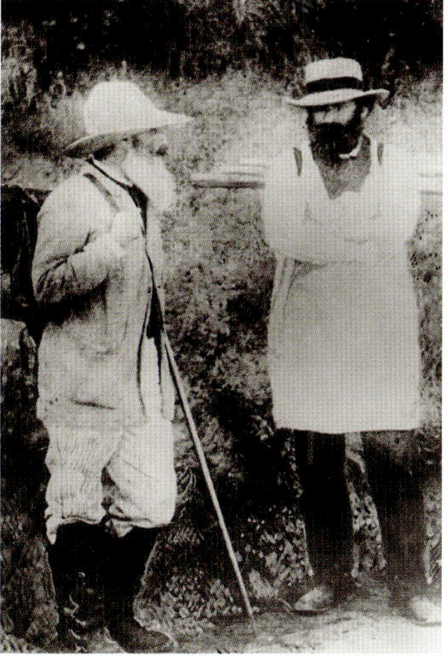

Far left *This affectionate portrait of Cézanne painted during the initial period of their close working collaboration poses the painter against a backdrop that includes one of Pissarro's own landscapes and two political prints; one of the government statesman Adolphe Thiers, the scourge of revolutionaries, and another of the socialist painter Gustave Courbet. Amusingly, Pissarro adjusted the original pose of Courbet so it looks as though he is toasting the young artist.*

Below *Cézanne's depiction of the forest at Osny, Près de Pontoise (1877), presents a typical forest motif favoured by Pissarro and himself during these years. By concentrating on the dense tonal relations and linear patterns of the trees in the foreground, the painter draws attention to his painterly treatment of the motif.*

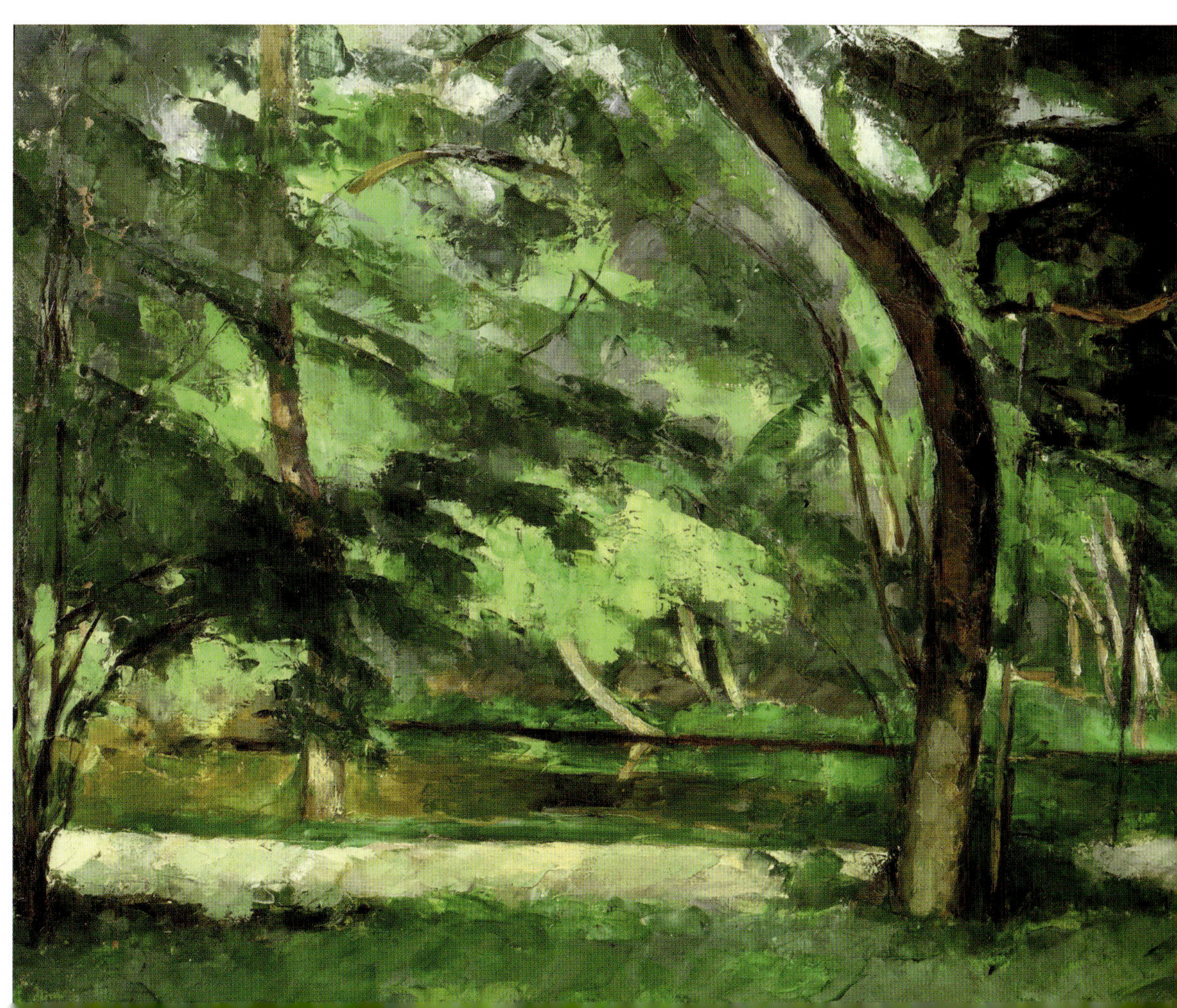

The First Impressionist Exhibition

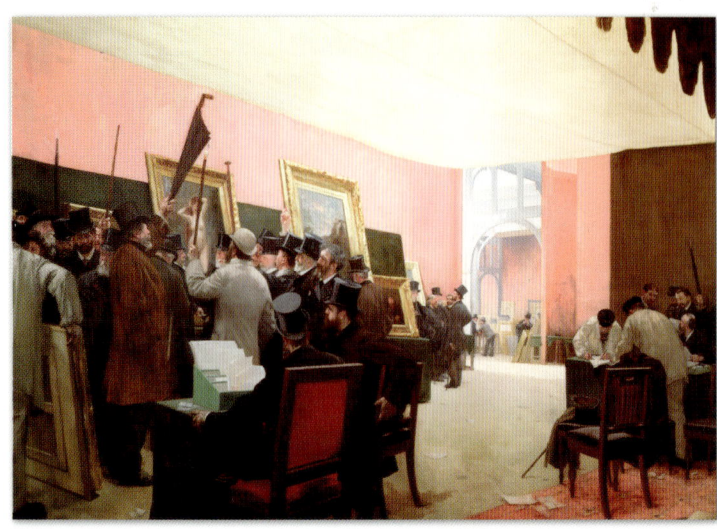

Paul Cézanne
1839–1906

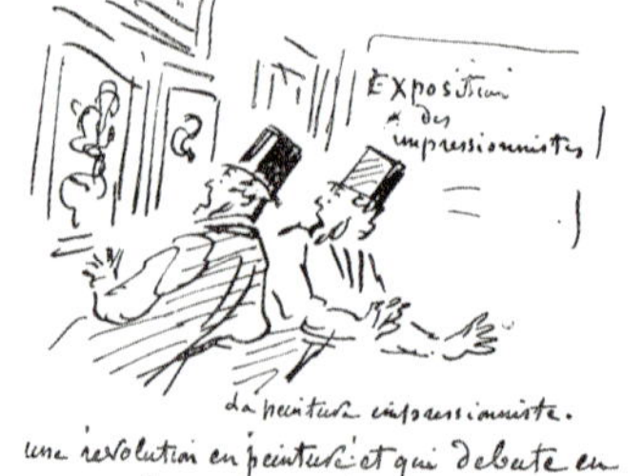

During the 1860s and '70s, Paul Cézanne established notoriety for himself as the enfant terrible of Impressionism, painting in a bold, "*cuillarde*" style, as he referred to it, that by contemporary Academic standards was regarded as wilfully incompetent and unintelligible. In his review of the Impressionist exhibition, Jean Prouvaire wrote, "Shall we mention Cézanne who, by the way, has his own legend? No known jury has ever, even in its dreams, imagined the possibility of accepting a single work by this painter." Indeed, Cézanne had 13 Salon rejections in a row before, in 1881, he finally had a work accepted.

The Impressionist Exhibition of 1874 is a landmark in the history of modern art. Frustrated by rejection from the Salon, the young Impressionists were keen to find alternative, more direct ways of bringing their work to the attention of the public. Moreover, during the early 1870s, Paul Durand-Ruel, their main dealer, experienced financial difficulties and the artists were forced to seek other outlets for their painting.

The prospect of an independent show had been discussed as early as 1867, but problems of funding the exhibition prevented its realization. In a letter from Frédéric Bazille to his parents dated May 1867, he wrote, "I told you about the plan of a group of young people to have their separate exhibition. With each of us pledging as much as possible, we have been able to gather the sum of 2,500 francs, which is not enough. We must therefore abandon our desired project. We will have to re-enter the bosom of the administration whose milk we have not sucked and who disowns us." Two years later, after having another picture rejected from the Salon, Bazille vowed, "I will never send anything again to the (Salon) jury," and spoke of "a dozen talented artists" who had decided together that "each year we will rent a large studio where we will exhibit our works in as large a number as we wish".

On 28 November 1870, Bazille died at the Battle of Beaune-la-Rolande during the Franco–Prussian war and it was not until four years later that the exhibition now known as the first Impressionist show opened on 15 April 1874 at the photographer Nadar's studio on the fashionable Boulevard des Capucines, a few steps away from the Garnier Opéra House. Organized by Pissarro, Monet, Renoir and Degas, the exhibition did not have a clear group identity as its original

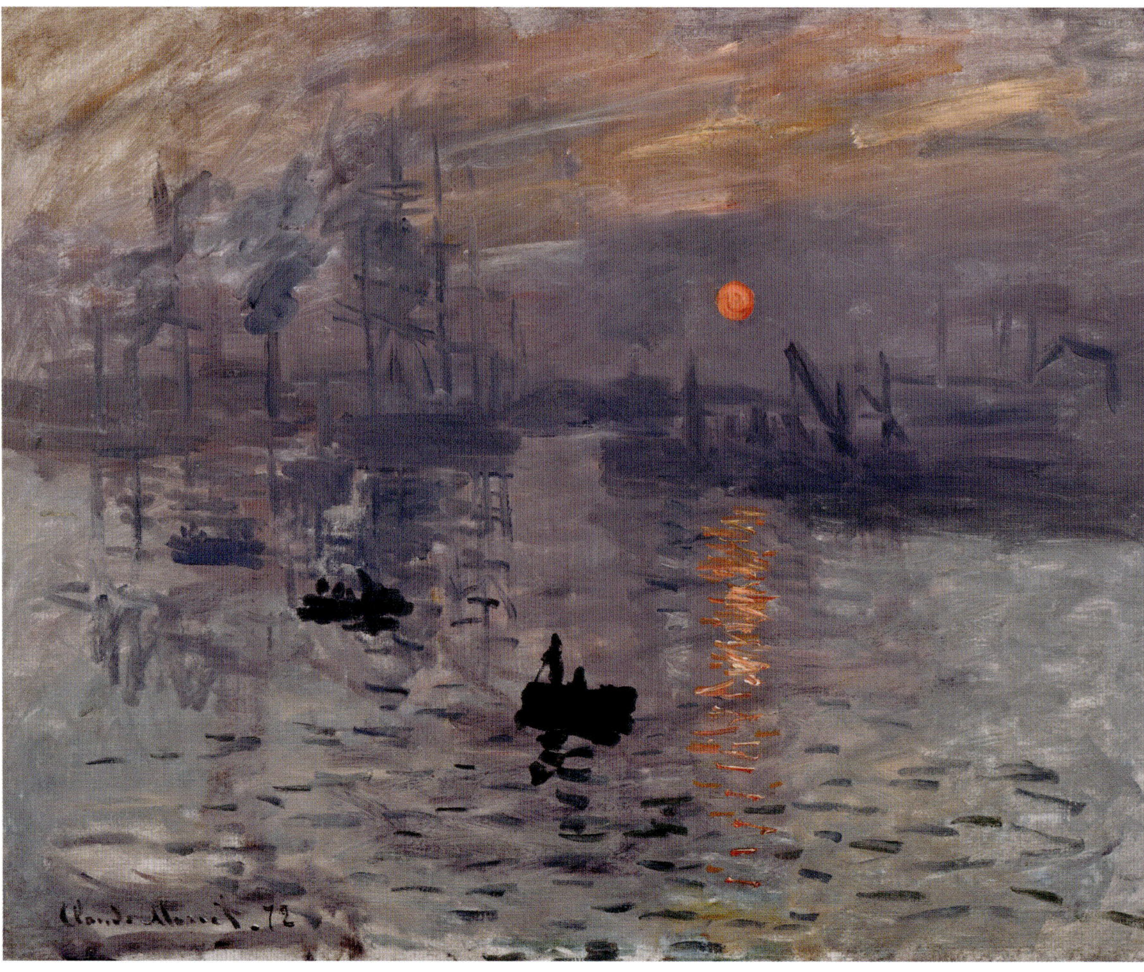

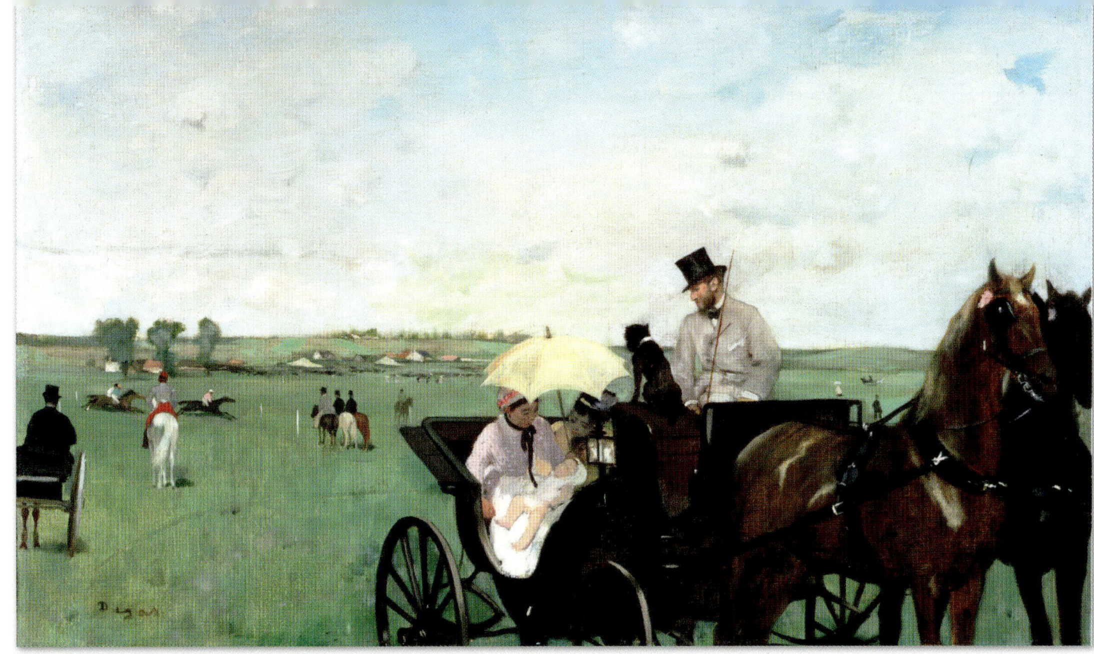

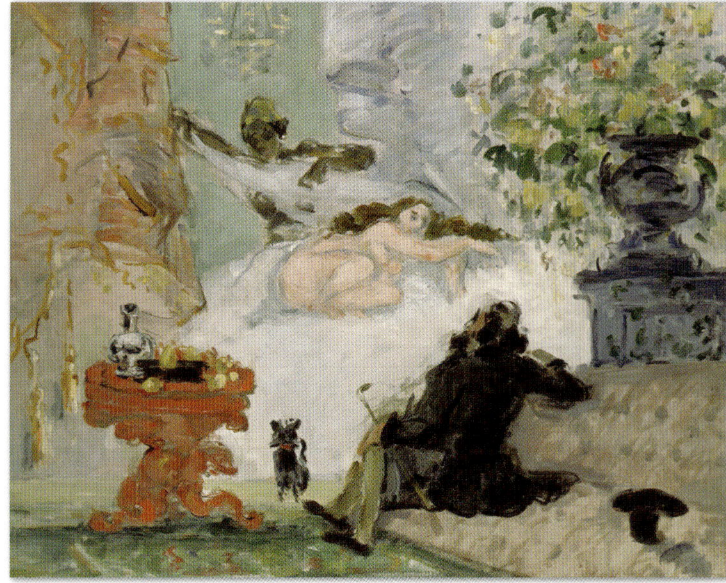

title, the "Société anonyme des artistes, peintres, sculpteurs, graveurs etc.", indicates and it included 36 artists who showed 156 works. Nevertheless, it was at this exhibition and those that followed over the next few years that the term "Impressionism" began to be applied to the group of young painters now known as the Impressionists. The critic and illustrator Louis Leroy used the phrase to describe the allusive, loose, painterly treatment of Monet's oil sketch *Impression: Sunrise, Le Havre* (1872) in a satirical review written for *Le Charivari*. Leroy parodied the exasperation of conservative critics who bluntly regarded the work on view as, in Emile Cardon's words, "quite simply the negation of the most elemental rules of drawing and painting". Cézanne bore the brunt of critical disapproval. Though praising the Impressionists' "quick intelligence" and attention to the "subjective sensation", Jules Castagnary referred to Cézanne's *A Modern Olympia* (1873–74) as an example of how Impressionism might fall prey to "personal, subjective fantasies without any echo in general reason".

Despite the strong tone of some of the criticism, many critics were responsive to the painters' technical innovations and their embrace of contemporary subjects. The unorthodox high viewpoint and vibrant suggestion of movement of Monet's *Boulevard des Capucines* (1873–74) drew special praise from respected critics like Ernst Chesneau. Despite his reservations about its lack of conventional finish and traditional draughtsmanship, he called the picture "a masterpiece" that "anticipated the painting of the future". Renoir's *La Loge* (*The Theatre Box*) (1874) was described as possessing "remarkable qualities of observation and colour". Armand Silvestre also wrote approvingly of the painters' renewal of French art, stating that "their impressions will immeasurably serve contemporary art". Though not a financial success – the Société anonyme was wound up only a few months afterwards – the show brought the painters to public attention and opened the way for future group shows over the next 12 years.

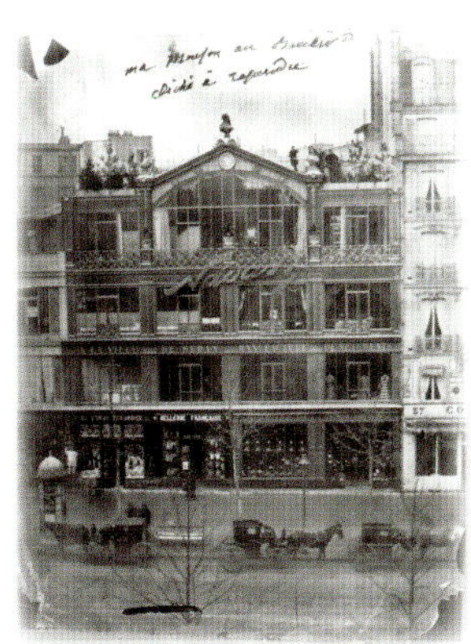

Nadar (Gaspard-Félix Tournachon) *1820–1910*

The "great Nadar", as Monet referred to him, was one of the most accomplished photographers of his generation. Famed for his memorable portraits of the cultural intelligentsia of his time, he was also known for his caricatures published in the journals *Le Charivari* and *Le Rire* and was an avid collector of Constantin Guys. The first Impressionist exhibition was held at his old studio at 35 Boulevard des Capucines and opened shortly before the Salon. Although Nadar did not have close connections with the Impressionists, his remarkable aerial photographs of Paris taken during his much publicized hot-air balloon flights influenced Impressionist depictions of the city.

Above left *Degas's* At the Races in the Country *(1872) provided a distinct contrast from the majority of landscapes exhibited in the Impressionists' first exhibition. It offers a pleasant view of Parisians at leisure.*

Above *Cézanne's* A Modern Olympia *(1874), one of a number of variations he did after Manet's* Olympia *(1863), reveals how important the example of Manet was to the development of his painting. The picture, which features Cézanne himself, stood out from the other exhibits and drew strong criticism. One critic called it a "bizarre sketch of the imagination" executed under the influence of Baudelaire, orientalism and hashish.*

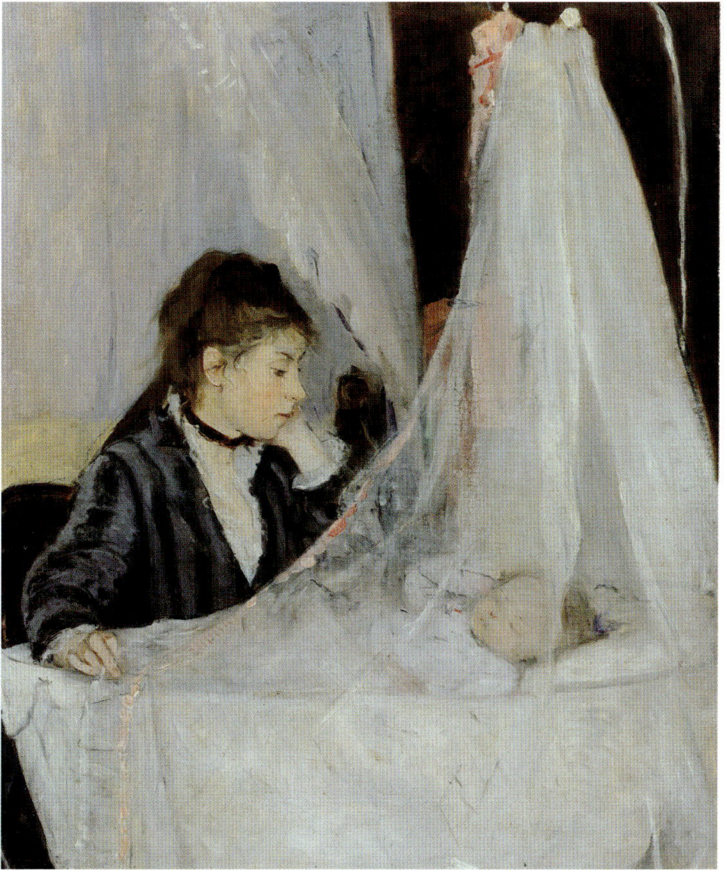

The Art of Sensation

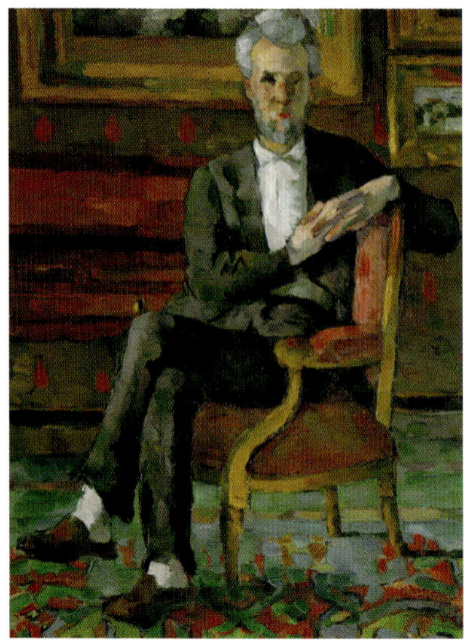

Left *This is one of a number of portraits Cézanne made of Victor Chocquet, one of the painter's few patrons, and demonstrates his experimentation with different ways of organizing and unifying his paintings by using a mosaic-like effect achieved by the deployment of a limited array of touches of colour distributed relatively evenly across the picture surface.*

Right *Cézanne's still lifes show his sensitivity to the complexities of perception. While contemporary critics often found the distortions of perspective in his paintings willful and incompetent, they are often explicable in optical terms. The refusal to correct these distortions indicates Cézanne's aim of remaining true to perceptual experience.*

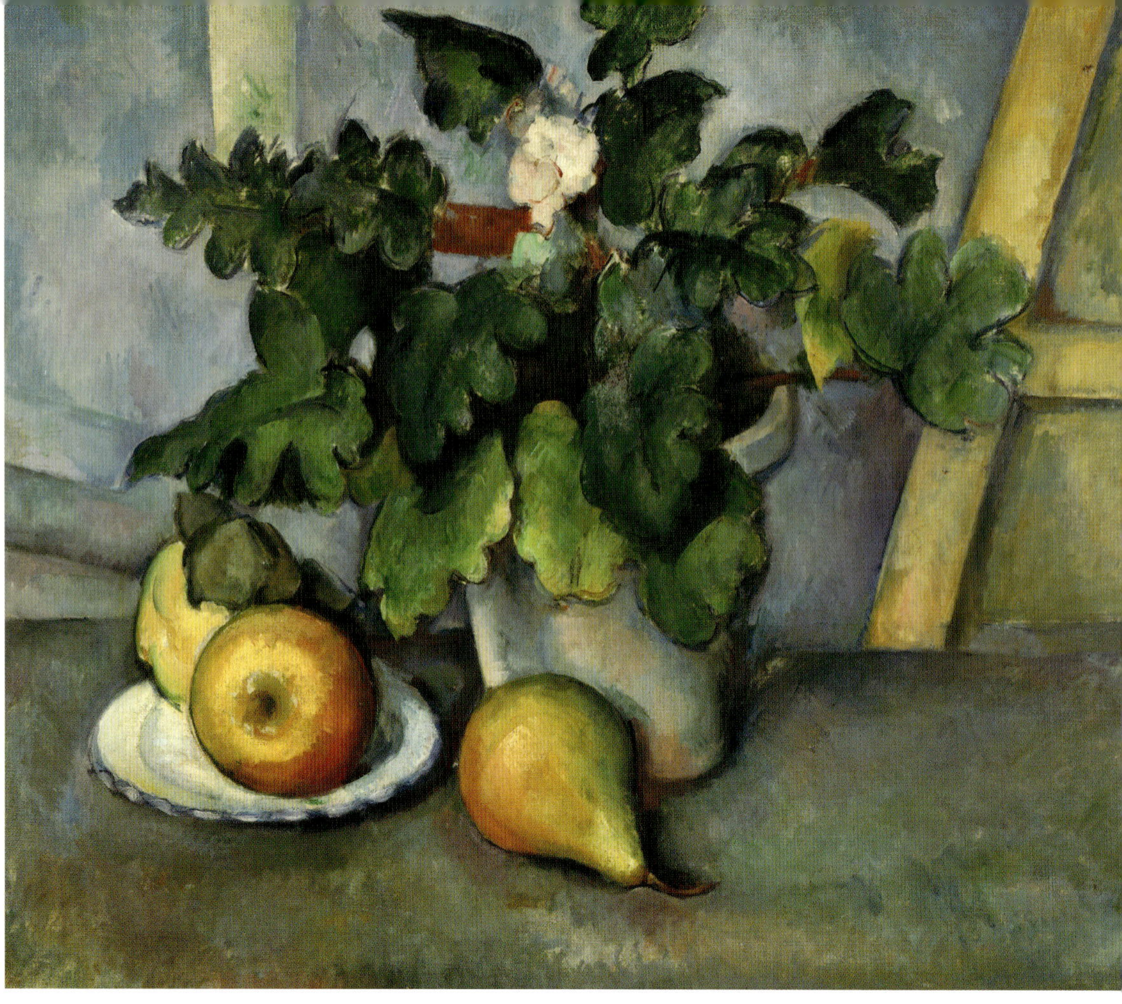

Impressionist artists were reluctant to theorize about their painting and most statements about their aims came from critical supporters. Those statements the Impressionists did make stressed their concern to paint with sincerity, spontaneity and naïvely, by which they meant to suspend preconceptions of the motif and paint as though viewing it for the very first time. Pissarro once characterized this as seeing the motif purely as colour stains or patches rather than as made up of discernible and distinct objects. They also spoke of expressing their *temperament* through their choice of motif and individualized manner of representing it. This testifies to the way Impressionists saw their painting as involving the unlearning of artistic rules and formulae in order to discover a more immediate relationship to nature, in short, to paint naturally. Monet even talked of his desire to paint as a bird sings.

Despite this, the letters of the Impressionists show that many were conversant with contemporary theories about optics and colour and had an intimate knowledge of the old masters in the Louvre. Reading their correspondence, key concepts emerge as the cornerstone of their painting and the framework in which their work was understood by their contemporaries. In his review of the first Impressionist exhibition, Jules Castagnary sought to clarify for his audience what Impressionism meant: "These painters are impressionists in the sense that they render not the landscape, but the sensation of the landscape." Castagnary distinguished between naturalism's aspiration to paint the natural world objectively, as it exists independently of human perception, and the personal or subjective rendering of it by Impressionists.

The terms "impression" and "sensation" were used interchangeably to express this subjective aspect of Impressionist painting. The painters

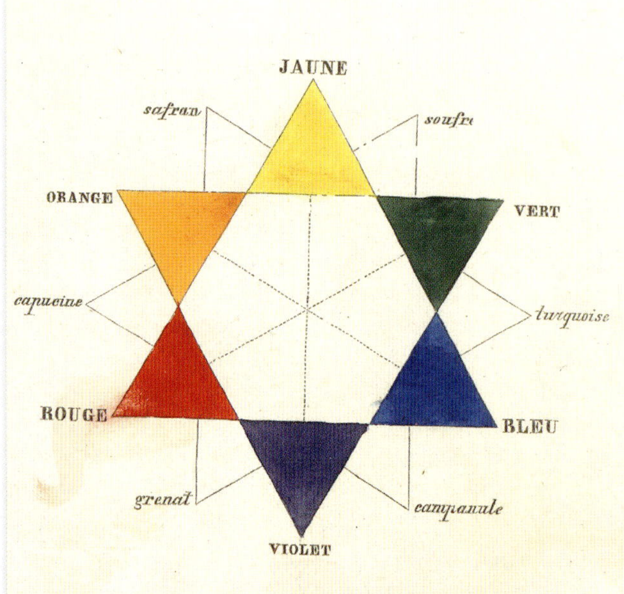

Colour Theory

Though Impressionists emphasized their responsiveness to nature directly perceived, their painting was influenced by contemporary colour theory. The publication of Eugène Chevreul's *On the Law of Simultaneous Contrasts of Colour* (1839) proved highly influential, though many of his discoveries had already been anticipated by the old masters. Chevreul's theory of the optical combination of colours encouraged the painters to employ touches of pure, unmixed pigment to achieve maximum luminosity, colour and harmony. Chevreul showed how the juxtaposition of colours optically influences their appearance, strengthening or weakening their properties of warmth, coolness and saturation. He also demonstrated how the combination of two colours can induce the appearance of another colour.

spoke of realizing or expressing their sensations or impressions of nature and how these sensations were the starting point for their work. This did not imply that Impressionism was an art of subjectivity alone. Théodore Duret emphasized Impressionism's truth to nature and accuracy, arguing that their brightly coloured palette and even some of the apparent "distortions" of their painting were derived from direct observation and could be objectively verified. The discontinuous line of the table in Cézanne's *Still Life (Pot of Flowers with Fruit)* (c. 1888–90) was an optical phenomenon that the scientist Helmholtz had written about in a work which the painter quoted in his correspondence. Helmholtz noted that where a straight line is interrupted by a vertical object the line may appear to fall and to be discontinuous. Cézanne appears to have been particularly sensitive to these optical distortions.

As this suggests the terms "impression" or "sensation", were used by the painters to refer both to an *effect of nature* and an *effect of the artist*. The Impressionists' employment of it drew upon two main sources: first, its use by art critics to refer to the first layers of an oil painting, which displayed the genesis of the picture in an immediate, primary and undeveloped fashion; second, the meanings it had in contemporary optical treatises and perceptual psychology. In perceptual psychology, the *impression* was seen as the point of intersection of subject–object relations and equated with the immediate effect of an experience or the "lively" and "raw" sensory data. Yet, it was generally argued that it was subjective in two key respects: first, because the impression was processed through the consciousness of the perceiving subject, and, second, because each subject had a unique psychological and physiological make-up, the impression of an object on any given observer would never be exactly the same, but would differ in accordance with their particular temperament, personality and emotional state. The development of perceptual psychology in the nineteenth century encouraged the painters to see visual perception as a field of exploration in its own right and regard any subject as of interest for the artist's way of envisaging it.

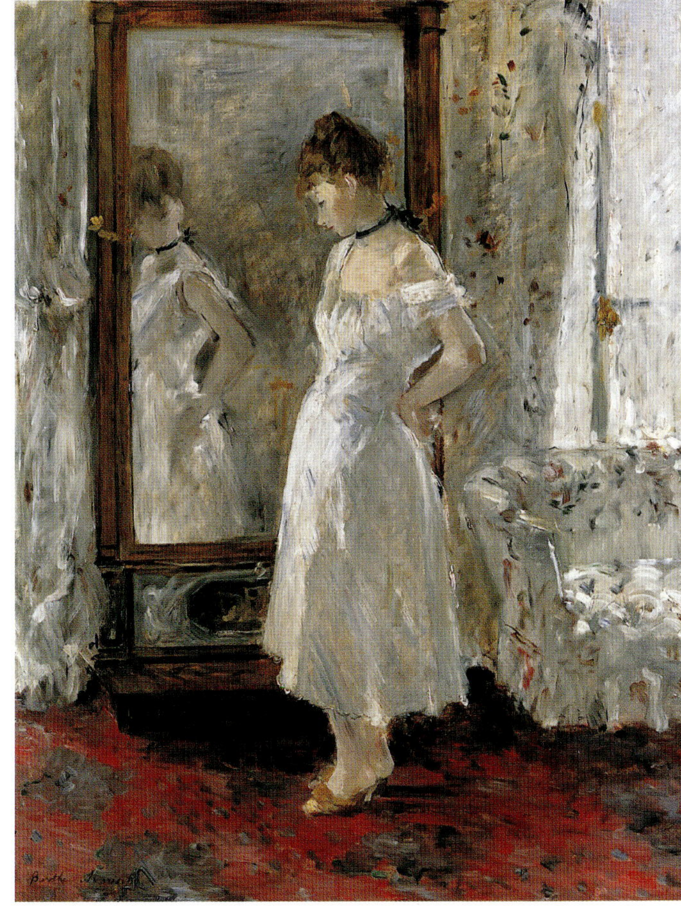

Right Morisot's combination of delicate, loose brushwork and alternately subtle or bold colour combinations established her reputation as one of the most experimental of the Impressionists. Like Monet, she often chose motifs that allowed her to represent a transitory moment. Her use of mirrors corresponds with these aims, but it also reflects her preoccupation with the theme of personal identity.

Bottom left Sunset at Lavancourt (1880) shows the kind of motif Monet was to favour throughout his career. His commitment to capturing a fleeting impression finds its most consummate expression in the river scenes in transitory lighting and climatic conditions. River motifs offered him the opportunity to exploit the spectacular reflective play of light across its surface.

Bottom right The most intellectual of the Impressionists, Camille Pissarro was well versed in contemporary theories of optics. He reflected on the moral and intellectual foundations of Impressionism. Pissarro saw the movement as providing painters with a "democratic" manner of painting that addressed itself to the material facts of the perception of nature.

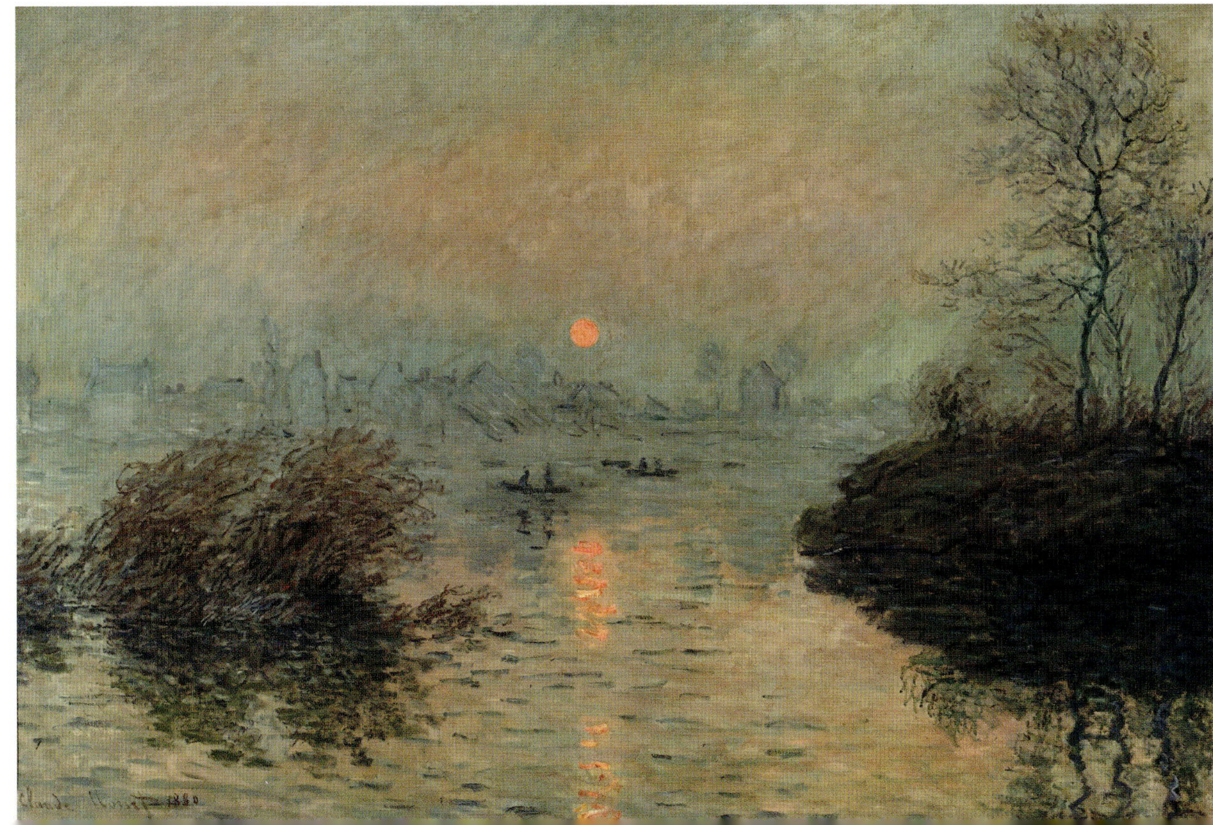

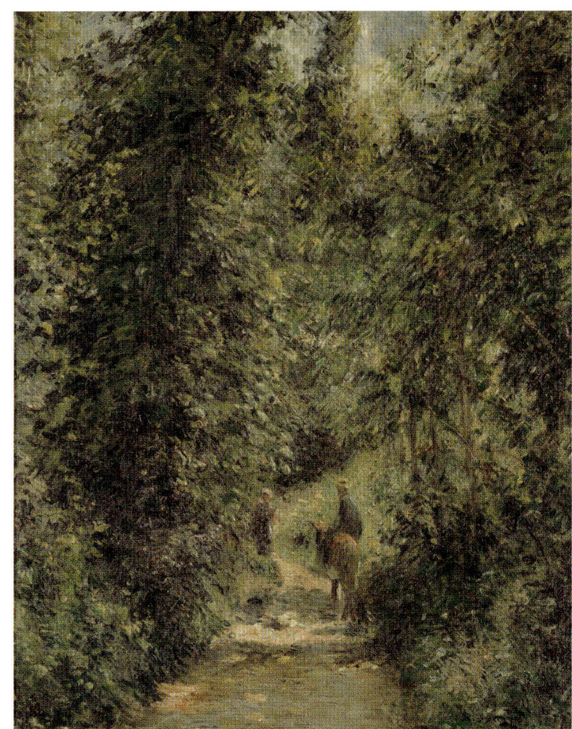

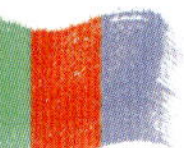

Impressionism and the Figure

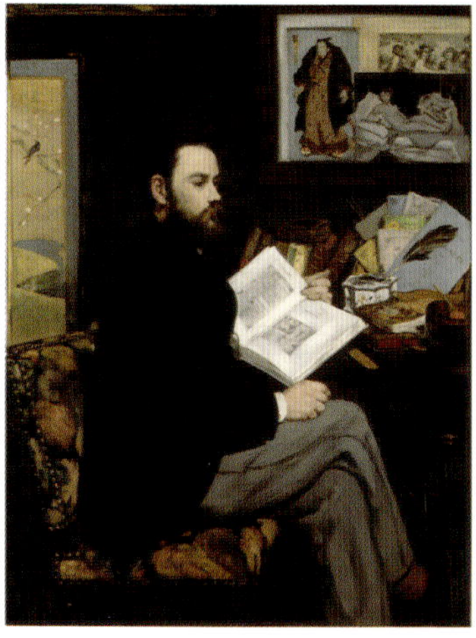

Impressionism is often regarded as primarily an art of landscape. It is sun-drenched pictures of the countryside and dappled reflections of light rippling across the surface of water that most immediately come to mind when we recall its imagery. This indicates how far Impressionism has come to be associated with Monet's painting, a connection that became established in the public's mind from as early as the late 1870s, when Monet began to be recognized as one of its leading exponents.

Although, in the 1860s, Monet had treated a broad spectrum of subjects, including ambitious figure paintings, from the late 1870s, he began to narrow his choice of subjects and to abandon the figure in

Left *Manet's portrait of the novelist and critic Emile Zola makes reference to the important article he wrote defending the painter in 1867, which is included in a blue pamphlet on the desk. On the back wall, Manet includes a Japanese print, a fragment of an engraving of Velazquez's* The Feast of Bacchus *(the source of his picture* The Old Musician, *1862) and a reproduction of his own* Olympia.

Below *Renoir's* Ball at the Moulin de la Galette *(1876) is one of the most memorable pictures of early Impressionism. This ambitious multi-figure composition, of which he made three versions, is set in a popular dancehall in Montmartre, on the fringes of Paris. Renoir frequented its Sunday balls that lasted from early in the day until late in the night. The radiantly sun-dappled picture conveys the hedonistic bohemian atmosphere of the place.*

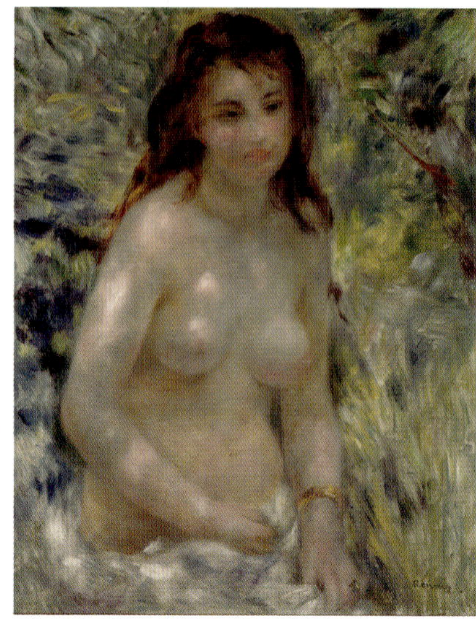

Torso of a Woman in the Sunlight

Torso of a Woman in the Sunlight, as the title suggests, represents Renoir's long-standing ambition to unite Impressionism's concern with the atmospheric effects of painting in the open air with the nude. The picture was criticized strongly when shown at the second Impressionist exhibition. In a much quoted review, the conservative critic Albert Woolf wrote, "Go ahead and try to explain to Renoir that a woman's torso is not a mass of decomposing flesh." While another critic wrote, "Let us throw a veil over (Renoir's) *Vénus* which he should have hidden behind a screen."

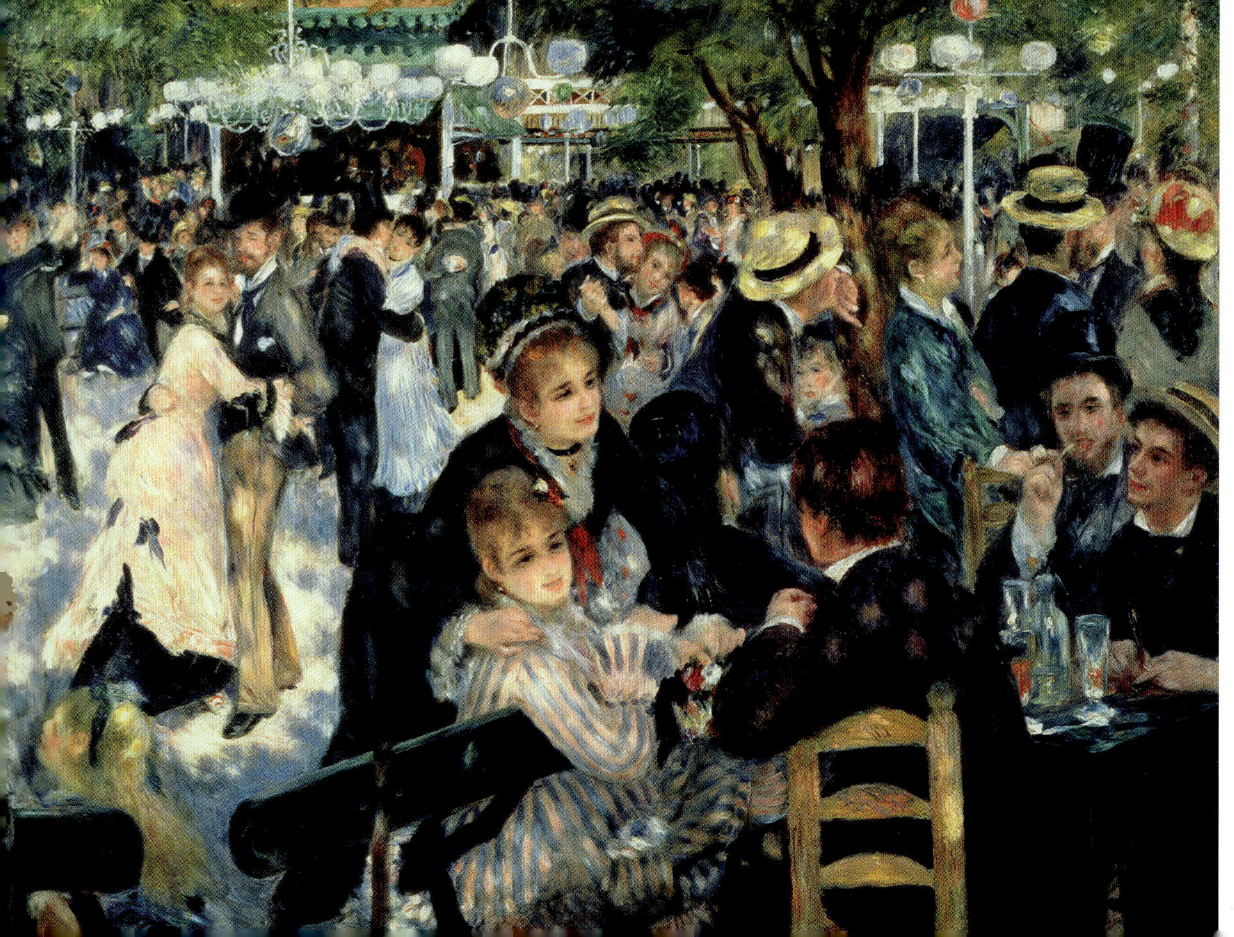

favour of solitary images of the countryside, where the artist's attention is devoted to the play of light, colour and atmosphere. Monet's abandonment of the figure reflected reservations about Impressionism's capacity to tackle the subject.

Camille and Jean on a Hill (1875), which portrays his wife and son, already marks Monet's ambivalence about reconciling his way of seeing his motifs as colour sensations that emphasized the treatment of all elements of the composition in the same manner with the demands of articulation and legibility required of the figure. The figure in Monet's paintings amounts to little more than a discreet punctuation mark in the landscape, an indicator of scale or a marker of the type of terrain (city, suburb or countryside) he is depicting. Apart from Sisley, who similarly eschewed the figure, most Impressionists regarded it as an integral aspect of their art.

While by the late 1870s critics acknowledged Impressionism's contribution to renewing French painting, praising the painters' scrupulous attention to the appearances of nature and development of new techniques and forms of composition, residual doubts remained about whether Impressionism was a suitable style for representing the human figure even among critics sympathetic to its aims. The "formlessness" that resulted from Impressionism's preoccupation with light and surface combined with its emphasis on the general effect over detail and refusal to differentiate the figure from other parts of the composition produced pictures that rarely suggest the deeper psychological features of the human

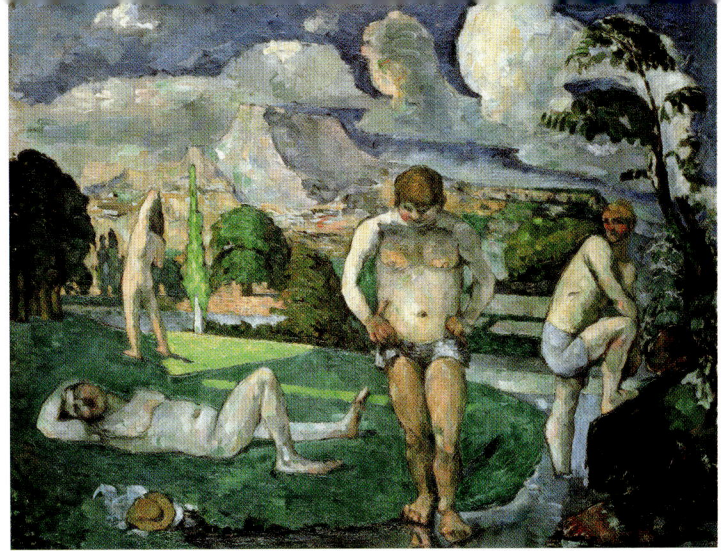

Criticisms of Impressionism's treatment of the figure were particularly strong when it came to the nude, which remained a key subject for French painters. While critics praised Renoir's modern life scenes like *Ball at the Moulin de la Galette* (1876) for representing the social types of Paris and the spontaneous pleasures of modern leisure pursuits, his nudes like *Torso of a Woman in the Sunlight* (1876) were subjected to harsh criticism. Nevertheless, Impressionists like Renoir and Cézanne saw the nude as an integral part of their *oeuvre* and in the mid-1870s the latter embarked on a series of bathers – a subject that was to preoccupy him throughout his career – with a view to showing that Impressionism could provide a new way of representing the nude harmonized with nature.

subject customarily expected. Only Degas and Caillebotte, whose work conformed more to these expectations, escaped censure.

When Manet exhibited his *Portrait of Emile Zola* (1867) at the Salon of 1868, Théophile Thoré wrote, "His present vice is a sort of pantheism that gives no higher value to a head than a slipper, which sometimes gives more importance to a bunch of flowers than a woman's face… which paints everything almost uniformly."

Impressionist portraits often implied the personality of the sitter through the setting in which they were placed, and suggested mood by the tonality or the objects included in the picture, but remained fixed on the visual impression, in general avoiding imposing psychological states of mind on their subjects or conveying the trappings of status, occupation and power.

Above left Bathers in Repose *(1876–77), was the centrepiece of Cézanne's submissions to the third Impressionist exhibition of 1877. It indicates his desire to make ambitious monumental nudes in classical poses, but rendered with an informal impressionist technique.*

Bottom left *Bazille was one of the few Impressionists to treat the male nude. His picture of male figures wrestling, swimming or sunning themselves by a stream may have encouraged Cézanne's enduring interest in the subject and was influenced by Courbet. Despite his premature death, Bazille's painting left an important legacy for Impressionism to build on.*

Right *Monet's picture shows his first wife, Camille, and son Jean walking in the countryside. Camille's pose, turning back to look at the painter, serves to convey the sense of a transitory moment captured and frozen for eternity. Despite the many figure paintings Monet produced in the 1860s and 1870s, Monet questioned his abilities as a figure painter and concentrated his attention on landscape from the 1880s onwards.*

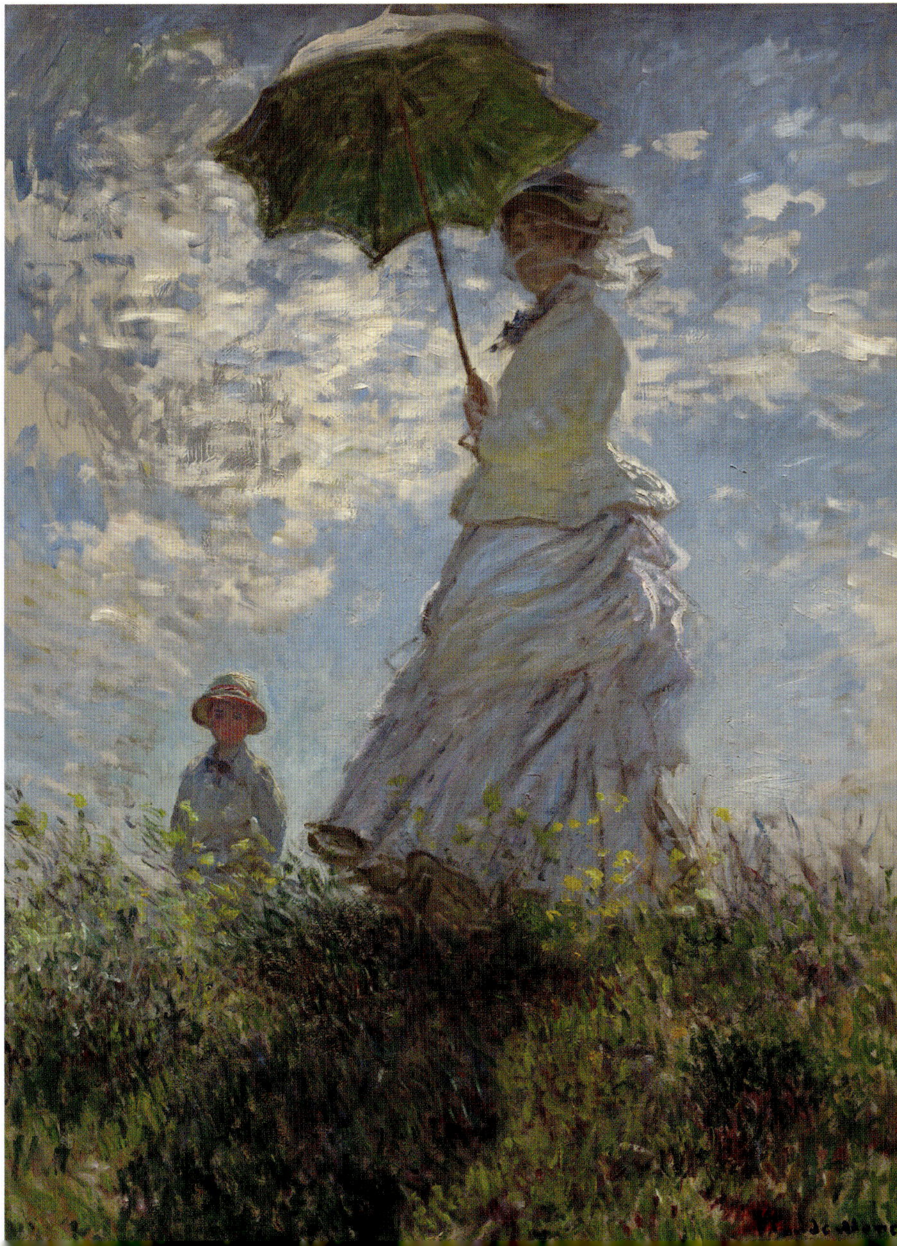

Degas and the Ballet

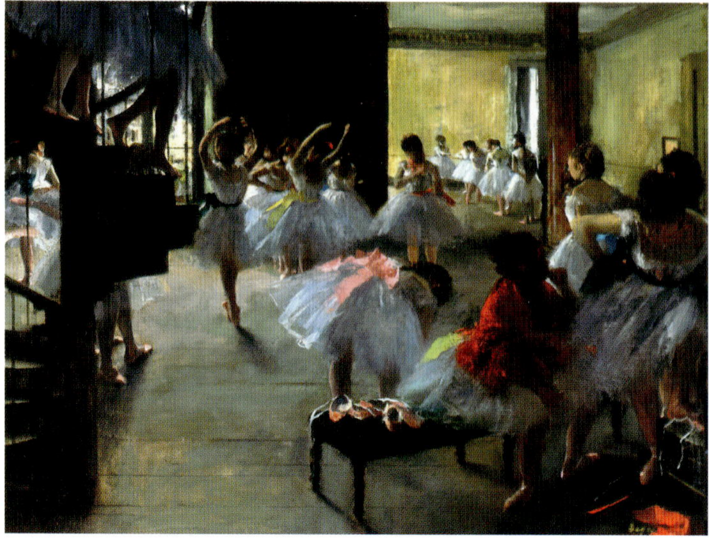

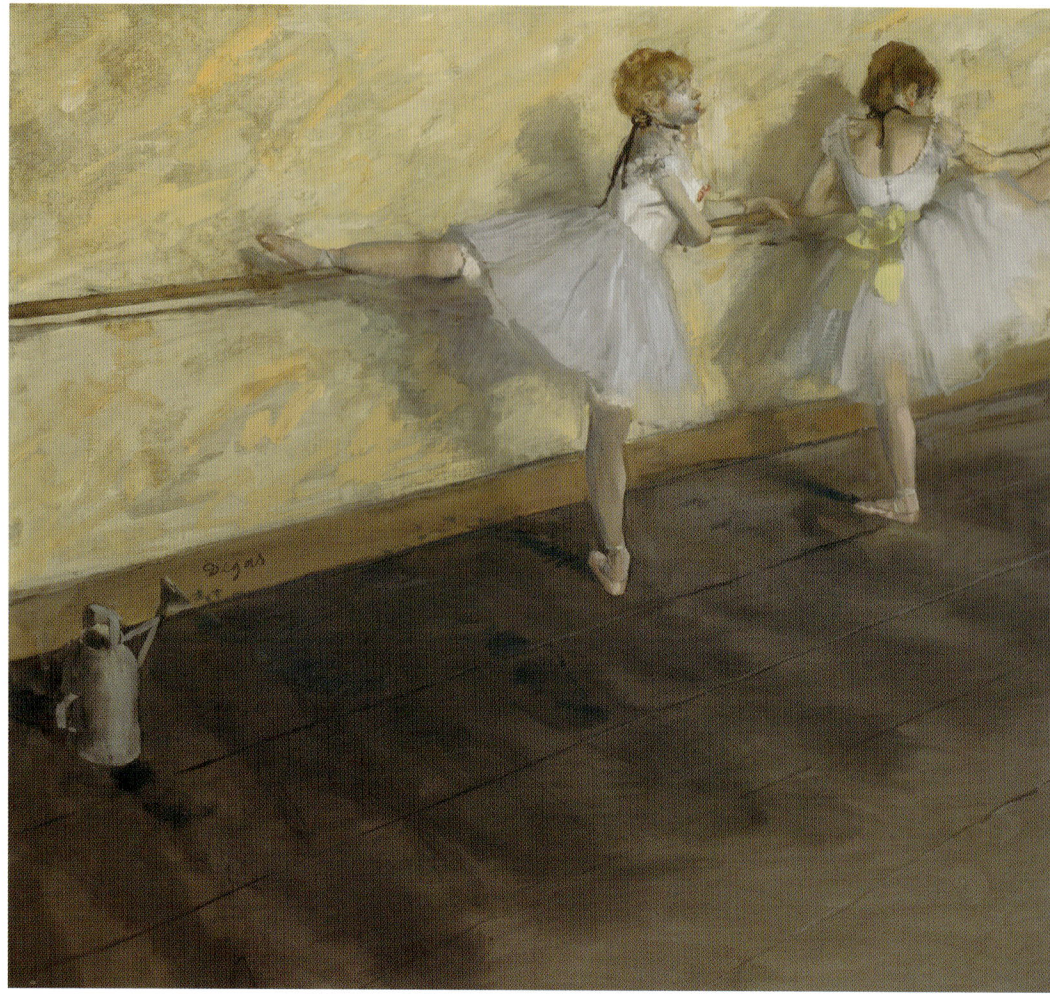

No subject held such a spell over Degas's visual imagination as that of the ballet dancer, a theme he represented on no less than 600 occasions in a variety of drawings, paintings and prints. His first images of the ballet appeared in the 1870s emerging out of his interest in modern life subjects dealing with *la vie élégante*, the tastes and pastimes of the Parisian *haute bourgeoisie*. The same bourgeois clientele that Degas depicts enjoying the pleasures of the racetracks of Longchamps or Deauville were among those who occupied the choicest opera boxes at the luxurious Palais Garnier, where ballet was presented as an accompaniment to opera. The theme of the ballet continued to preoccupy him for the next 40 years. As the most traditional minded of the

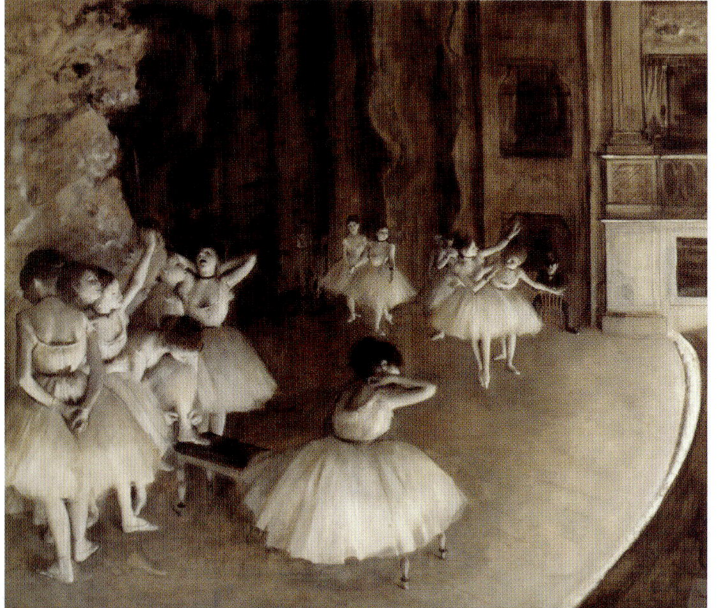

Above left *Degas's images of the rehearsal room are untypical of the normal imagery of the ballet in focusing on the instruction of the dancers in learning their art. Degas was clearly fascinated by the craft of the dancers, the artfulness and grace encapsulated in their choreography, and the tough training their bodies had to endure to master their metier.*

Above *Although Degas had a strong admiration for the grace and beauty of the dancers, he also approached the subject with an eye for wit and humour. In Dancers at the Bar (1876–77), he draws an amusing comparison between the pose of the ballerina on the far right going through her warming up exercises with the watering can on the far left.*

Left *The Rehearsal of the Ballet on Stage (1874) again shows the mixture of grace and satire of Degas's ballet imagery. While the dancers on the far side of the stage are shown practising their dance steps, those in the left foreground are shown scratching, yawning, stretching or adjusting the straps of their shoes. Degas's eye for comic juxtaposition is also evident in the way he conflates the legs of the seated ballerina with the carved wooden legs of the bench.*

Impressionists, Degas viewed the dance as a subject that allowed him to combine his interest in modernity with references to the antique. Asked by Louisine Havemeyer, who owned one of his series of *Two Dancers*, why he painted the ballet so frequently, he replied, "Because… it is all that is left to us of the combined movements of the Greeks."

While these nostalgic sentiments indicate the deep seated meanings the theme had for him, Degas seems to have first taken up the subject after the collapse of the family bank following the death of his father, which left him with heavy debts. Degas's initial ballet pictures were targeted at a connoisseur market for such subjects. The commercial and artistic success of his portrayals of ballerinas fast established his reputation as a specialist in this genre. Subsequent pictures in the mid-1870s explore the full spectrum of the life of the dancer in ways that reveal the depth of his engagement with this subject.

Many of his early images of the ballet show him vitally alive to the opportunities of presenting the scene in novel ways from different vantage points offered by the theatre auditorium. Often the picture's point of view suggests one of the exclusive *loges* (opera boxes), implying not only a particular location but the status of the onlooker who occupies that position. Likewise, the artificial ambience and distortion suggested by the modern theatre lighting was a marked feature of these ballet pictures.

However, it was the life of the rehearsal rooms and the ballerina's metier that became the quintessential themes of Degas during the later 1870s and early 1880s, and it is this preoccupation with life behind the scenes that sets his imagery apart from his contemporaries. In 1877, one critic wrote, "For those who are partial to the mysteries of the theatre, who would happily sneak behind the sets to enjoy a spectacle forbidden to outsiders, I recommend the works of Monsieur Degas. No one has so closely scrutinized the interior above whose door is written, 'the public is not permitted here.'"

Though from the perspective of the audience the ballet was a glamorous spectacle, from that of the performers it was a world of labour and craft. It is this private world of the preparation for performance, the dancer's taxing exertions in bringing her art to perfection, and the fatigue and struggle this involves, that is the focus of Degas's attention. Not

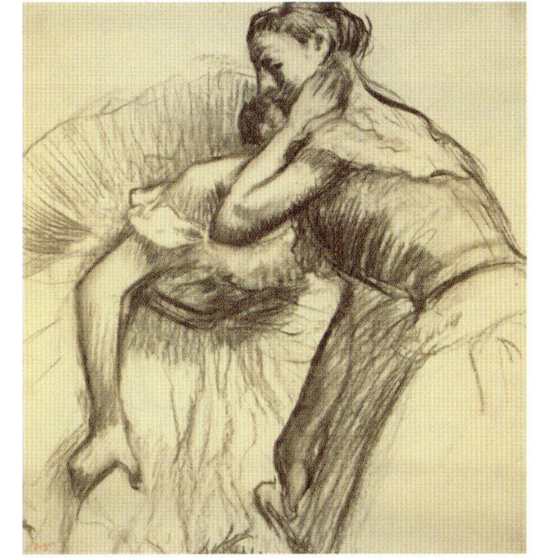

Below In his compositions of rehearsals Degas subtly interweaves dancers performing their choreography with others stretching and resting, playing on the way the poses of each echo one another. Here Degas shows the dance master orchestrating some of the dancers, while another well dressed man sits passively in the distance watching the dancers. In the foreground we see the neck of a cello from the orchestra pit, which serves both to counterpoint the forward thrusting arms of the dancers, while also positioning the viewer obliquely to the stage.

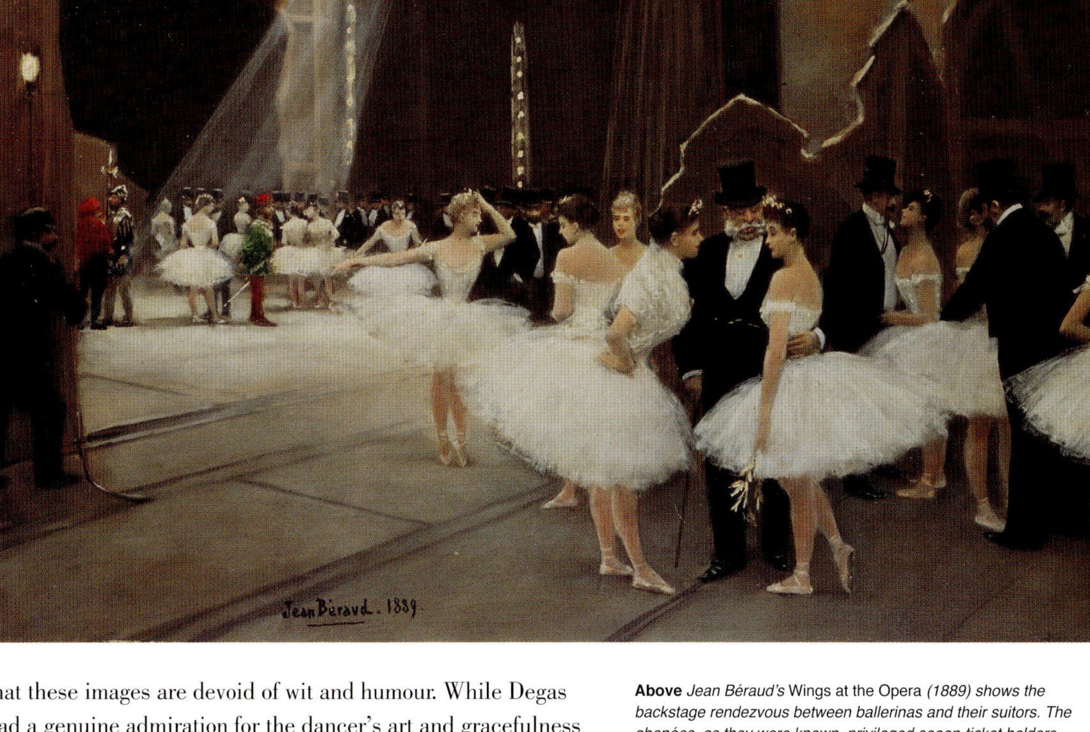

that these images are devoid of wit and humour. While Degas had a genuine admiration for the dancer's art and gracefulness and an appreciation of her toil, the artist is also responsive to the comic potential of the subject and often suggests something of the gaucherie of the dancers. In some pictures, a watering can or some other inanimate object serves as the prosaic visual counterpart to the dancer's elaborate posture and this penchant for visual puns was a much-remarked-upon feature of his painting.

Above Jean Béraud's Wings at the Opera (1889) shows the backstage rendezvous between ballerinas and their suitors. The abonées, as they were known, privileged seaon-ticket holders who had access to the Opéra's private quarters, the "foyer de la danse" and the "coulisses" (the wings and the practice rooms backstage), often took ballet dancers as their lovers.

Left Degas produced a large body of preparatory drawings of dancers rehearsing. These show him exploring the expressive poses and compositional groupings of his figures. Degas was particularly fascinated by poses in which the bodies of the dancers overlap and intertwine, alluding to how ballerinas lose their individuality in the collective motion of the performance.

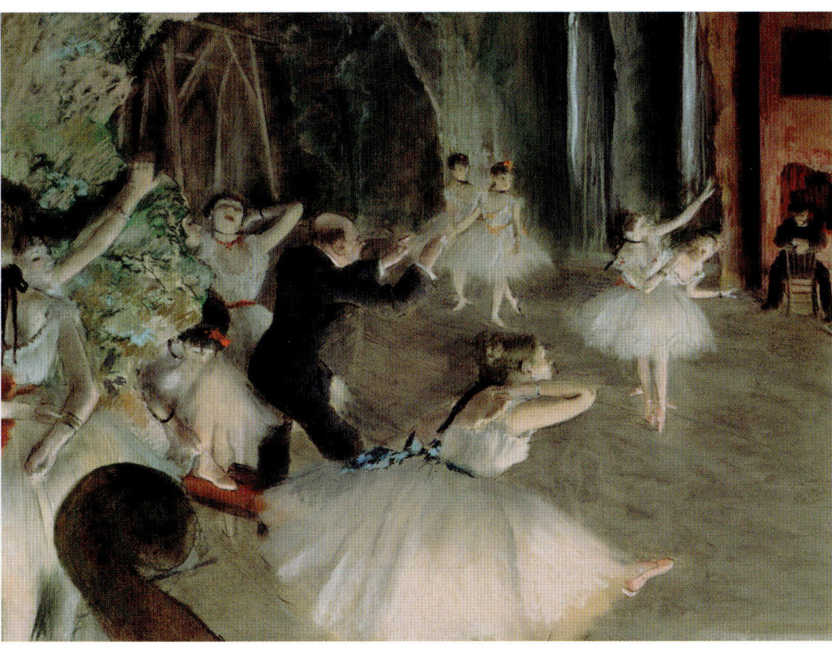

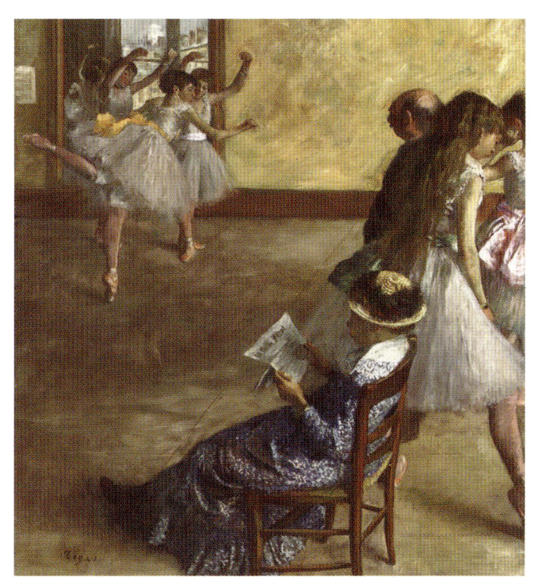

Stage Rehearsals

In many of Degas's images of the backstage rehearsals we also see the dancers' mothers who accompanied their daughters to rehearsal and performances as guardians. In contemporary literature, such as Ludovic Halévy's La Famille Cardinal, which Degas illustrated with a series of monotypes, they were represented as gold diggers, brazenly seizing opportunities to match their daughters with eligible season-ticket holders. Degas's depiction of mothers in these pictures is more matter of fact, showing them adjusting their daughter's costumes, offering encouragement or simply whiling away the time, subtly alluding to the passage from performer to maternal companion of the life of the dancers.

Women Impressionists

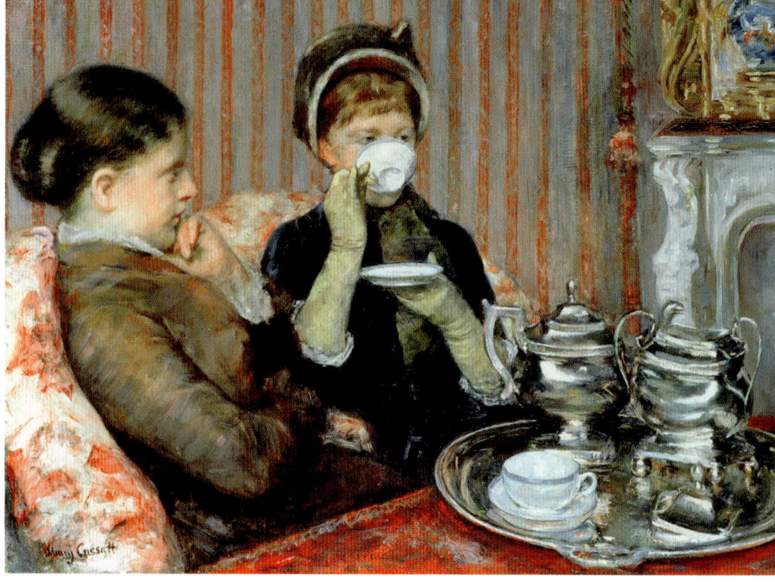

While many women pursued artistic careers in the nineteenth century, few enjoyed success at the highest level. Deprived of the opportunity to study at the Ecole des beaux-arts, or in the life class, their work often reflected a lack of training and traditional skills, particularly in relation to the figure. Consequently, most women chose subjects in lower genres that often inhibited their success at the Salon. It is no coincidence that those who were successful came from backgrounds that gave them privileged access to artistic training. Berthe Morisot, Mary Cassatt and Eva Gonzalès shared in common that they either came from artistic backgrounds or that marriage and family connections brought them into contact with established artists who were sympathetic to their ambitions.

Morisot's status within Impressionist circles was enhanced through her association with Corot, Daubigny and Manet, and she became a mainstay of the group; her weekly soirées were regularly attended by most of the Impressionists and by leading writers such as Stéphane Mallarmé and Emile Zola. As Degas's pupil, Cassatt was able to show at the Impressionist exhibitions, where her work was well received. As this suggests, within Impressionism, women artists found a favourable context

Below left *Morisot's* On the Balcony *(c.1871–72) was inspired by Manet's* The Balcony *(1868–69), but Morisot entirely transformed the theme, reversing the sight lines. The picture is set in the suburbs of Passy, with a woman and her daughter looking out across the river onto the vista of Paris beyond. Here the balcony serves to define the circumscribed life of middle-class women and the divisions between the private domestic realm and the public realm of the city.*

Below *Morisot's subject matter often focuses on the private aspects of women's lives, moments of reflection or preparation at their toilette. The soft, often delicate brushwork and refined harmonies, which parallel those of Whistler, encouraged critics to see her work as an expression of her femininity.*

for their work. The Impressionists' choice of informal subjects, such as landscapes or scenes of everyday life, combined with untraditional techniques far removed from academic painting enabled them to integrate into this artistic milieu.

While much of their imagery mirrors that of their male counterparts, it offers significant differences of accent and scope. In some respects this was dictated to them by circumstance. Most of the sites and spectacles that made up the early imagery of modern life that Morisot's and Cassatt's impressionist colleagues depicted were off limits to women artists. Women were discouraged by social convention from wandering the city unchaperoned. The artist Marie Bashkirtseff complained of her inability

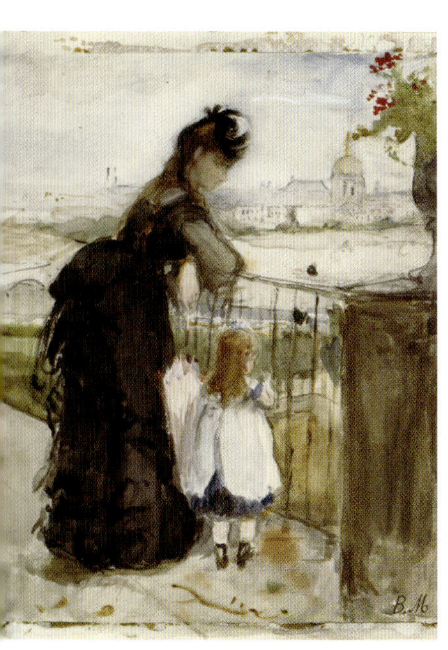

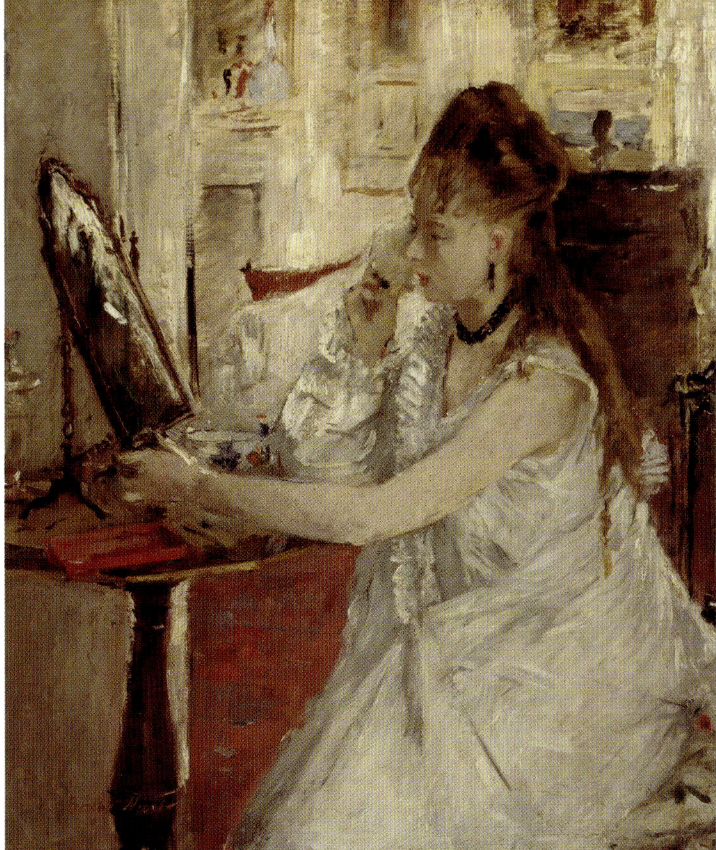

Eva Gonzalès
1849–83

Gonzalès was the daughter of a fashionable novelist and Manet's only pupil. His portrait of her was painted in the year of her first Salon success, a painting of a boy soldier reminiscent of a subject of Manet's that had been rejected four years before. By presenting her painting at the easel, Manet asserts Gonzalès' status as an artist, but other aspects of the picture compromise perhaps the serious image of a professional painter. Manet emphasizes her femininity through the fashionable way she is dressed, the detail of the flower by the hem of her dress and by the way the palette is made to resemble a fan, the quintessential female fashion accessory of the nineteenth century.

to enjoy the freedom of male artistic counterparts in being able to roam freely. As a result, many of the ultra-modern motifs of Impressionism are absent from the paintings of women Impressionists. The subjects Baudelaire associated with the painting of modern life – the imagery of the street, café-concerts and the prostitute's boudoir – do not feature in their work. The paintings of Morisot, Cassatt and Gonzalès often point to this lack of access and allude to the social constraints on women's artistic aspirations. Their images chart the everyday life, rituals and relationships that structured the domestic milieu, and which defined the existence of middle-class women in the nineteenth century, introducing themes of motherhood and child rearing that are, with the exception of Renoir, rarely depicted by their male peers.

Not all the sights and spectacles of modernity are absent from women artists' work. The Opéra was one spectacle of the new Paris that women had access to. Cassatt tackled the subject on eight occasions. While many of these pictures closely resemble Renoir's, others, such as The Woman in Black at the Opera (1879), are quite different. In Renoir's *La Loge* (*The Theatre Box*) (1874), the artist's lightness and spontaneity of touch in conveying the shimmering play of light on fabrics contributes to the sensuousness of the scene that sets up a flirtatious encounter between the viewer and the woman in the foreground. By contrast, Cassatt eschews all the decorative embellishment of the Renoir. Her painting is dominated by the sober, silhouetted figure of the woman whose gaze is averted from the viewer onto the stage. The woman's austere black-and-white costume and the undefined contours of the body, unlike the Renoir, do not invite lingering inspection. Rather than being an object of visual delectation, the spectacle is something she is shown viewing.

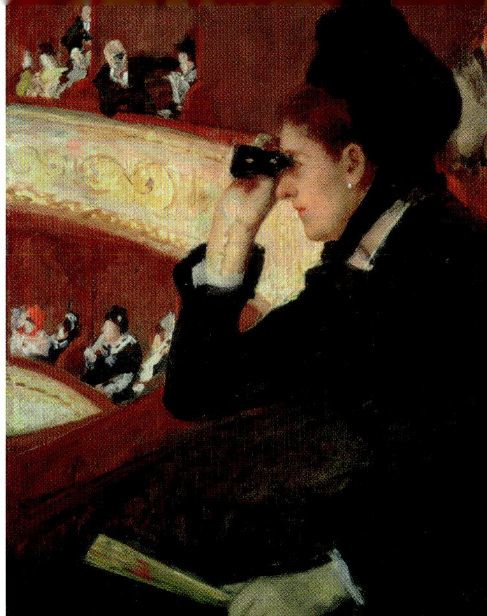

Above *Cassatt's gentle wit and satirical eye are both in evidence in* Woman in Black at the Opera *(1879). Cassatt's pictures show her often challenging the stereotypical ways of representing women. Inventive compositionally and technically, her work received strong support from critics at the Impressionist exhibitions.*

Left *From the 1880s onwards, Renoir became principally known as a painter of French women. His art celebrates women's beauty and sensuality but pays little attention to the more intellectual aspects of their lives, picturing them only as objects of desire or as nurturers of children.*

Berthe Morisot
1841–95

Berthe Morisot came from a wealthy middle-class family. With her sister, Edma, she studied painting with Joseph Guichard, a friend of Corot and on the latter's advice began painting at Auvers and Fontainebleau, where she met Daubigny. In 1868, she became friends with Manet, posing for a number of pictures, including *The Balcony* (1869). Six years later, she married his brother Eugène, but unlike her sister, defied convention by continuing to pursue her artistic career. From 1864 to 1873 Morisot regularly showed at the Salon and exhibited at all the Impressionist shows. At the time of her death in 1896, she was regarded as one of the leading Impressionist artists.

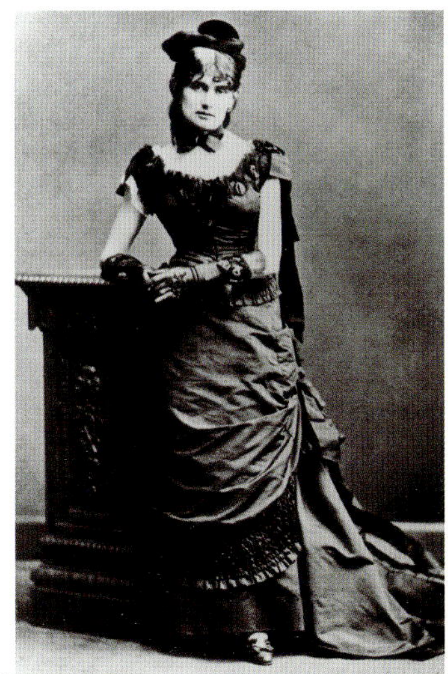

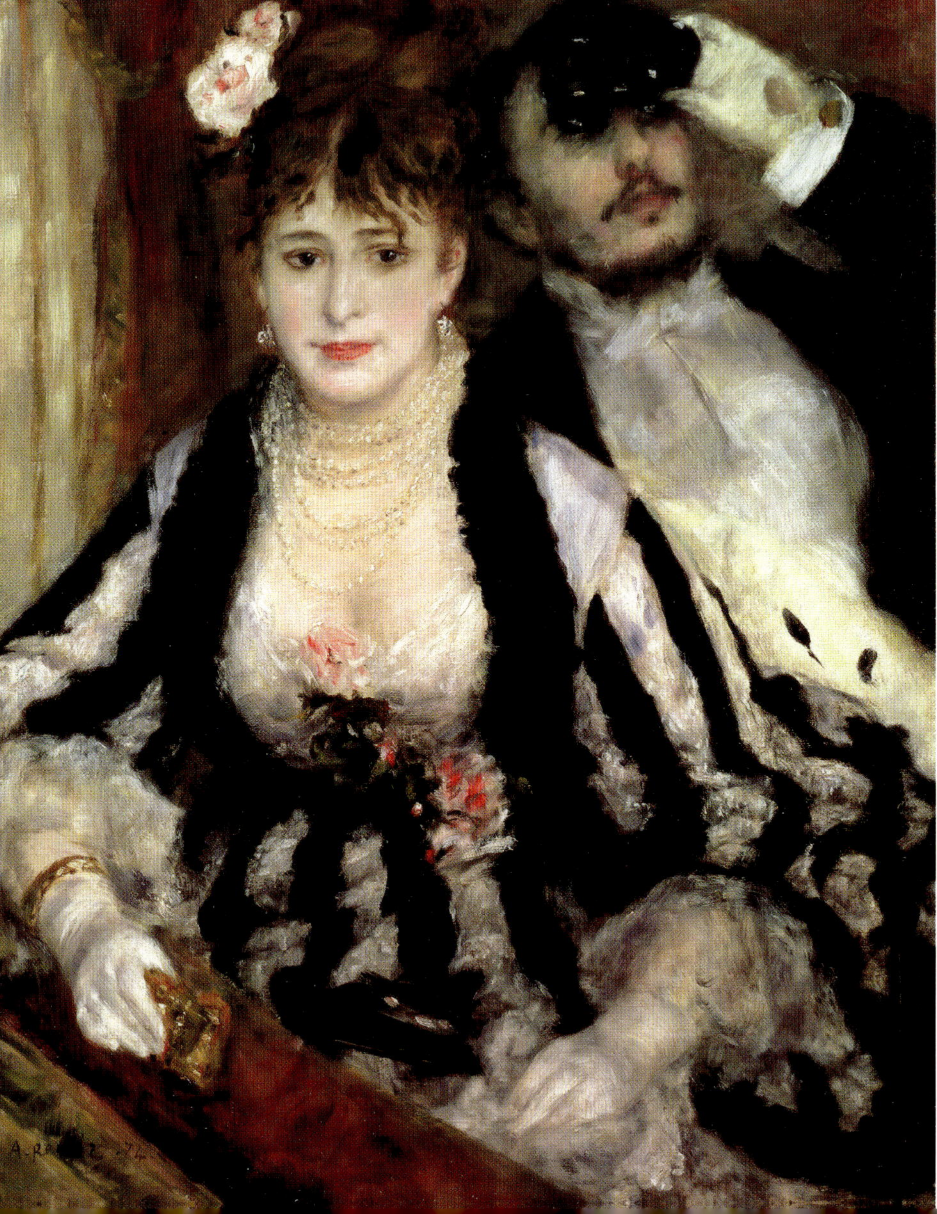

Impressionism During the 1870s and 1880s

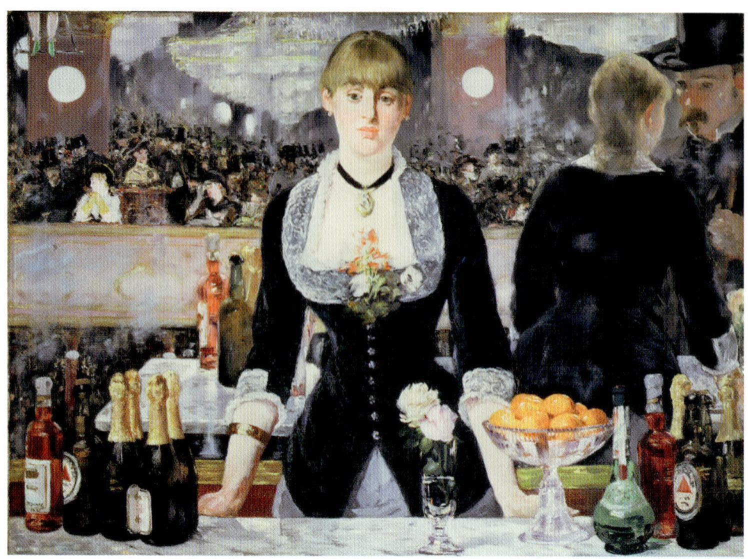

Left A Bar at the Folies-Bergère *(1882)*, was one of Manet's last ambitious paintings before his premature death. *The Folies-Bergère was a fashionable Parisian muscic hall, which offered an array of entertainments, including singers, dancers and even acrobats: the green boots of the acrobat Petit Bob of the Hanlon Lees company can be glimpsed in the upper left margin of the picture. Manet's pyschologically complex picture contrasts the detachment and ennui of the bar maid with the hedonistic ambience reflected in the mirror behind her.*

Below Oarsmen at Chatou *is set in one of Renoir's favourite riverside towns. His Luncheon at the Boating Party is also set here on its adjacent island. During the 1870s and 1880s, many of the Impressionists visited and painted the region, drawn to its pleasures of boating, restaurants and promenading in the countryside. In the 1870s, Renoir and Monet often chose similar motifs, but Renoir remained more focused on the figure and the portrayal of middle-class leisure pursuits.*

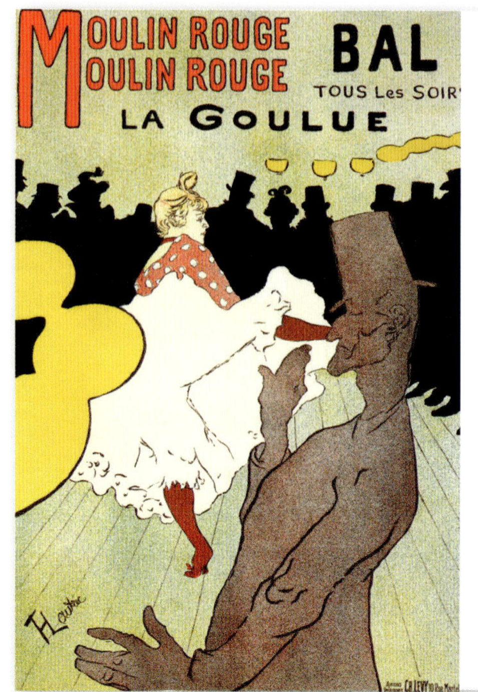

Music Halls

Cafés, café-concerts and music halls became an increasingly prominent feature of Parisian life from the 1840s onwards and thus a popular subject for modern life painters during the latter half of the century. Toulouse-Lautrec was an habitué of the music halls of Paris and his huge colour lithograph poster – measuring 2 x 1 metres wide (6.5 x 3 feet) – for the Moulin Rouge's 29th June Ball shows La Goulue (Louise Webber) and her dance partner, Valentin le Désossé. La Goulue was famed for her bizarre, lewd dance that involved kicking the hats off members of the audience.

The decade between the 1870s and the early 1880s was a crucial moment for the Impressionists, the period in which the mature styles of the painters and their abiding preoccupations were formed. It was also the period when the group identity of the Impressionists emerged from the series of independent exhibitions they staged and the close-knit associations they had established with each other. During this time, the Impressionists began to abandon any vestiges of traditional techniques that remained in their work, minimizing their use of *chiaroscuro*, earth colours and black, in order to paint with a brighter, lighter palette, largely composed of primary and secondary colours, which gave freshness and vibrancy to their work. Monet, Morisot, Sisley and Renoir characteristically sought to convey atmospheric effects and the fugitive aspects of nature, and accordingly de-emphasized pictorial structure in favour of the suggestive impression. They sought to "naturalize" their painting by establishing flexible conventions that corresponded to qualities they saw nature as possessing, such as transience and flux. Their use of fluid and broken brushwork provided a cursory, notational, artistic vocabulary that quickly captured their sensations, allowing the painters the freedom to respond "indiscriminately" to visual stimuli and render their motifs in terms of the shifting play of light and colour.

By contrast, the paintings of Pissarro and Cézanne displayed a greater concern with form and less interest in the fleeting play of light and reflection. Though these effects can sometimes be found in their work, both painters generally preferred even and stable lighting and Cézanne, in particular, avoided fugitive, climatic effects. He tended to select motifs with strong structural components, often focusing on foreground elements.

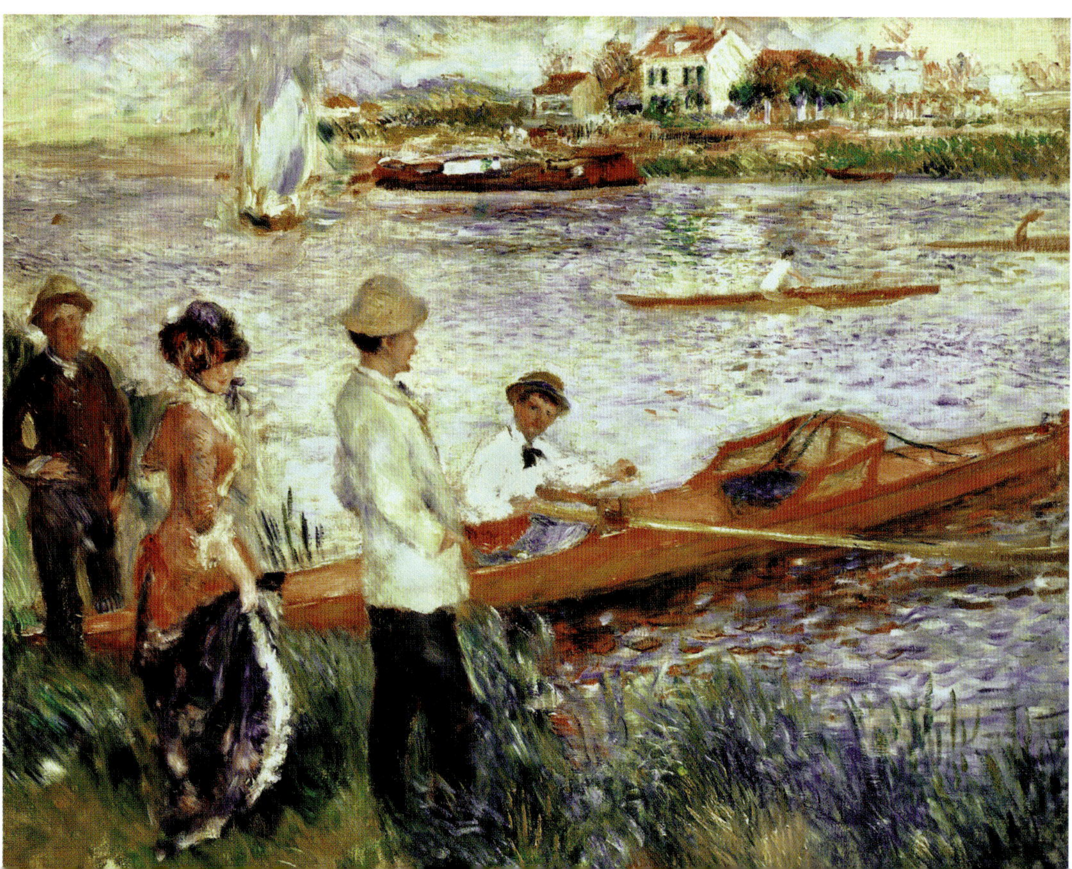

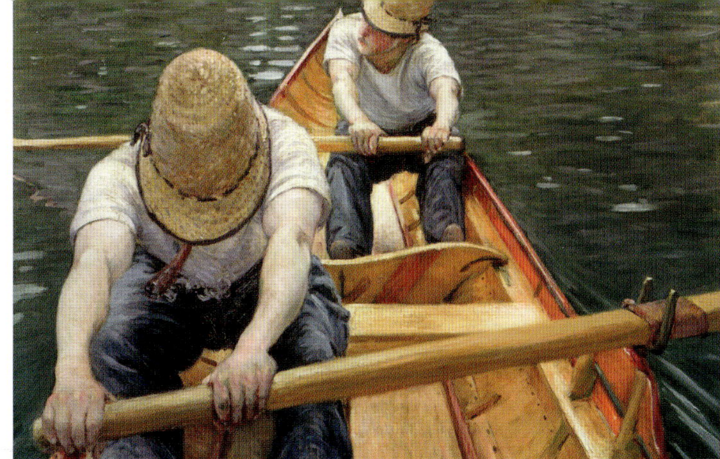

The differences in conception between Cézanne's painting and that of the other painters points to divisions within Impressionism as to whether the painter sought to capture an impression of the contingencies of nature as instantaneously and spontaneously as possible, or render a more reflective synthesis of impressions through prolonged scrutiny, which implied memory and analysis and a concentration on the underlying structures inherent in nature.

During this period the artists redefined or expanded the range of subjects that they tackled. In the late 1870s and 1880s, Monet, who began to be recognized as the leading landscapist of the group, turned his attention to remote landscape subjects often favouring seascapes that make much of the dramatic and monumental rock formations along the northern French coastline of Normandy, to which he continued to make lengthy visits over the period 1880–86, as well as the countryside around Giverny where he settled in 1883. In this decade, Monet travelled extensively across France in search of contrasting types of landscape motifs, adjusting his palette and treatment in response to the varied kinds of landscape and conditions he encountered. At the beginning of 1884 he visited Provence, painting in Antibes, Menton and Bordighera situated on either side of the border with Italy. In 1886, he painted the Brittany coastline, depicting the extraordinary granite formations of the Belle Ile and, in 1889, he painted a series of melancholic views of the bleak landscape of the Massif Central, depicting the monumental hills situated along the confluent rivers of the Creuse and Petit Creuse.

While Monet turned his back on the modern motifs he had favoured in the early 1870s, Renoir, Degas and Manet continued to pursue modern life subjects. These often concentrated on the new forms of leisure and entertainment in Paris, which saw an explosion of cafés and café-concerts. Manet's *Bar at the Folies-Bergère* (1882) was his last major statement about modern life before his premature death in 1883 as a result of complications arising from a syphilis infection. It portrays a barmaid at a bar on the second-floor balcony of one of the most spectacular music halls, with its array of operettas, comedians, acrobats and dancers. Degas was also drawn to such subjects, but concentrated on the female performers at the Ambassadeurs and its nearby rival, the Alcazar d'été, where the singers Emélie Bécat and Thérésa (Emma Valadon) performed.

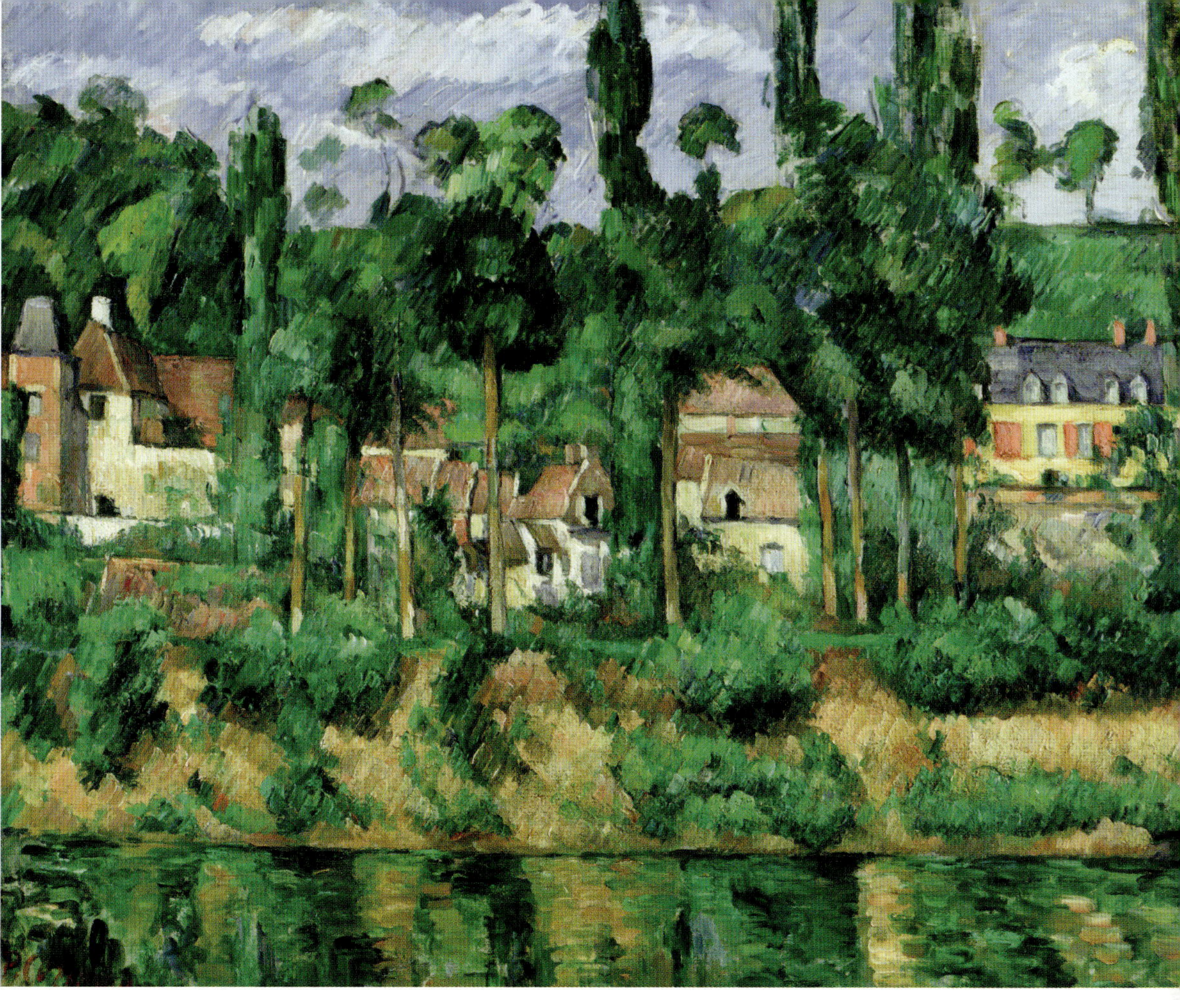

Above left *The Caillebotte family owned a house at Yerres, south-west of Paris. Yerres was famed for its boating, a motif depicted by Caillebotte in a number of paintings. Here, he depicts the "périssoires", a type of flat-bottomed skiff propelled by a two-bladed kyak paddle that could achieve very fast speeds. The composition, which places the viewer close to the rowers shows his experimentation with point of view.*

Below *Degas's images of Paris's café-concerts capture the strange charm, vulgarity and splenetic performances of the leading stars of the day. In* Aux Ambassadeurs *(1876–77), shown at the third Impressionist exhibition, the singer dressed in red is probably Victorine Demay, whose performance contained "an echo of the boulevard lifes".*

Above *From the late 1870s Cézanne was experimenting with ways of organizing his pictures. In* The Château de Médan, *featuring a house owned by Zola, whom Cézanne had known since childhood, he divides the canvas into five bands each containing a different type of brushwork, using a range of simple, directional strokes to give definition and establish spatial intervals.*

Below Snow Effect at Vétheuil *(1878–79) was begun shortly after Monet and his family moved to the town in Autumn 1778. From the mid-1870s onwards, Monet began to explore a range of climatic effects in his painting. His use of small touches of broken brushwork captures the glimmer of the winter light, the reflections on the icy surface of the river and the fragility of the snow on the surface of the town.*

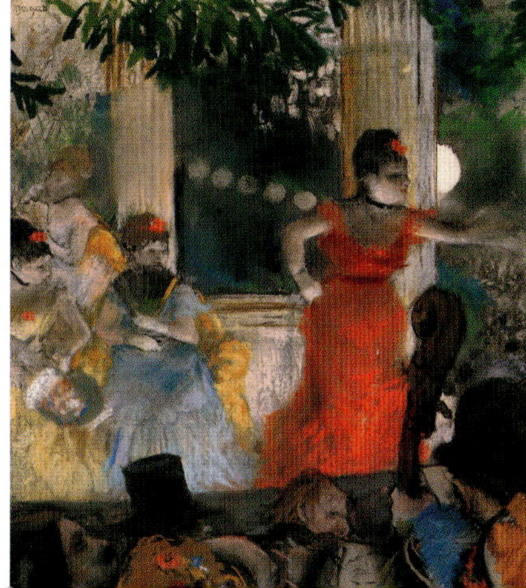

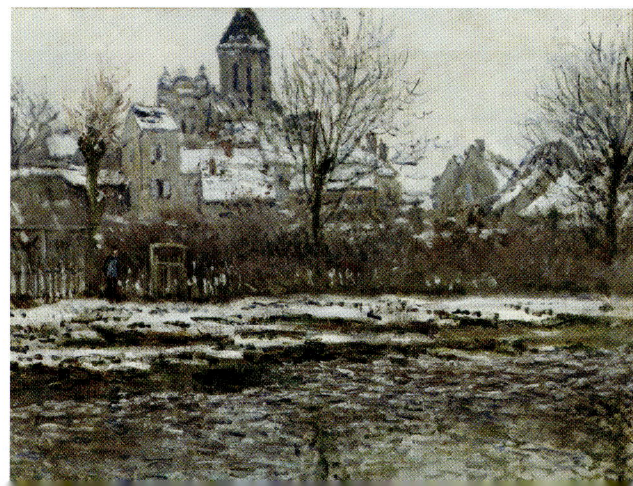

Salon Success and Group Shows

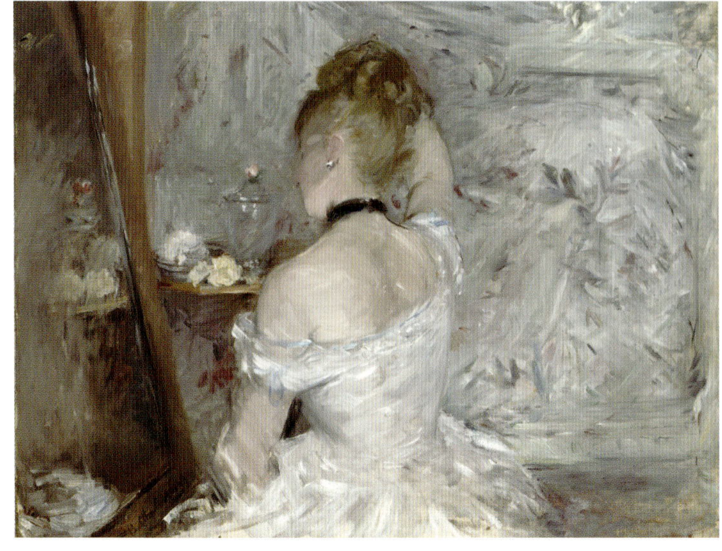

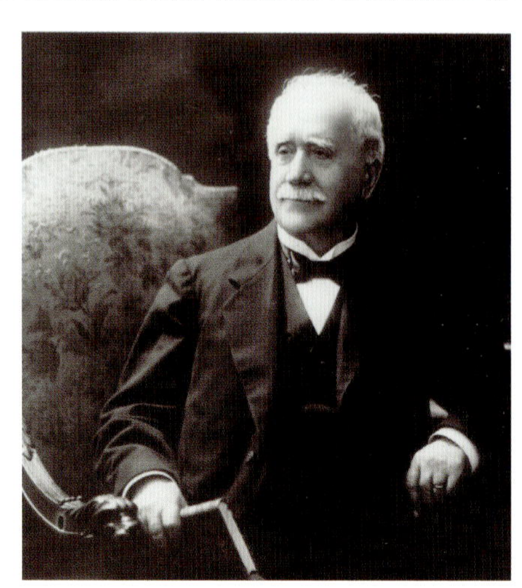

Paul Durand-Ruel
1831–1922

The son of a picture dealer, Paul Durand-Ruel became the main art dealer of the Impressionists and his acumen and deft touch for public relations were instrumental in their success. His first contact with them was in 1871, when he met Pissarro in London, and he staged an exhibition of their work there the following year, marketing them as the successors of the Barbizon painters. In 1876, he provided the financial backing for the second Impressionist exhibition, which was held in his gallery on the centrally located rue le Peletier. Though relations with the painters were not always cordial, he provided them with financial and moral support believing, in his own words that "the true picture dealer should also be an enlightened patron".

Although the first Impressionist exhibition was intended as a one-off event, the continual problems that many of the painters experienced in gaining success at the Salon led to further group exhibitions. Between 1874 and 1886 eight shows were staged, though the titles of the exhibitions, their aims and the artists who participated all fluctuated. Despite a core of exhibitors that included Pissarro, Caillebotte, Morisot and Degas, the contributors differed from exhibition to exhibition, and only the third show was called the exhibition of Impressionists. Monet and Renoir were only occasional, and sometimes even reluctant, exhibitors with the group, showing regularly in the 1870s but only rarely after 1880, having gained the strong backing of several leading art dealers. From this point on, they sought to enhance their reputations at the Salon, which remained the most important exhibition forum, or in dealer-backed, one-man shows that presented the artists not as representatives of a general tendency but as unique individuals.

The cultural, political and economic conditions of the Third Republic initially provided a volatile context for artists working outside the official system of rewards. The humiliating defeat at the hands of the Prussians had left France in financial ruin and the country was run more or less under martial law until the liberal

Above Woman at her Toilette *(c. 1875) shows Morisot's subtle colour harmonies and vibrant impressionistic brushwork. It was exhibited at the fifth Impressionist exhibition to much critical success. Armand Silvestre singled it out as one of the most impressive works of the exhibition, praising its novel composition and subtle handling of light.*

Right *During his visit to Etretat, Monet executed a number of views of the Manneporte, exploring its physiognomy from a variety of different vantage points. Here, he emphasizes the monumentality of this giant rock formation with its natural arch, using the lighting and the storm-tossed sea to dramatize his motif.*

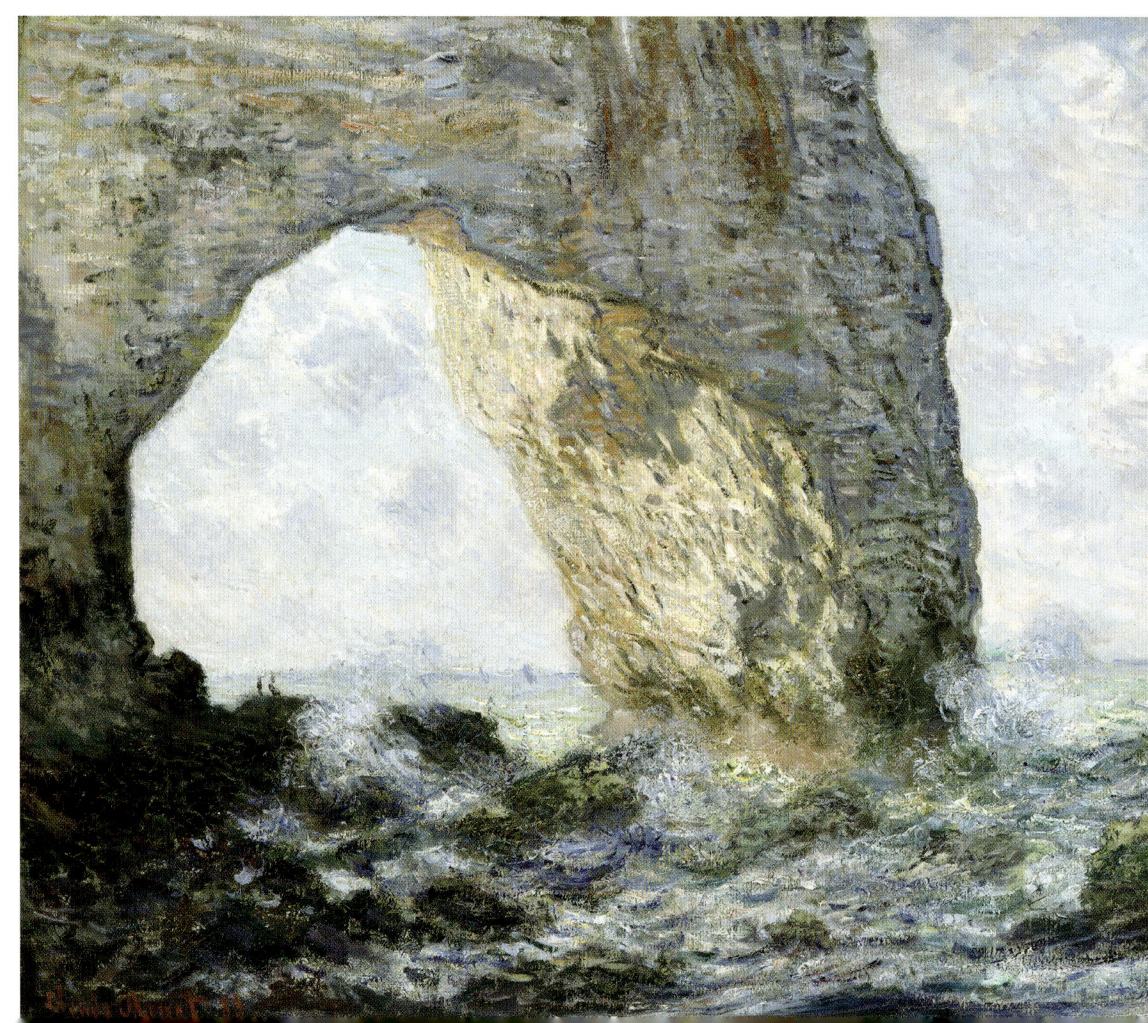

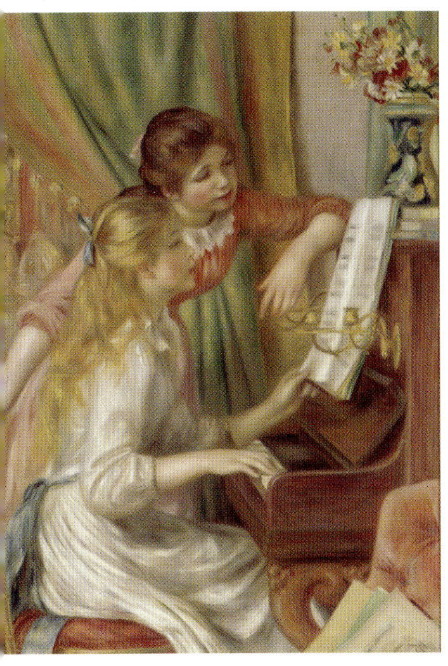

reforms of the late 1870s. At the second show in 1876, critics used the term "*intransigeants*" to describe the most innovative paintings on view. It was a term that suggested the radicalism of the painters in abandoning the traditional skills and pictorial values that most critics conventionally expected from painting, such as a high degree of pictorial finish, the self-containment of the picture space and clarity of compositional design. However, it was also a term that had political overtones. In Spain, in 1873, the anarchist wing of the Spanish Federalist party, known as *Los Intransigentes*, was instrumental in the downfall of the Spanish Constitutional Monarchy that plunged the country into civil war. The incident set off alarm bells in neighbouring France. The term "Impressionism" was adopted for the third exhibition 1877 in large measure to defuse the ready association of radical painting with radical politics.

Contemporary critical reviews of the exhibitions distinguished between the impressionist tendency that they primarily associated with Monet, Renoir, Morisot, Sisley and Pissarro, and a realist grouping of Degas and his followers, such as Zandomeneghi, Cassatt and Forain. The distinction occludes much that they shared in common, such as modern subject matter and innovative compositional techniques, but drew attention to different accents in their work. Throughout the 1870s, Degas and his followers focused on figures set in Parisian contexts and chose less ephemeral subjects than their colleagues. For all their innovation, their work displayed more traditional artistic skills of line drawing, as critics frequently noted. Artists like Monet, Sisley and Pissarro concentrated on landscape subjects, rendered with a broad, painterly effect and with an eye for the atmospheric qualities of light and colour.

These artistic differences exacerbated personal ones and the organization of subsequent exhibitions led to many acrimonious exchanges, particularly between Caillebotte and Degas, as they wrestled for control over the shows' contents and objectives. Degas's insistence that exhibitors did not send work to the Salon continually rankled with other contributors. At the eighth exhibition in 1886, Pissarro's determination to include two young artists, Georges Seurat and Paul Signac, led to arguments and withdrawals and eventually their work, alongside that of Pissarro and his son Lucien, was shown in a separate room. These arguments put paid to any further group exhibitions, but in many ways the Impressionist exhibitions had already run their course. By the late 1880s, Impressionist artists had begun to gain public recognition and enjoy success at the Salon, which in 1881 was privatized and placed in the hands of artists. In May 1892, the State purchased Renoir's *Young Girls at the Piano* (1892) and followed this by buying one of Monet's pictures of the Rouen Cathedral façade. When Caillebotte, who apart from his artistic affiliation with the movement had also been one of its chief patrons, died in 1894, his bequest to the Musée Luxembourg of his collection of Impressionist pictures was, after protracted negotiations, eventually accepted. These events announced Impressionism's official endorsement and its recognition as an important artistic movement.

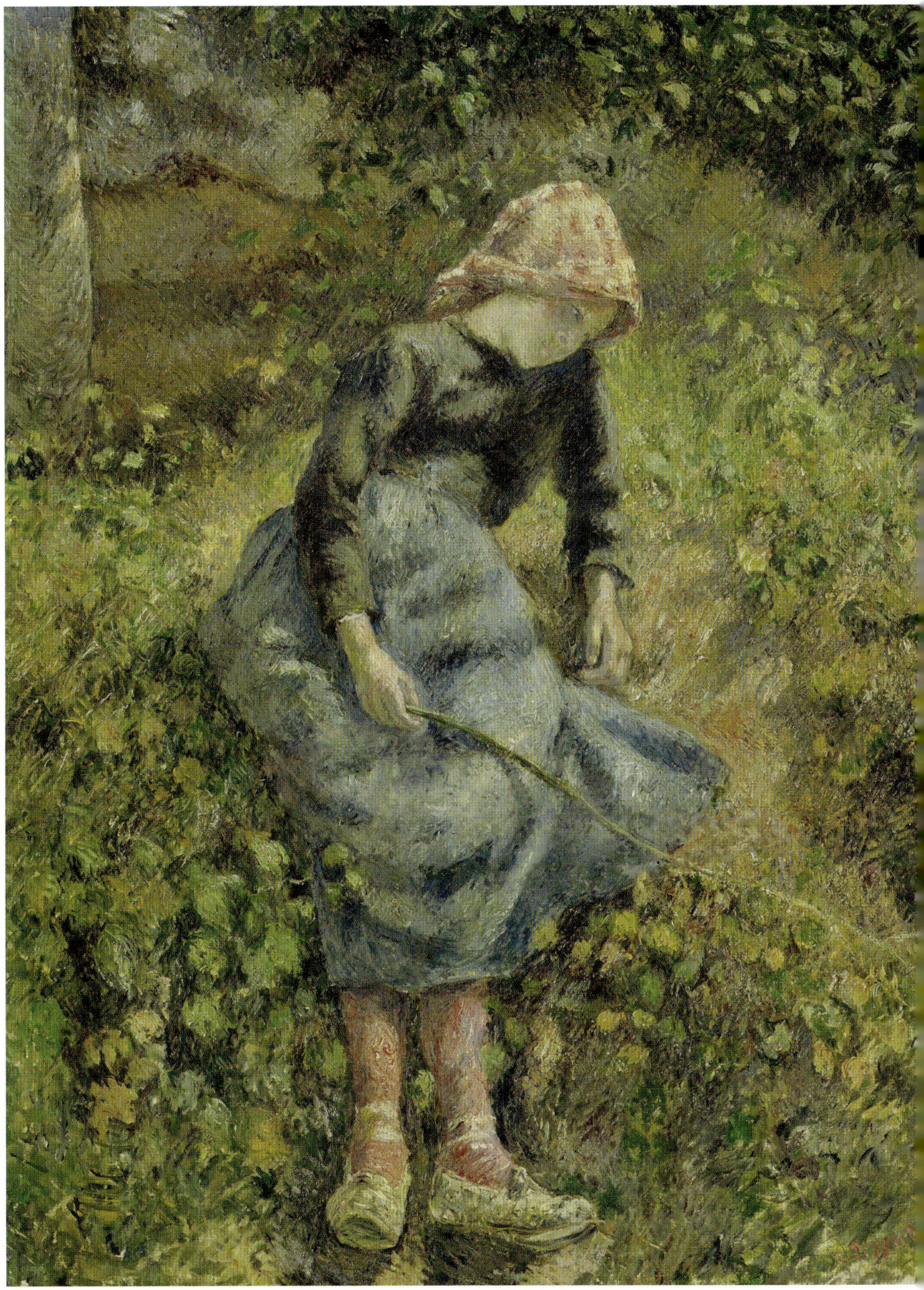

Above left *Renoir produced several versions of this motif, which was one of his favourite subjects. He produced a large number of preparatory sketches in developing the composition. Though he used two sisters as models, he presents them as types rather than individuals. This type of genre painting had clear reference points in the work of eighteenth-century French artists.*

Above The Shepherdess *(1881) evokes the quiet melancholy of many of Pissarro's paintings of the countryside. Despite the close viewpoint, the depiction of the girl remains objective and detached. Pissarro constantly questioned himself about whether he had succeeded in giving form to the distinctive beauty of the working classes, and sought to avoid the sentimentality of Salon representations of the peasantry.*

Neo-Impressionism, Pissarro and the Critique of Impressionism

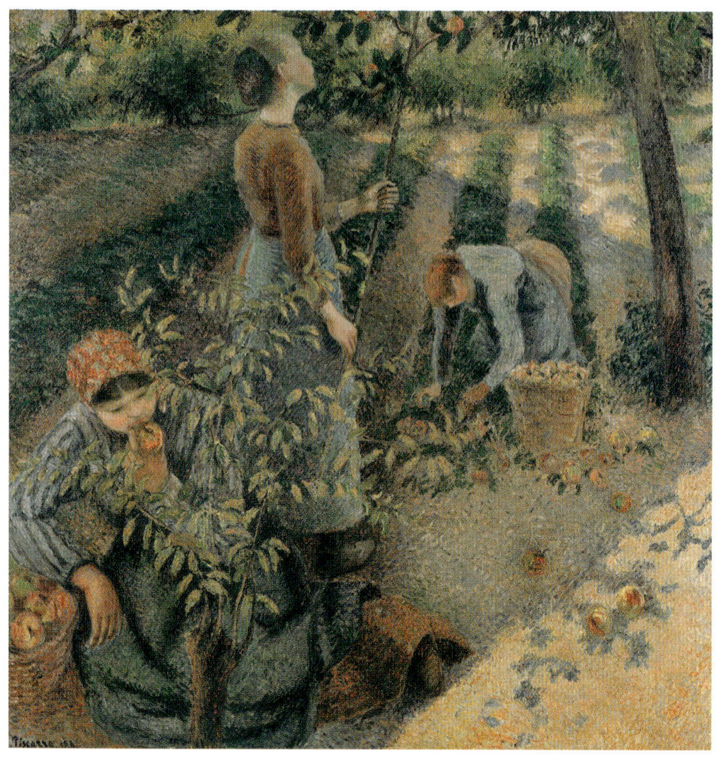

Camille Pissarro *1830–1903*

The importance of Camille Pissarro for Impressionism extends far beyond the considerable artistic achievement of his work. As the most articulate and intellectually minded of the Impressionists, he had a major role in setting up the Impressionist exhibitions and conceptualizing its artistic aims. A radical in politics, he sought to express in painting his deeply ingrained feeling for nature and humanity. Most of his imagery focuses on the life of the countryside, which for Pissarro represented an inalienable relationship between man and nature. Apart from his paintings, Pissarro was an enthusiastic engraver, watercolourist and painter of porcelain designs.

Far left *Pissarro's short period of neo-Impressionism produced many lyrical and idyllic masterpieces, including* Apple Picking *(1886), a subject he treated many times over several decades. Two female figures pick apples from the ground while a third shakes them from the branches. The painting was one of his most critically successful in his lifetime.*

Below *Seurat's* Bathers *(1884) was his most ambitious work to date. Executed on a large scale, it sought to combine Impressionist subject matter with references to the classical tradition. The picture was strongly inspired by the poetic harmony, tonality and classical poise of Puvis de Chavannes, though the choice of modern subject was far removed from the subjects Puvis favoured.*

At the eighth and final Impressionist exhibition, two new young artists appeared in the catalogue, Georges Seurat and Paul Signac. Their inclusion, at the insistence of Pissarro, sparked controversy and led Renoir to pull out of the show. Although Seurat and Signac could be regarded as broadly working within the general aims of Impressionism, their painting was seen as critiquing the freely improvised and subjective style favoured by Impressionist painters. The term Neo-Impressionism was quickly coined to describe the indebtedness but also departure of these young painters from the principles of Impressionist painting.

At the 1886 exhibition, Seurat, widely regarded as the leader of the emerging Neo-Impressionist group, exhibited nine works, including the monumental *A Sunday Afternoon on the Island of La Grande Jatte* (1884–86), which, in its formality, size and style, was out of character with the small scale and informality of the other works on view. The painting, which mixes references to Impressionism with allusions to classicism, Egyptian art, popular prints and fashion plates, took over a year to complete and involved many preparatory drawings and oil studies. It was the first picture in which Seurat began to employ the distinctive *pointilliste* or *divisioniste* technique that became the hallmark

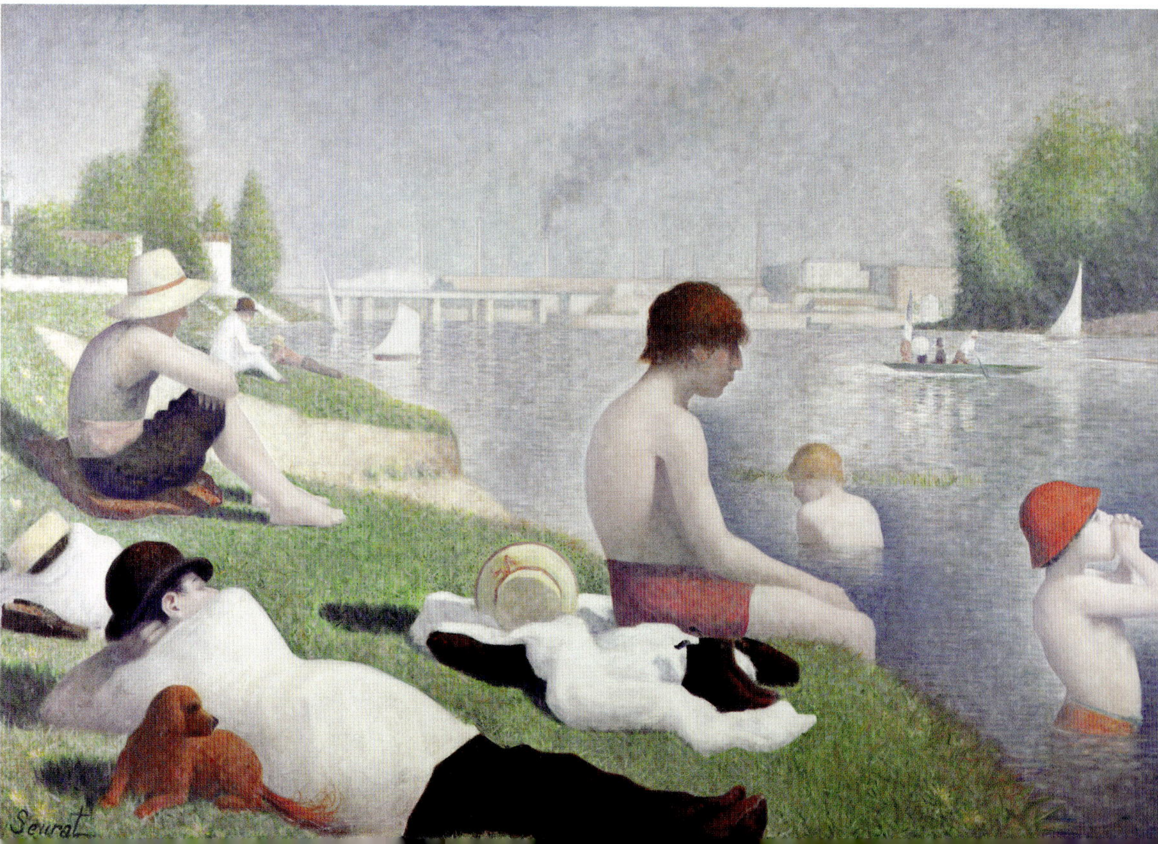

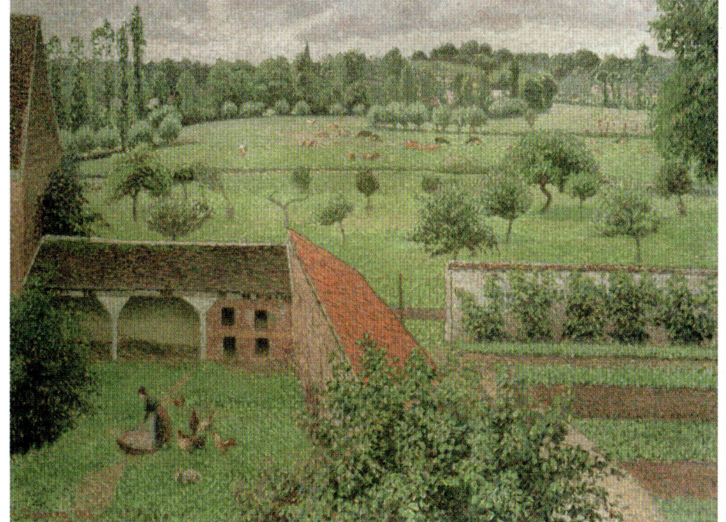

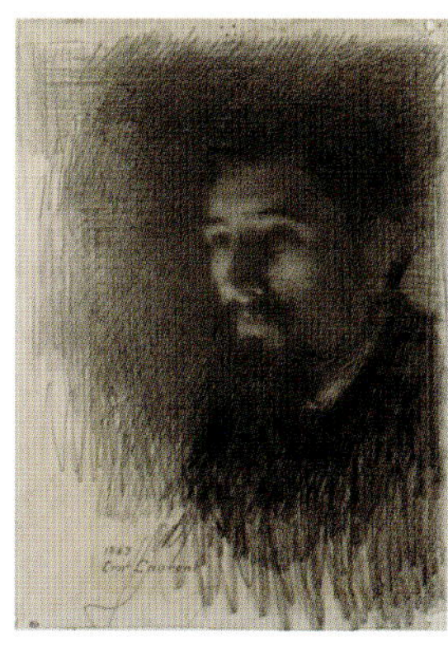

Georges Seurat
1859–91

Born in Paris, Seurat studied at the Ecole des beaux-arts and spent much of his student days copying in the Louvre. His earliest works already attest to the passion for analysis that would ultimately lead to the development of the Neo-Impressionist style of divisionism. He immersed himself in the theories of Chevreul and other scientists dealing with visual phenomena, and also read Charles Blanc's influential treatise "The Grammar of Painting". Seurat died prematurely, aged 32, from an infection, and therefore did not live to see the influence of his work, nor realize the full implications of his theories.

Far left *Pissarro's* View from my Window, Eragny-sur-Epte *(1886–88) shows a meadow in the village of Bazincourt. Pissarro's rustic themes and the subtle, grey-violet harmonies of his skies proved less popular with Durand-Ruel who rejected the picture. Nevertheless, Pissarro felt it was an important work, and singled out the vibrant red roof and naïve drawing as the hallmark of his painting's modernity.*

Below *Measuring 2.1 by 3.1 metres (6.9 by 10.1 feet), Seurat's ambitious multi-figure composition,* Sunday Afternoon on the Island of La Grande Jatte *(1884–86), which features over 50 figures of varying ages, class and occupation, was meticulously worked out through a large series of preparatory drawings and oil sketches. It was clearly intended as a major statement about modern life, and is one of the first pictures in which he developed his pointillist technique. The critic Jules Christophe described his work as a "mechanical ballet", that critiqued the "sterile conformism" of the bourgeoisie.*

of Neo-Impressionism. While the Academically trained Seurat admired the technical innovations of Impressionism, particularly the painters' adoption of modern subjects and their acute scrutiny of light and colour, he felt their compositions lacked the structure, harmony and clarity associated with the old masters and contemporary classicists such as Puvis de Chavannes. Impressionism, in his view, was devoid of method and too preoccupied with the individual artist's vision, an art that for all its renewal of the technical means of painting, lacked the poetry and intellectualism that he sought in painting. Seurat's more systematic pointillism, building up of the surface entirely out of small dots of pure pigment, provided a more uniform, unified and disciplined artistic vocabulary than the varied range of impressionist brushstrokes. Seurat saw pointillism as a highly rationalized technique that allowed for a more objective, analytical and scientific approach to the recording of optical phenomena.

La Grande Jatte was the companion piece to his *Bathers at Asnières* (1884), pictures that are set on adjacent banksides of a suburb located on the edge of Paris along the Seine. The two works contrast the alternate milieus and lifestyle of the workers and the middle classes. Much of Seurat's imagery of the period revisits the subject matter that had preoccupied Impressionism in the 1870s, but which many of the painters were now dispensing with, and might be seen as reviving Baudelaire's original vision of the painter of modern life, re-connecting Impressionism with the painting of the city and the suburbs.

Aside from *La Grande Jatte*, the centrepiece of his exhibits, Seurat showed three drawings, executed in his atmospheric *conté* crayon style, and five landscapes set at Grand-Camp and Courbevoire. The spare, solitary, coastal pictures of Grand-Camp, executed on a small scale in a meticulous pointillist style, intentionally invite comparison with Monet, whose choice of motifs they closely resemble.

Pissarro, the most theoretical and radically minded of the Impressionists saw Seurat and Signac's pointillism as offering a new direction at a time when the absorption of Impressionism into mainstream painting led him to question its continued viability. His

own submissions to the exhibition, such as *Apple Picking* (1886) and *View from My Window, Eragny-sur-Epte* (1886–88), display a tauter and more uniform network of brushstrokes and greater decorative conception that reflects his adoption of the more disciplined style of the younger painters. The association of Neo-Impressionism with anarchist politics may also have encouraged him to view Neo-Impressionism as a more democratic and egalitarian style of painting. Pissarro's conversion to Neo-Impressionism did not last long, however, and within a few years he had returned to his earlier Impressionist style.

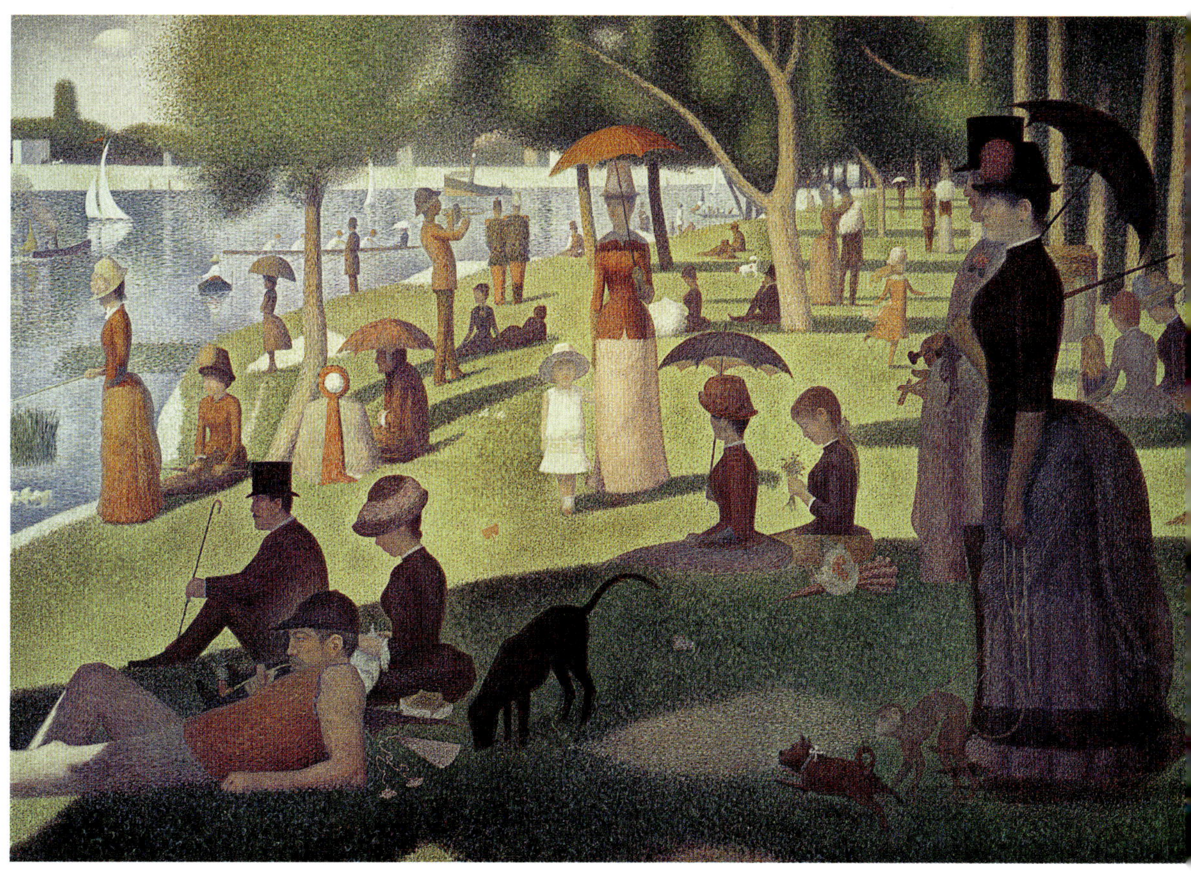

Degas's Nudes

During the 1880s, Degas began an ambitious series of female nudes at their toilette. Although he had tackled the nude before, most ambitiously in his *Young Spartans* (c.1860–61), during the 1870s he had generally avoided the subject, preferring modern life scenes set in the Parisian milieu. With the exception of his ballet pictures, these now receded as he turned his attention to images of women bathers. The centrepiece of his contribution to the eighth and final Impressionist exhibition was to be ten works, listed under the comprehensive title "Suite of Female Nudes, Bathing, Washing, Drying, Wiping, Combing Themselves and Being Combed". Only six or seven of these were actually exhibited, but the choice to present a series of nudes was a declaration of a new direction in his art. He followed this up with a show two years later of nine bathers at the Boussod & Valadon Gallery on Boulevard Montmartre.

These nudes announced a more overt engagement with traditional subject matter but, as always with Degas, in a way that renewed the subject by re-presenting it in a modern fashion, setting his figures in

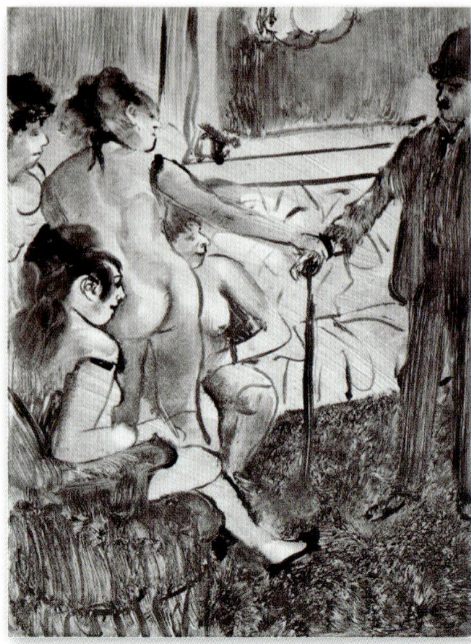

Degas's Monotypes

In the 1870s, Degas began experimenting with print media and produced a large number of monotypes, most of which feature scenes of prostitution. These pictures have more in common with the earthy representations of prostitution in low art media than the glamorous or sentimental image of the prostitute's life in high art imagery. They are often sexually explicit and the figures unidealized, but these prints are also witty. Some feature clients rather timidly being led to the bedchamber, while others show prostitutes idle and bored, waiting for clients. These monotypes were mainly made for private consumption. Degas exhibited very few during his lifetime and many were destroyed after his death.

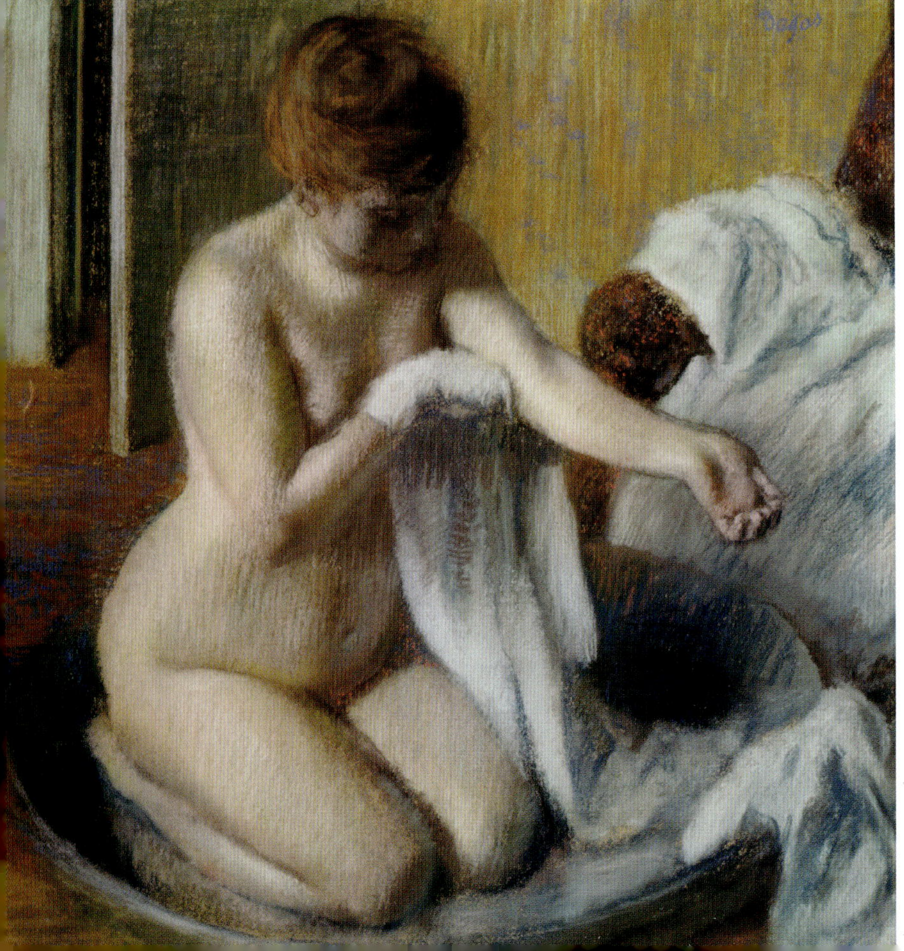

contemporary apartments or the artist's studio. *Woman in a Tub* (1884) (now in the Burrell Collection) alludes to a statue from antiquity, the famous *Crouching Venus* in the Louvre, while others make reference to the nudes of Rembrandt, Ingres and the old masters. The close proximity of the figures to the viewer, most of which are seen from the back, heightens the intimacy and voyeurism of these images. Gustave Geffroy wrote, "[The artist] wanted to paint a woman who did not know she was being watched, as one would see her hidden by a curtain or through a keyhole."

The lack of idealization and affectation of these nudes, described by one observer as "frank representations of the imperfections of the flesh", led some to see them as inspired by misogynistic feelings. The critic Octave Mirbeau caught the general mood when he remarked, "These are admirable works and their composition is utterly extraordinary. There is a wonderful power of synthesis and abstract line in them… (They) have not been done to inspire passion for women nor sensual desire. Degas has not sought beauty or grace… on the contrary there is a ferocity that speaks clearly of a disdain for women and a horror of love."

The Suite of Nudes also marked Degas's preference for working in pastel. Pastel was a medium that was associated with French, eighteenth-century, rococo artists and his attraction to it reflected the revival of interest in their work. Pastel,

Far left *Degas's subtle use of pastel technique in hatching strokes imaginatively conveys the tactile experience of a woman washing and drying herself. Always alert to the possibility of visual puns, Degas draws a visual parallel between the outstretched arm of the woman and the arm of the armchair draped with towels.*

Opposite bottom right The Tub *(1886) is one of a number of pictures Degas made of women crouching or bending while washing themselves. These bathing scenes offered him the opportunity for exploring complex and unorthodox figure arrangements, often from high vantage points. Degas used boxes in his studio to achieve these high viewpoints.*

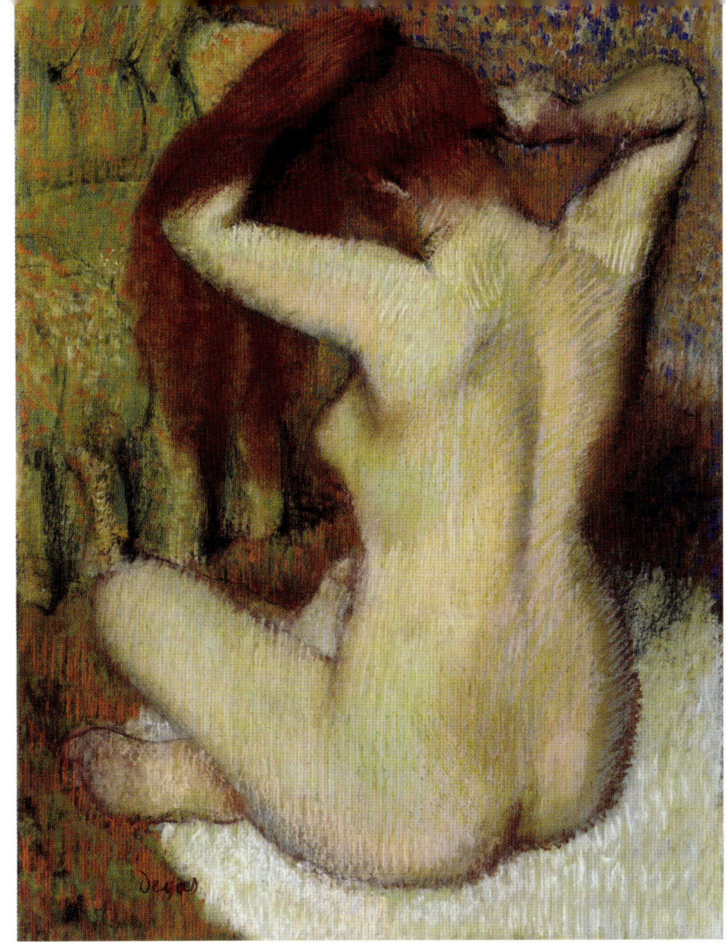

Left *In this vibrantly coloured pastel the representation of the body in short hatch strokes dragged across the picture surface parallels the action of the woman pulling a comb through her hair. In this way Degas intensifies the viewer's tactile experience of the picture. The pastel is a good example of Degas's adaptation of classical poses to modern settings.*

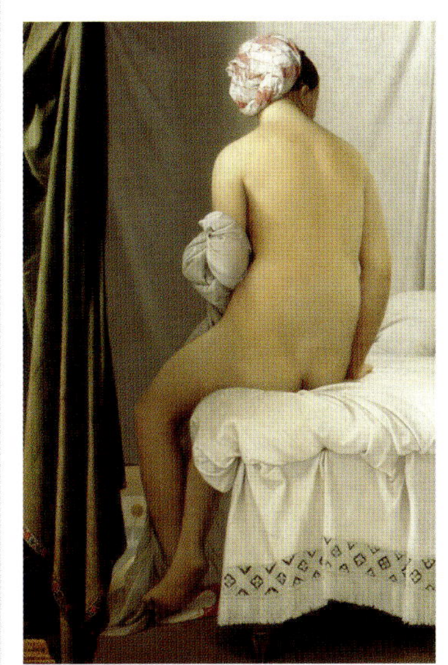

Jean-Auguste-Dominque Ingres
1780–1867

Although the neo-classical painter Ingres was a staunch traditionalist, who famously declared there was only one true artistic school, that of the antique, he was recognized, even by his opponents, as a peerless draughtsman and one of France's greatest artists. Degas much admired Ingres and as a young man even once visited him. He later recalled the artist advising him "Study line… draw lots of lines, from memory or from nature". Degas particularly revered Ingres's masterpiece *The Valpinçon Bather* (1808), a female nude seen from behind at her toilette, the memory of which is continually revisited in Degas's own nudes.

long out of fashion, became *à la mode* and in 1885 the Societé des Pastelistes was formed attracting artists of all allegiances. In using pastel, Degas was able to fuse his linearity with the vibrant colour effects pastel afforded and to blur the boundaries between preparatory sketches, for which most artists restricted their use of pastel, and exhibition pictures. The flexibility of pastel allowed him not only to delineate and model the figure at the same time, but also rapidly to work up the surface of his pictures layer by layer in fluent fashion, making adjustments as he went along. Degas may also have been attracted to pastel for other reasons. In the 1880s, his eyesight further deteriorated, leaving him with hypersensitivity to bright light, myopia and an irregular field of vision. The amplitude and breadth of pastel made it a more convenient artistic medium for him to work in, allowing him to dispense with preliminary studies. Working in pastel, Degas emphasizes the tactile qualities of the body, in a way that departs from the smooth, glossy surfaces of academic painting. The web of hatching strokes, which echo the weave of the canvas, and smudgings of pastel draw the viewer's attention to the artist's act of marking the surface of the canvas. In this way a parallelism is established between the artist's intense activity of touching the surface and the women's action of rubbing and drying themselves and this parallelism heightens our attention to the physical quality of touch.

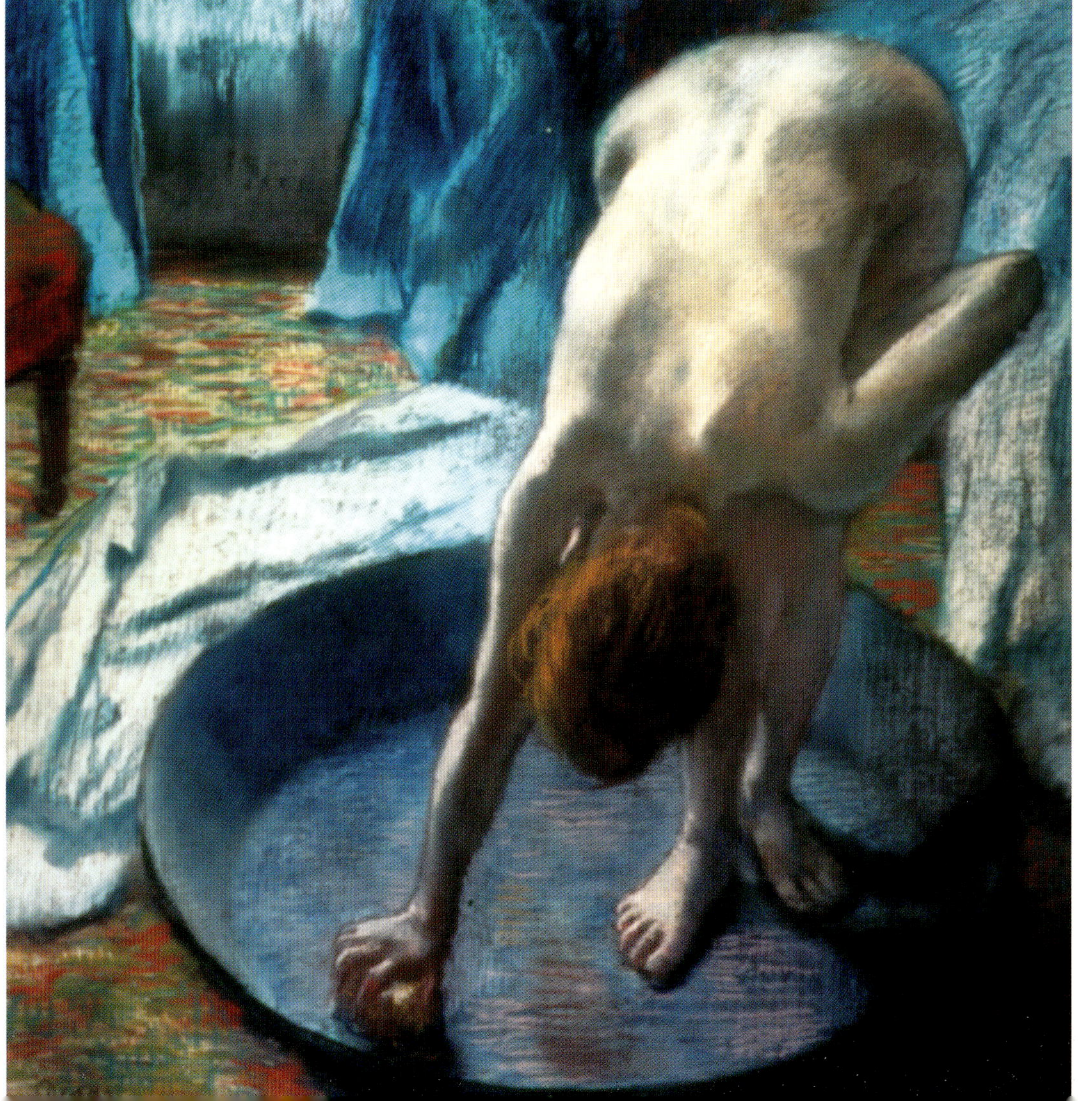

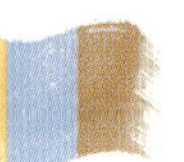

Monet's Series Paintings

The 1880s had seen Monet become a painter of the diverse regions of France. Monet tended to work en plein air, making a number of freely worked views of the same motif from closely related viewpoints, and working up these paintings in his lodgings or studio. The idea that a single motif, viewed under different lighting and climatic conditions, or by way of small adjustments of vantage point, could be the subject for many different paintings seems to have been consolidated in his mind at this time, and in the 1890s he began to work methodically on landscape motifs conceived as series. Later, Monet would explain to the critic Gustave Geffroy and his dealer Paul Durand-Ruel how he was driven by a desire for "instantaneity", attempting to capture the fugitive appearances of his motifs under altered lighting conditions.

This necessitated working on many pictures at the same time, rapidly changing canvases in response to the changes in the light and atmosphere. Monet recalled sending his daughter Alice back to his studio to fetch new canvases as he struggled to respond to the ever-changing light and weather conditions."

Over the next decade, Monet concentrated on four ambitious series of motifs all of which expressed aspects of traditional France. The first of these was his series of pictures of grainstacks, humble agrarian motifs that are given monumentality and pictorial interest by his vibrant and variegated palette, followed immediately by a series of poplars, his most decorative pictures to date. Monet exploited to the full the possibility of treating a single motif in decidedly different ways, sometimes presenting

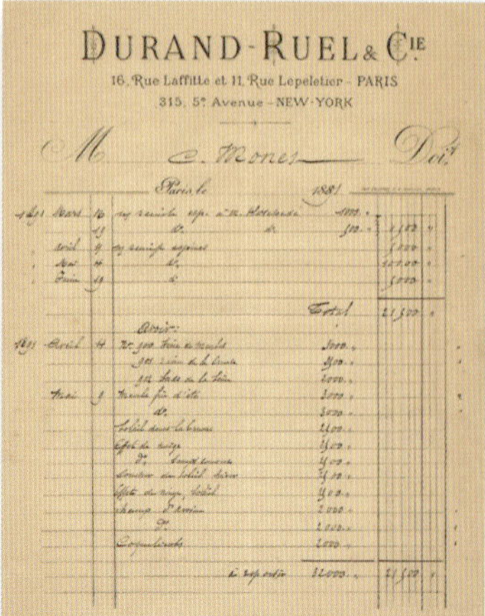

Monet's Fame

Though Degas and Pissarro dismissed much of Monet's recent work as too commercial and decorative in conception, the success of the series paintings consolidated Monet's reputation as one of the leading artists of his day and coincided with major one-man exhibitions at the galleries of George Petit and Durand-Ruel. The latter's expansion of his activities into America with his New York shows in 1896 was dominated by Monet's pictures and assured an international following for the artist. Monet's paintings began to fetch high prices, particularly in America. While Clemenceau's attempt to persuade the State to purchase the entire Rouen Cathedral series floundered, it did purchase one of the paintings, capping Monet's newfound wealth and fame.

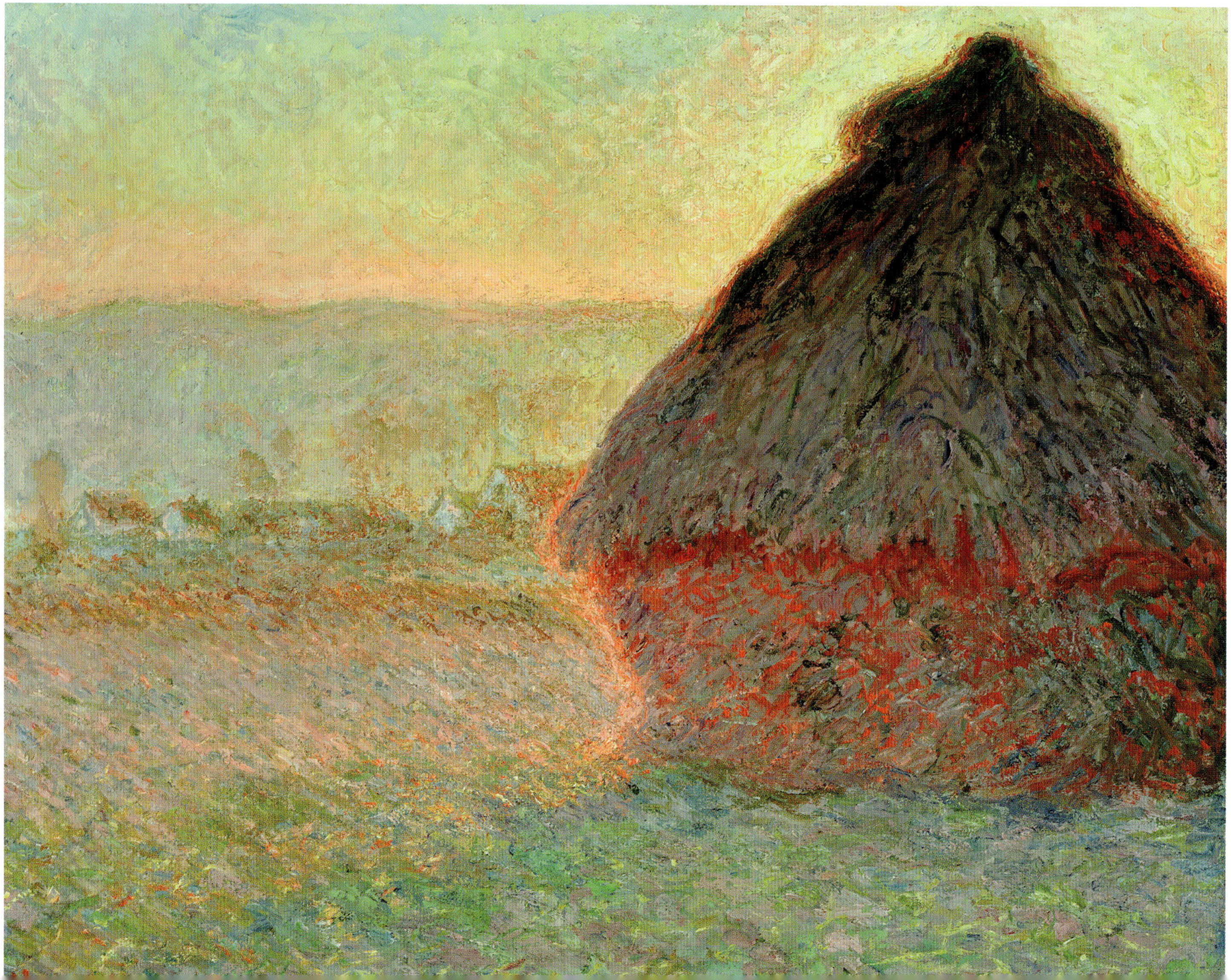

Left The glowing red and golden hues of Grainstack: Sunset (1891) illustrate how Monet intensified his palette in order to suggest his sensations of, or feelings towards, a motif, rather than simply what he saw. While attempting to convey qualities of light, Monet was also conscious of the expressive possibilities of his motif.

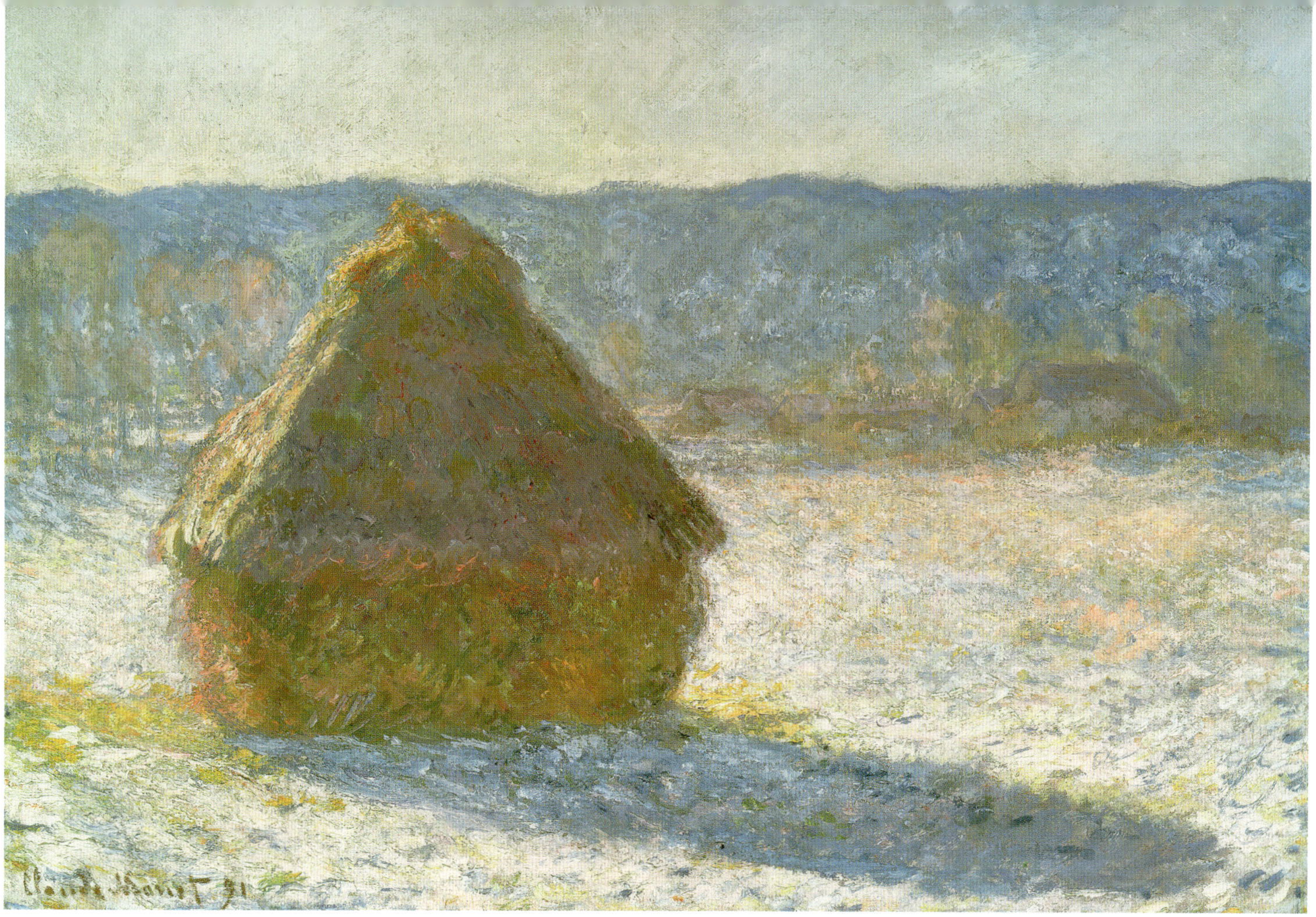

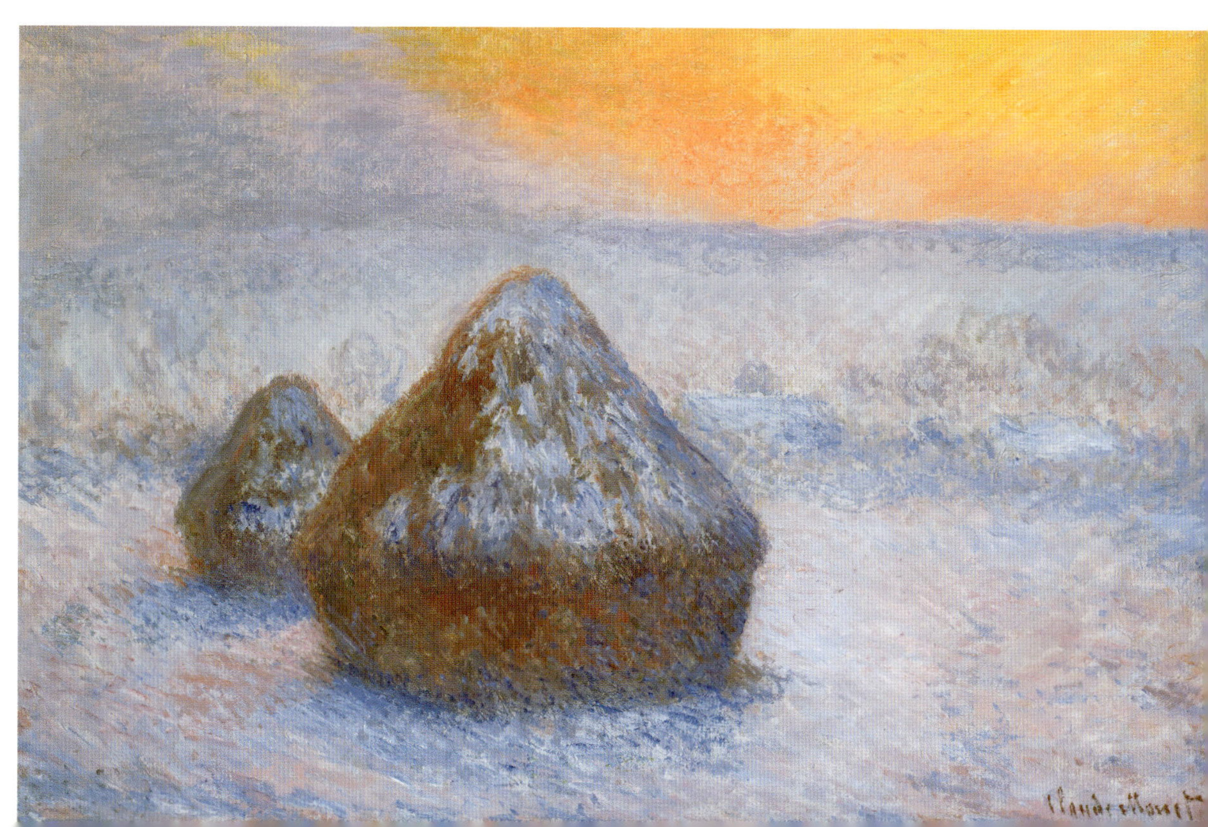

it in dramatic climatic conditions or in a more subdued, understated fashion, drawing attention to the painter's versatility by way of his varied ways of representing the motif.

During the winter of 1892, he embarked on a new series of pictures of the façade of the medieval Rouen Cathedral, returning in April the following year to continue the project. The paintings portray Monet's impressions of the cathedral's rough, pitted exterior under the full spectrum of lighting conditions from early morning to dusk, in bright sunlight and drizzling rain. The pictures set up a contrasting relationship between the enduring monumental architecture of the cathedral and Monet's attention to the fugitive and ephemeral effects of nature. Immersed in the dense welter of painterly brushstrokes, the solid structure of the cathedral often looks as if it is melting in the sunlight or dissolving in the rain and mist, conveying a haunting visual power.

As his letters testify, the problems posed by such an intricate motif as the Rouen Cathedral were taxing on Monet. "Each day," he wrote to Alice Hoschedé, his new wife, "I add something and subtract something I had not known how to see before." In another letter dated 3 April 1892, he wrote, "I am broken, I can't do anymore," and in mid-April returned to Giverny temporarily dejected and unhappy with what he had achieved. In his next major series, he returned to more familiar terrain, the banks of the Seine. However, this time he avoided the modern features of the river that he had treated in his earlier pictures. The modernity of these pictures rested solely on his innovative style. Monet's increasing emphasis on the envelope, the atmospheric diffusion of the light, is most pronounced in this elegant series of pictures of the Seine, a subject made famous by Camille Corot. These delicate and lyrical paintings, painted from the same flat-bottomed boat he had used in painting his poplars, capture the calm but mysterious atmosphere of the dawn's breaking light, just as Corot had favoured, and were rapturously received when exhibited in 1898 at Georges Petit's gallery in Paris. Guillemot described the series as "a marvel of contagious emotion and intense poetry".

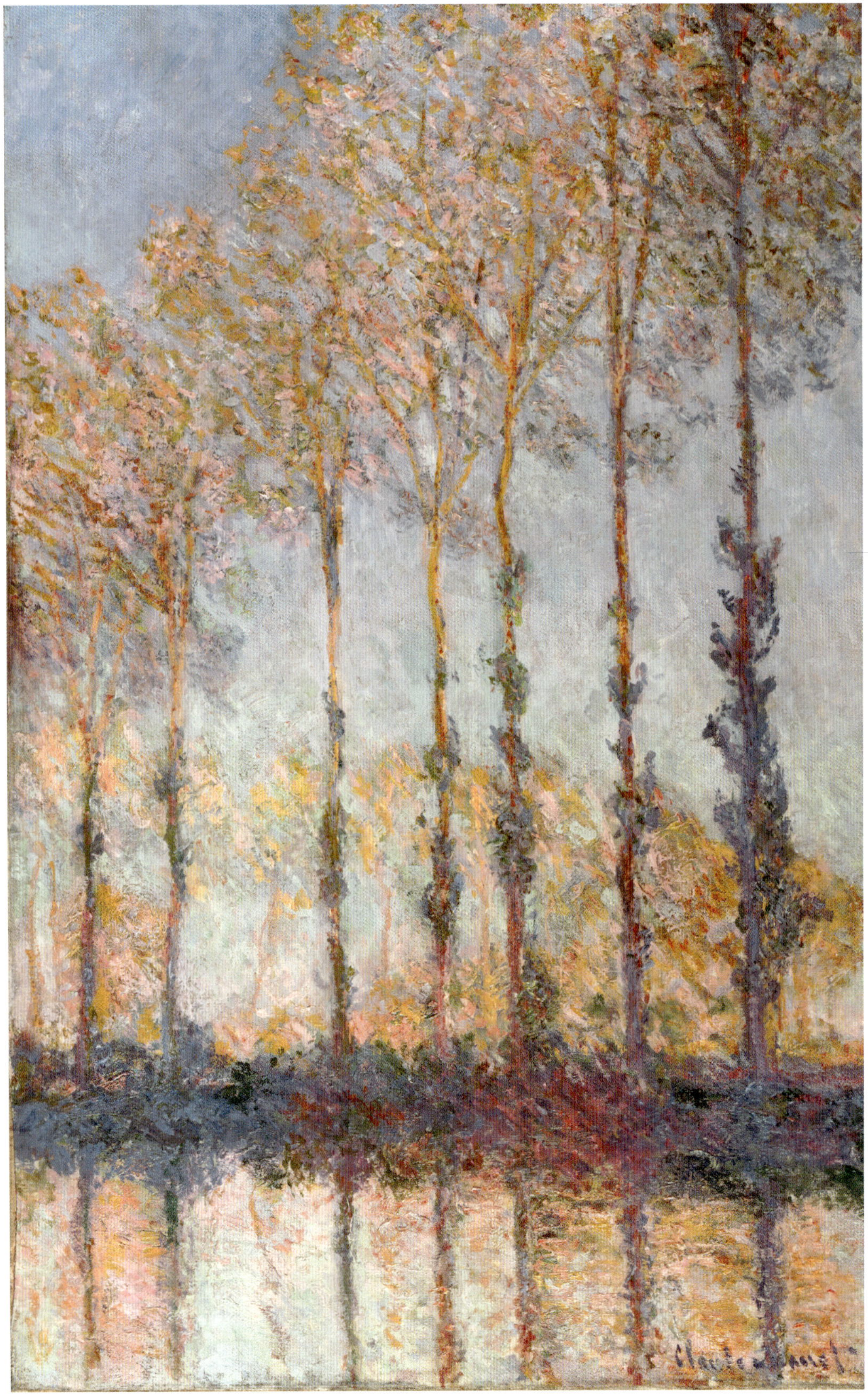

Rouen Cathedral

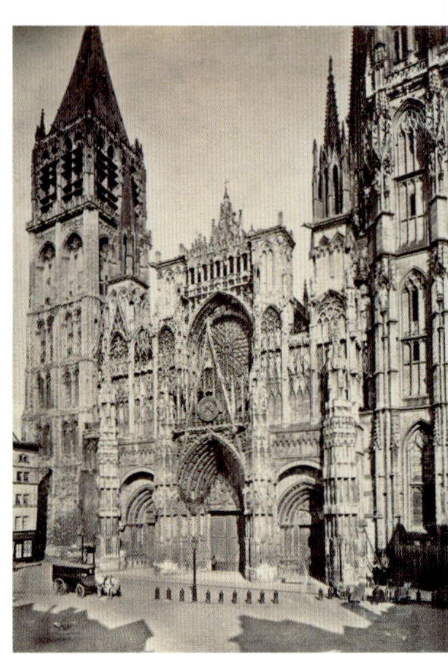

Monet's choice of such a traditional national symbol as Rouen Cathedral has been interpreted as a call for unity at a time when France was deeply divided over the Dreyfus affair, which re-opened the wounds of the Franco–Prussian war and intensified the political struggles that destabilized the Republic in the 1890s. It may, however, simply reflect a concern to bring the "serious qualities" to his painting that critics accused his work of lacking. Renting a room above a shop located across the square, he charted his impressions of the cathedral façade's changing appearances. Twenty of these pictures were shown at Durand-Ruel's gallery in 1895 to great critical acclaim.

Left *Monet began his series of poplars around the Spring of 1891, purchasing the trees, which had been planted on communally owned property, at auction to prevent them from being cut down. In these Japanese influenced compositions Monet accentuates the "S" curve of the tree formation, subtly contrasting the elegant lines of the trees with their shifting, wavering reflections.*

Opposite left *Rouen Cathedral, with its complex ornamented façade was perhaps Monet's most challenging motif to date. In this version, Monet suggests the misty, nebulous atmosphere of morning light half-obscuring the cathedral's monumental form. The evocative quality of the motif is enhanced by the subtle harmonies of lavender and grey.*

Opposite top right *In this version, Monet views the cathedral under strong sunlight. The effect is a glowing study in orange and violet tonality. Monet's changing responses to his motif are evident not only in his palette but also in his touch. Here the paint is deeply encrusted on the surface to suggest the masonry of the cathedral façade.*

Opposite bottom right *This is one of the most impressionistic and least finished of the Rouen Cathedral pictures. Here, the raking sunlight almost obliterates the motif, which seems to be dissolving before the viewer's eyes.*

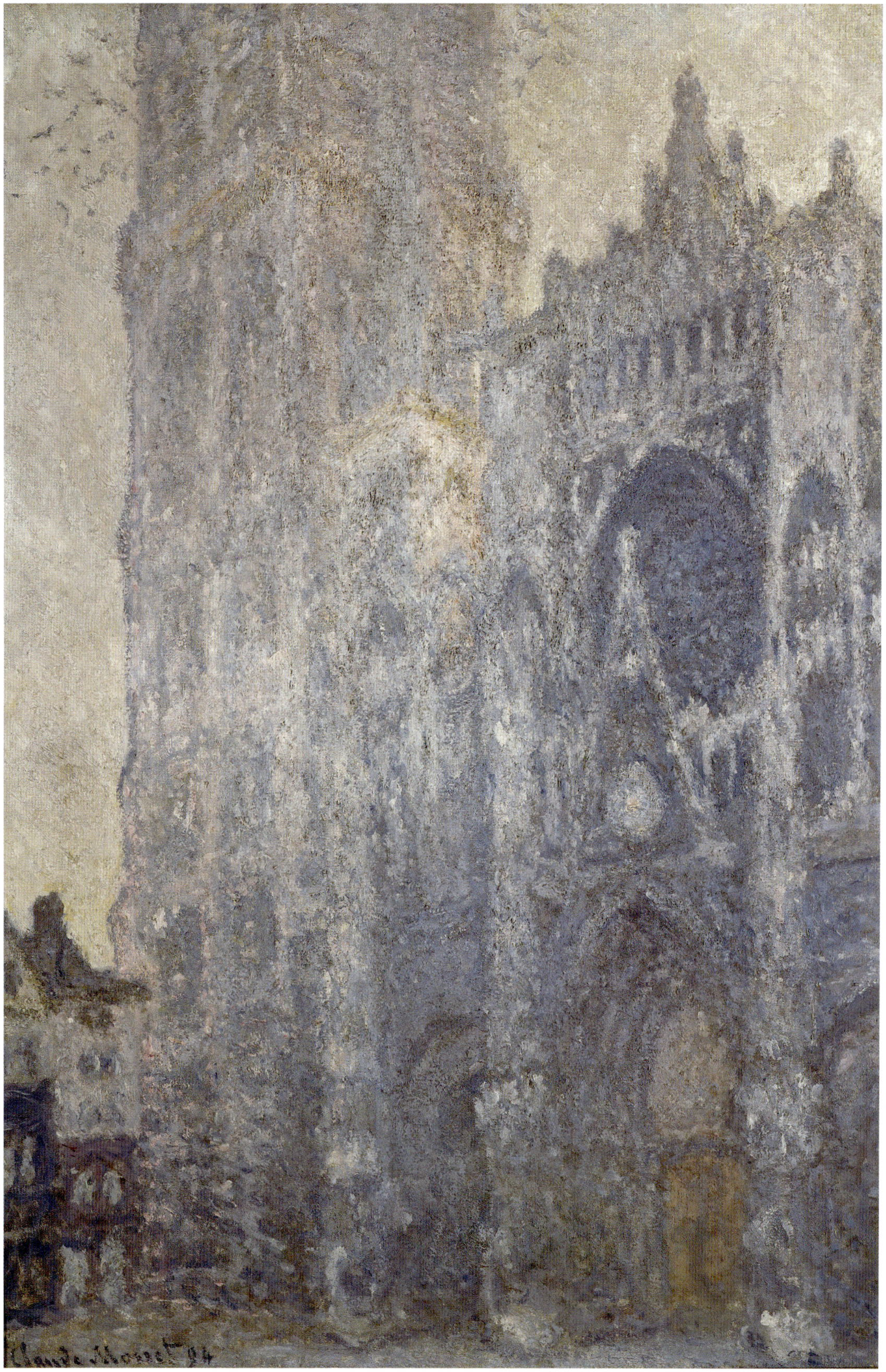

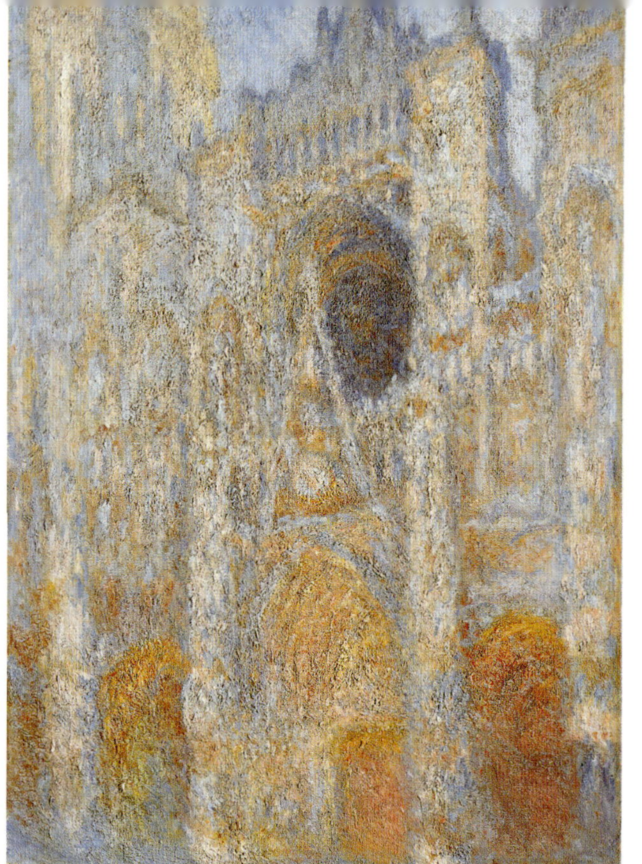

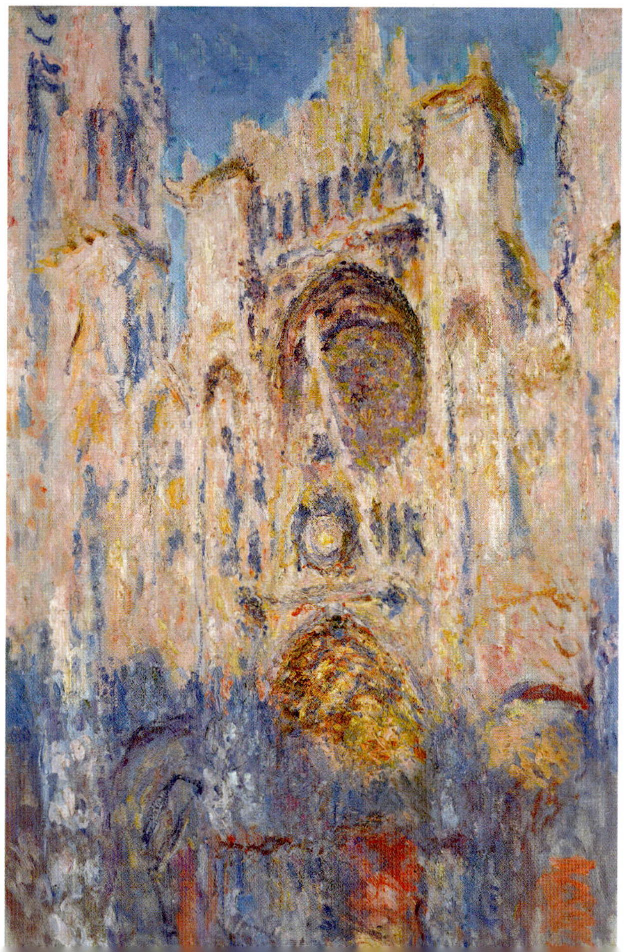

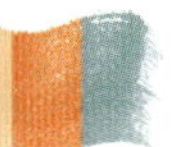
Renoir's Bathers

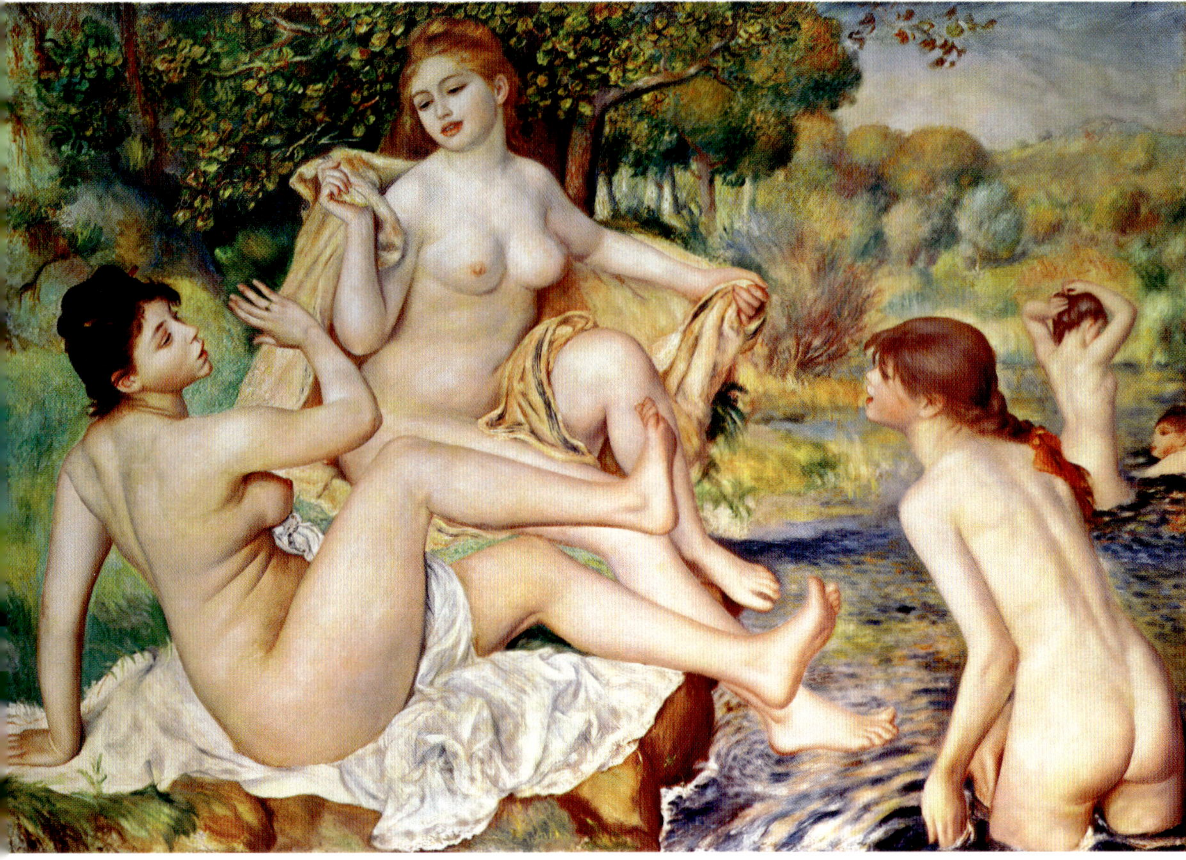

Above *A key work in his oeuvre, Renoir's Bathers (1887) announced his intention to revise his work in line with the example of the old masters. In technique, subject-matter and composition, Renoir moved away from the fleeting and transitory pictures of the previous decade, abandoning the impressionist instant in favour of something more timeless and monumental.*

Right *The subject of a seated bather, which he first executed in Italy in 1881, was one Renoir continually returned to over the last four decades of his career. This version, dating from 1892, is framed against a marine background. While earlier pictures had absorbed the figure into the landscape, the central foreground position of the figure and drawing serve to make the figure dominant, while rejecting the harsh linear contouring of the bathers of 1887.*

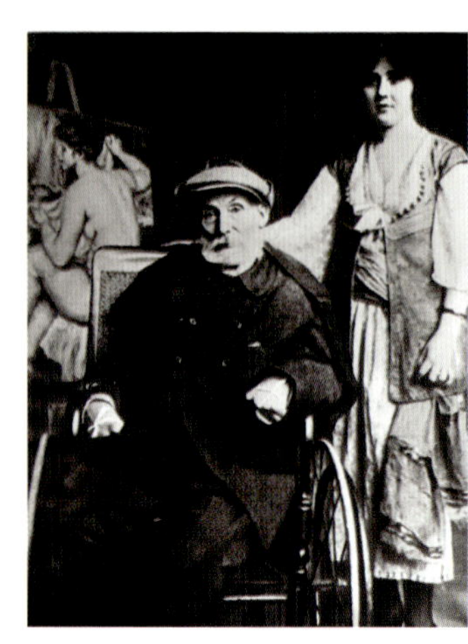

Pierre-Auguste Renoir, born in Limoges, the son of a tailor and a dressmaker, began his career as an apprentice porcelain painter, which gave him a masterful understanding of pigments. In 1861, he entered Gleyre's studio and studied at the Ecole des beaux-arts. Although one of the greatest Impressionists, he participated in only four of the group shows preferring to show at the Salon or in one-man exhibitions. From the late 1870s, he began to enjoy the patronage of the affluent Charpentier family, for whom he produced numerous portraits. His later pictures focus almost exclusively on images of women and, in particular, the female nude.

During the 1880s, many of the Impressionists went through a period of critical re-evaluation of their work that resulted in changes in approach, style and subject matter. None more so than Renoir, whose *Bathers* (1887) in the Philadelphia Museum of Art seems to reject almost everything that had previously characterized his art to date. Compared with the improvised, painterly qualities of his *Ball at the Moulin de la Galette* (1876) with its casual modern subject, sun-dappled play of light and soft impressionistic treatment, his *Bathers* seems altogether more formal, traditional and even theatrical. It combines vivid, brightly lit colouring with, for Renoir, an unusually strong contouring that circumscribes the figures. The nudes, pictured resting by the bankside or swimming in the river, are amply proportioned and placed in a generalized country setting. Despite the informality of the scene, their gestures seem mannered and artificial and draw attention to their sources in the generic repertoire of classical poses.

The *Bathers* and the works that followed afterwards mark a more conservative turn in Renoir's art and ideas that reflected a loss of confidence in his technique and approach to painting and a

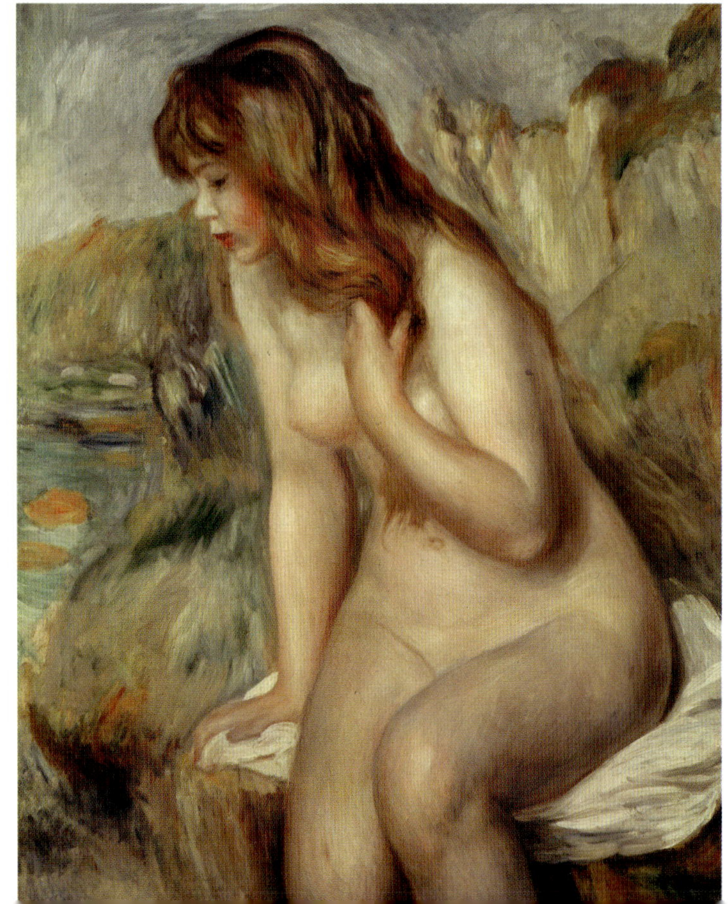

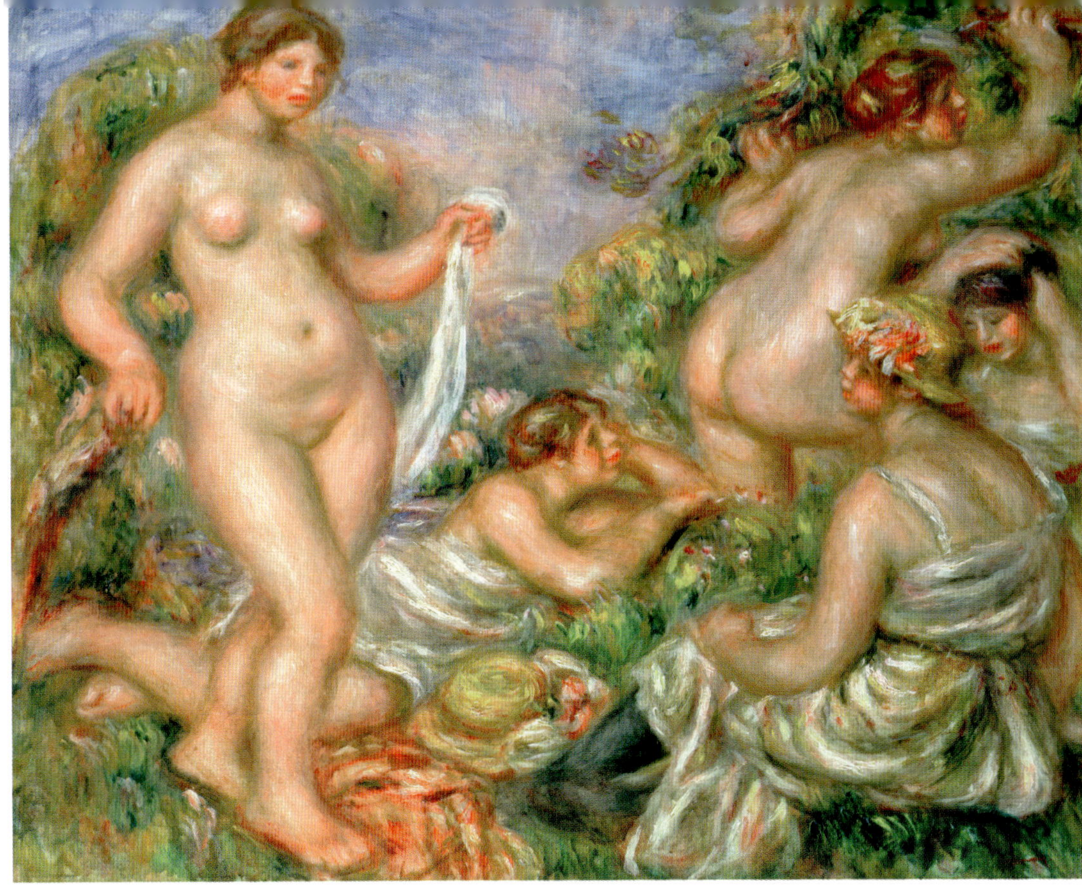

perfection which mean the drawings of the engineer are becoming the ideal". Renoir's painting from the late 1880s onwards shows the marked influence of the free brushwork and decorative sensibility of rococo artists such as Boucher and Fragonard, to whom in a letter dating from autumn 1888, he compared his latest work.

While retaining the influence of rococo artists, Renoir's later monumental nudes at the turn of the century reach back further in time to evoke the tonal palette and lush, sensuous brushwork of Venetian masters of the sixteenth and seventeenth centuries, such as Titian, Tintoretto and Veronese, and, in their monumental proportions, they make particular reference to the voluptuous nudes of Flemish artists, like Rubens, who was regarded at the time as one of the greatest artists in the canon.

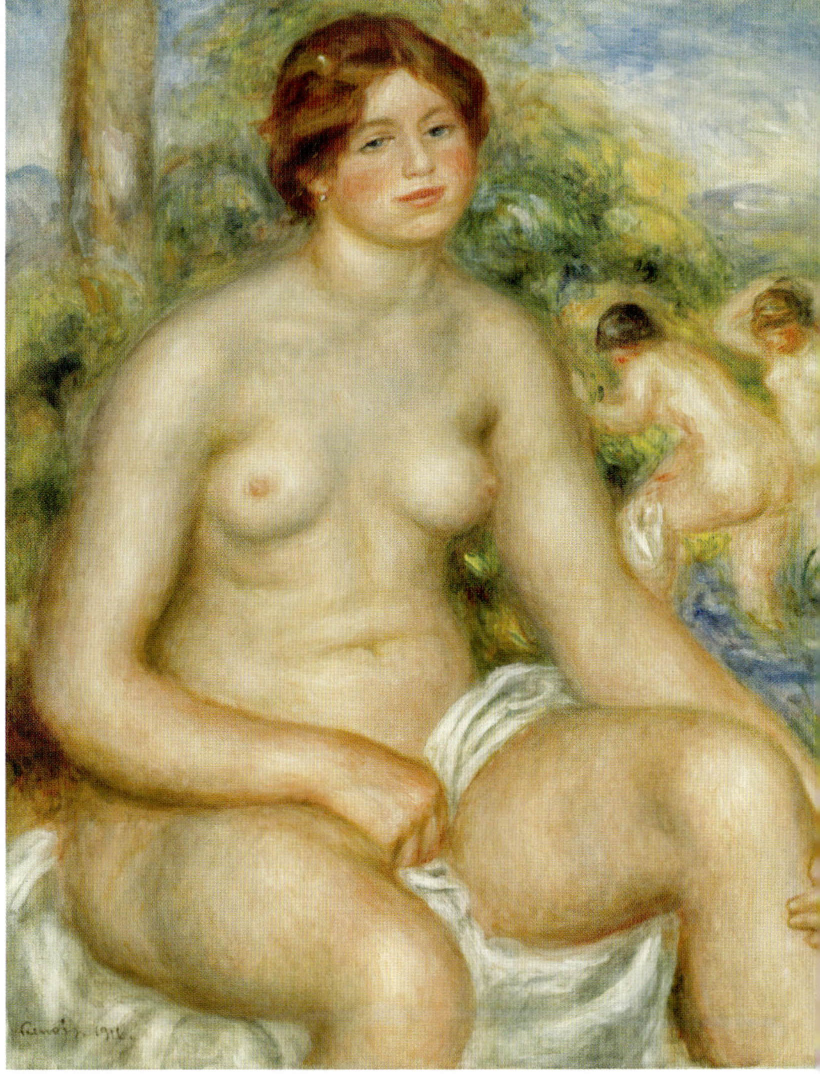

disenchantment with the modern city subjects that had been the staple of his art to date. In the autumn of 1881, he travelled to Italy to see the work of Raphael and his letters convey his strong admiration for the latter's frescoes in the Villa Farnesina in Rome, which confirmed in him the need for a change in artistic direction. He also travelled to Venice and Naples, where he was much impressed by the frescoes at Pompei. At the same time, he was also studying after Ingres and the figures and drapery of the *Bathers* contain echoes of Ingres's figure drawings. Henceforth, Renoir would increasingly embrace more traditional, timeless and universal values in art. This sea change in his painting went hand in hand with his rejection of the Third Republic's progressive political programme that fostered a modernized, technologically advanced and more democratic society, and, as part of the extension of these policies, of bringing art, science and industry into closer alliance.

Renoir now began to look nostalgically to the past both socially and artistically, regarding his own age as a period of decadence and loss of true artistic quality. Henceforth, it was to the artists of the seventeenth and eighteenth century that he looked for inspiration and the subtitle of his *Bathers*, "An essay in *peinture décorative*", made explicit reference to the decorative tradition of rococo painting in the eighteenth century. In the manifesto that he drafted in May 1884 for his planned but unrealized Society of Irregularists, he singled out the French rococo artists as exemplary, contrasting their "penetrating charm and exquisite fantasy" with the "dryness" of the art of his own age with its "mania for false

Above The Bathers *of 1918–19 demonstrates the large monumental nudes of Renoir's final years. Renoir conceived the picture as his final grand statement on the nude and his sons presented the picture to the State. The colour scheme is warm and vibrant and the handling of the nude and landscape energetic and fused together into an overall harmony. Andée (Dédée) Hessling, Renoir's favourite model in his later years, was used for both figures in the foreground.*

Right *In the last two decades of his life Renoir produced many of these amply proportioned and voluptuous bathers. In many of these compositions a dominant foreground figure viewed from close-up is contrasted with a small group of nudes seen in the distance, treated in a sketchier and more improvised way. Though these nudes have always received a mixed reception, during the 1920s Renoir's bathers were to exert a powerful influence on avant garde painters like Picasso and Braque.*

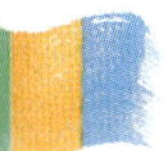

Late Impressionism and the Question of Style

While Impressionists' accounts of their painting emphasized a preoccupation with representing nature as directly as possible, this ignores expressive and aesthetic qualities of their painting that cannot be explained in this fashion. Impressionist artists made little distinction between the act of seeing and the act of painting motifs using the terms "sensation" and "impression" to refer to both, but it is clear from their correspondence that, on occasion, the artists felt a tension between their *recherches sur nature*, which often led to unorthodox paintings, and what in their judgement made for a satisfactory or successful picture.

While seeking to remain true to their perceptions of nature, Impressionists were prepared to adjust and reorganize these perceptions in order to make them accord with their ideas of pictorial unity or to express more forcefully a particular emotional feeling or effect that arose in response to the motif. This did not imply a renunciation of the sensation, which remained the starting point of their paintings, but the recognition that it needed to be transposed into an intelligible form.

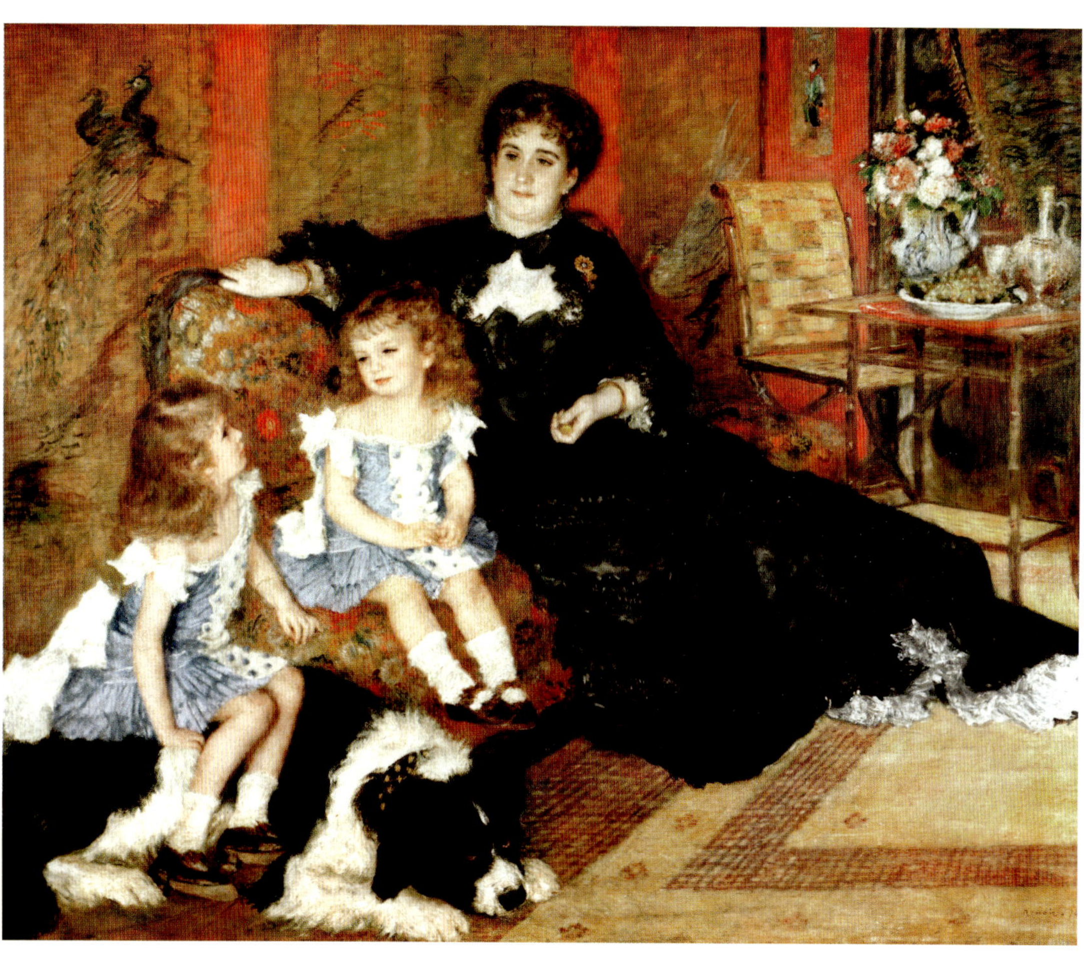
Right Madame Charpentier with Her Children *(1878) was a great success at the Salon of 1879. The charming, informal grouping of the figures and the vibrant colour scheme, derived from Delacroix, are typical of Renoir's work from the late 1870s onwards. The patronage of the wealthy and influential Charpentier family did much to secure the success of his career. Proust later referred to the painting in* Le Temps Retrouvé.

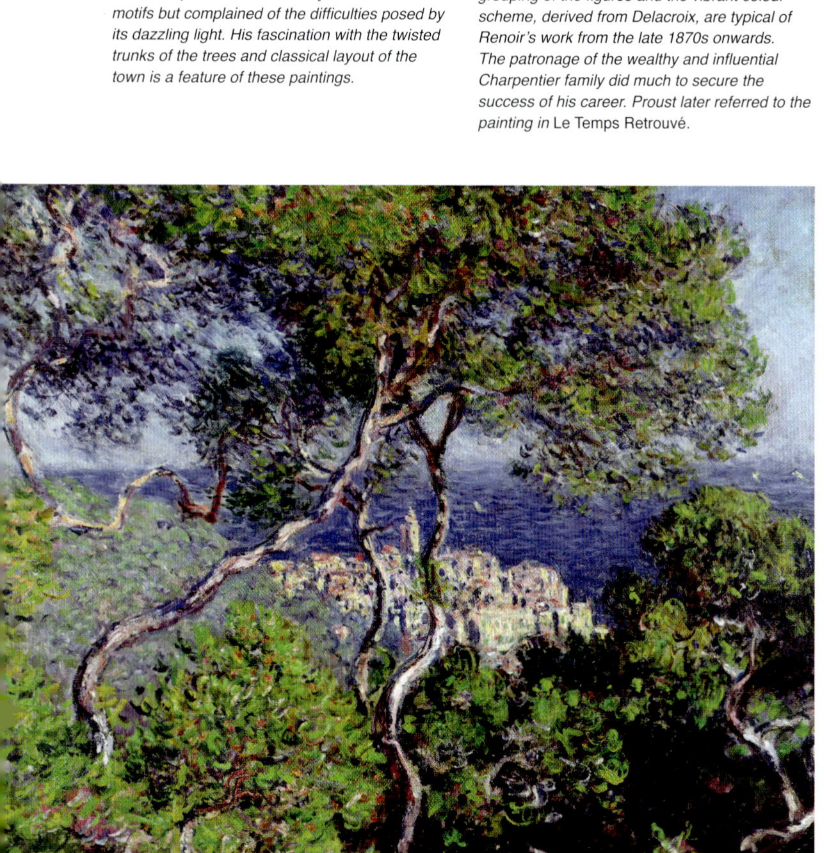
Below *During his two spells of painting on the Mediterranean in 1884 and 1888, Monet tested his painting against the brilliant light and colour. Monet responded to the beauty of these southern motifs but complained of the difficulties posed by its dazzling light. His fascination with the twisted trunks of the trees and classical layout of the town is a feature of these paintings.*

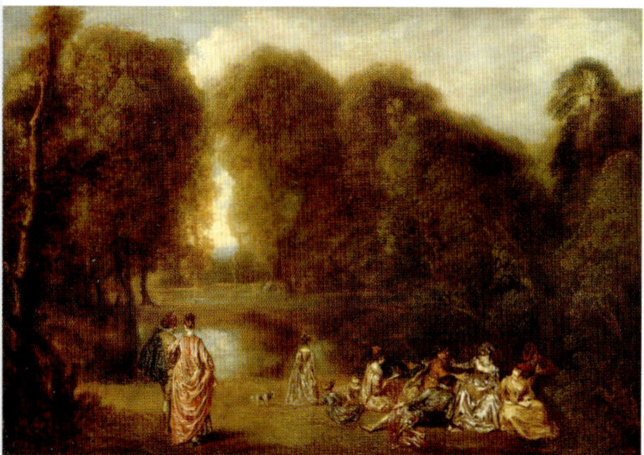

Rococo Artists

Though much reviled at the beginning of the century, from the 1860s a growing taste for the rococo artists, particularly Watteau, Greuze, Fragonard and Boucher, led to a significant revival in their work. The publication of the Goncourt brothers' *Eighteenth Century French Painters* (1856–75) consolidated this re-assessment and encouraged the view of rococo painting as the true national style of France. Rococo painting increasingly became a visual resource for Impressionist painters. Renoir, whose style and subjects continually made reference to their work, drew comparison between his painting and Watteau's, though his brushwork was often compared with Boucher's.

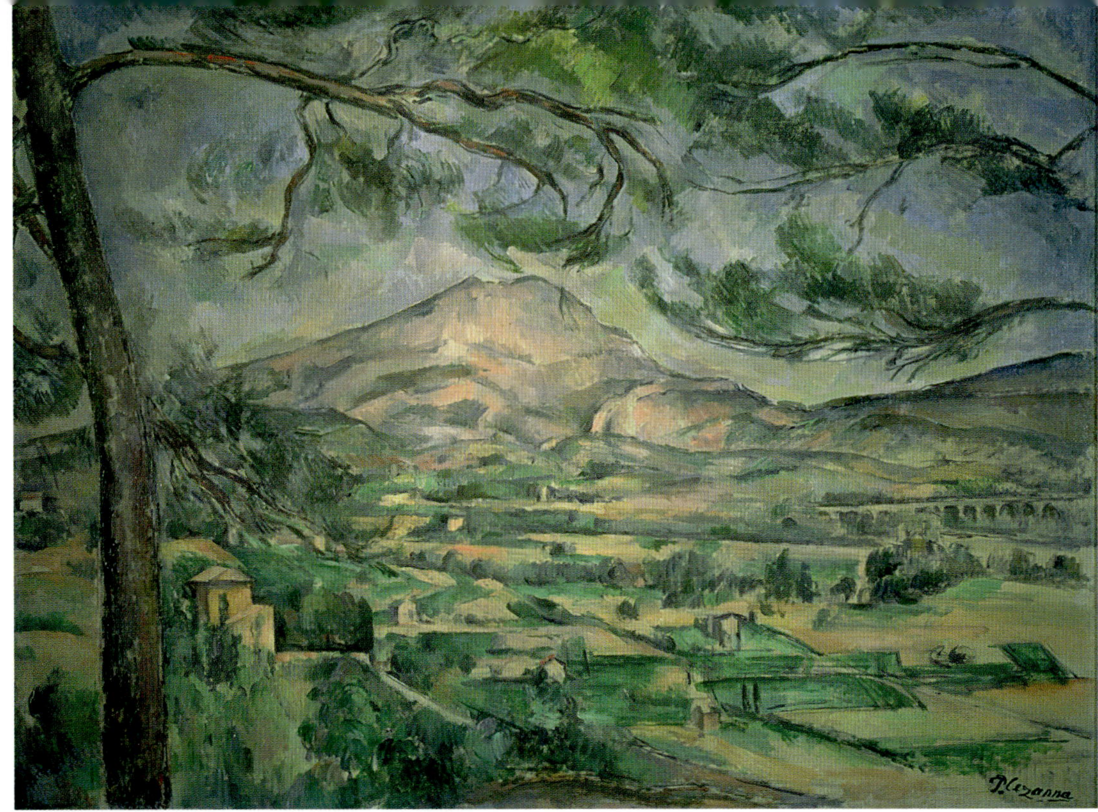

The painter, no matter how committed to remaining faithful to his impressions, had to establish a relationship between visual perceptions and the possibilities and limitations of the medium of painting. Impressionists were conscious that the effects in nature they sought to represent could not simply be imitated but had, at some level, to be expressed or suggested. Natural sunlight, for instance, could not be reproduced, for the colours available to a painter were both less intense and less numerous in register than those in nature. The artist had therefore to communicate such effects by way of establishing an equivalence between the range of colour contrasts available in his palette and the colour relationships perceived in nature, finding pictorial effects to stand in for those perceptions. Similarly, though it was an article of faith among the Impressionists that they should make their works *sur le motif*, in practice most paintings were completed in the studio, and thus were, to varying degrees, the product of memory and contrivance.

In the latter part of their careers, the artists frequently stated their concern to harmonize all the relations within their paintings and to achieve greater compositional unity, and they also brought a higher level of finish to their work. The new accent on harmony and unity in their painting is gradually evident in their colour and drawing from the 1880s onwards, where more balanced contrasts of warm and cool colours prevail or where pictures are harmonized by the choice of a dominant tonality. There is no doubt that by the end of the century, with Impressionism increasingly recognized as having made a major contribution to modern painting, the Impressionists were also becoming conscious of their place in the history of art. Their pictures accordingly begin to make clearer references to traditional sources. They also began working on ambitious large-scale pictures sometimes on a mural scale.

As their painting evolved, the artists emphasized precisely those features of their pictures that we associate with their style and aesthetic effect. Monet's late style draws attention to his robust and virtuoso brushwork and eye for brilliant colour effects, while Pissarro and Cézanne's paintings show a greater pictorial finesse and stylization. Parallel developments can be found in Degas, who became increasingly preoccupied with technical experimentation and the artifice of painting. Impressionism often seems to encourage the viewer to think about the artist's act of fabricating the picture and lays bare its processes of construction, and this is an increasing theme in the artists' late works.

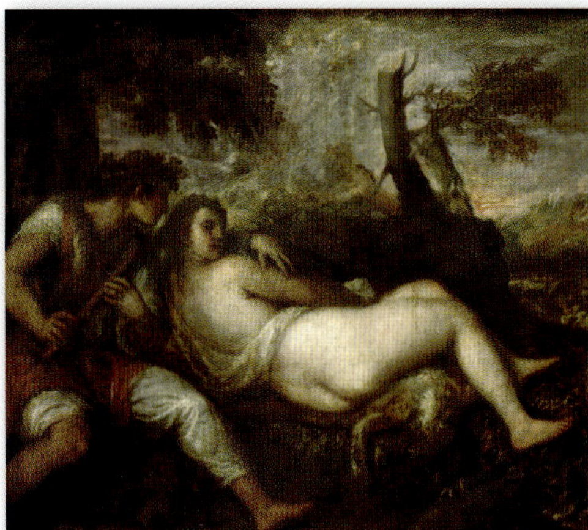

Venetian Artists

The colour schemes, painterly effects and representations of landscape subjects made Venetian artists popular with Impressionist painters. Cézanne counted Titian, Veronese and Tintoretto among his favourite painters and the Impressionists' use of a dominant tonality to unify their later pictures owes much to their example. Nineteenth-century interpretations of Venetian art emphasized their decorative concerns and preoccupation with musical motifs to the exclusion of meaning and narrative. These features found their parallel in the Impressionists who, in their later careers, were fond of analogies drawn between the vibrant tonality of their palette and that of music.

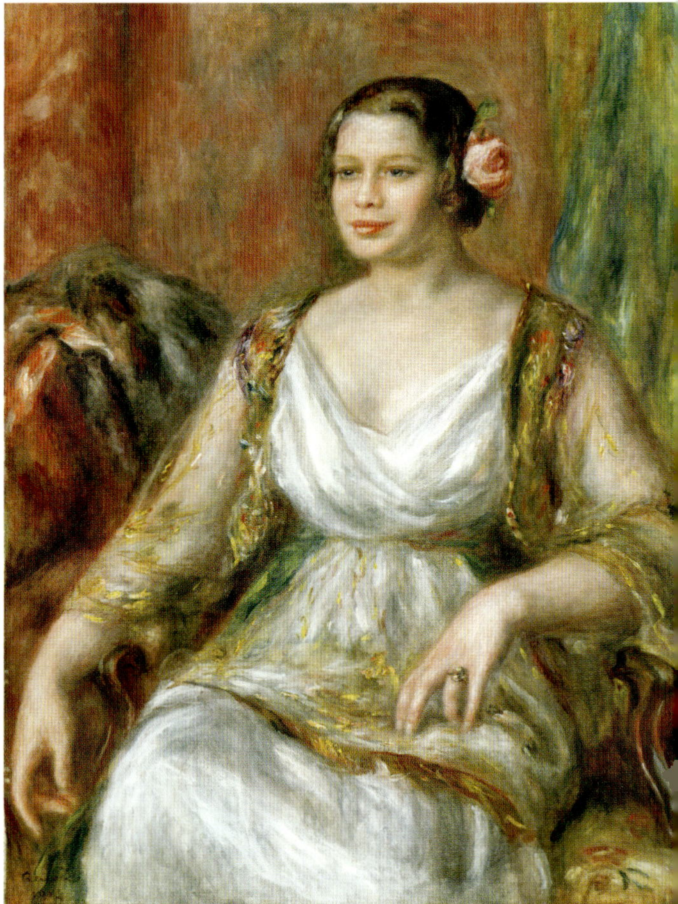

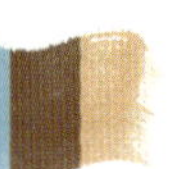

Impressionist Sculpture

Although Impressionism was primarily a tendency in painting, Impressionist sculpture had a comparable influence on the development of modern art. In a period characterized by modernization and change sculpture could seem moribund and remote from contemporary life. In an essay in 1846, Baudelaire even wondered whether it would survive. Degas's sculpture with its discreet references to classical sculpture in the Louvre combined with a feeling for a freer and more modern treatment pointed the way towards a new approach to the medium. His desire to have sculpture embrace the exacting poses and preoccupation with movement found in his painting led him to work in the fluid medium of wax, but posed many problems of execution, particularly when transposed into bronze. To his frustration, his sculptures often broke apart while being fired in the kiln and many only survive as fragments. Nevertheless, Renoir, who also took up sculpture in the latter part of his career, was to call him the greatest sculptor of his age.

At the sixth Impressionist exhibition, in 1881, Degas showed his most audacious work to date, a tinted wax sculpture entitled *Little Dancer of Fourteen Years* (1878–81), for which the young Marie van Goeten modelled. Degas meticulously planned the work, producing numerous preparatory sketches and a number of maquettes over a three-year period. He listed it in the catalogue of the previous year's Impressionist exhibition, but the glass case reserved for it remained empty. When finally shown, the work drew great attention from critics and public alike for its astonishing naturalism, enhanced by the satin ribbon adorning her horsehair wig and the actual silk bodice, gauze skirt and pink slippers that the original version

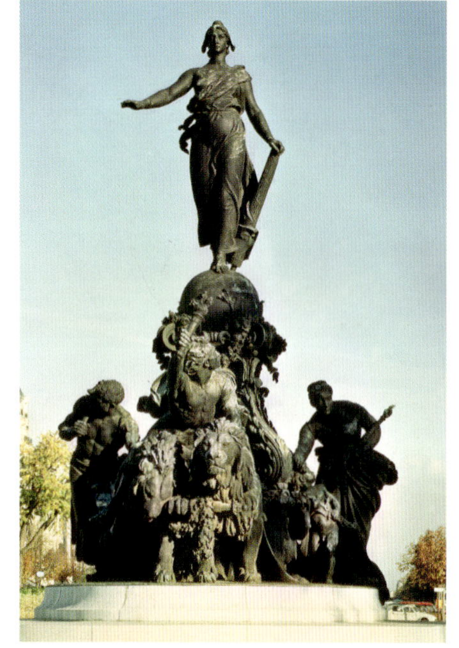

Left *Degas's sculpture paralleled his interests in painting, translating into a three-dimensional medium the complex poses of his dancers. These sculptures reveal how much his painting was influenced by his study of antique statuary in his choice of poses and also Degas's concern to develop the language of sculpture to embrace the themes of contemporary art.*

Above *Jules Dalou's* Triumph of the Republic *(1899), located on the Place de la Nation, is typical of the monumental public sculpture promoted by the Third Republic. The statue, who wears a Phrygian cap and carries a bundle of rods symbolizing "strength in unity", represents the republic. She stands on a globe supported by a chariot drawn by two lions, symbols of the people, which is guided by allegorical representations of Liberty, Industry and Justice.*

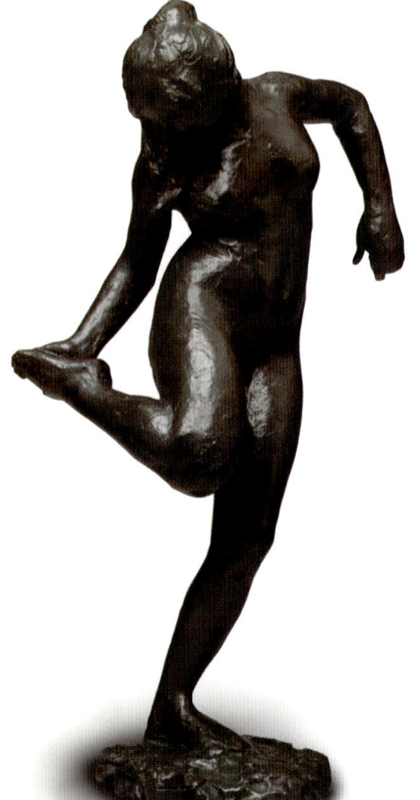

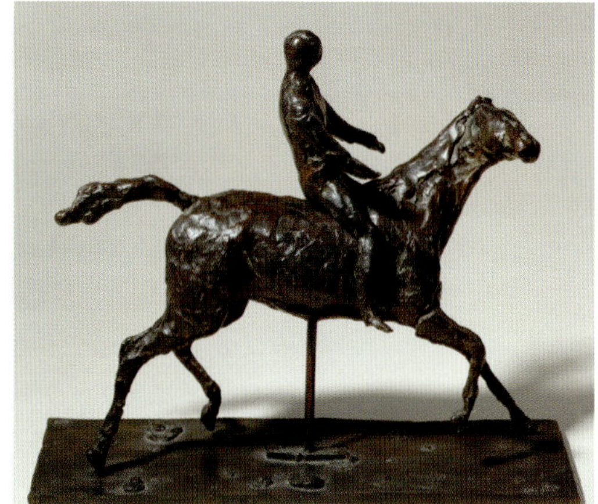

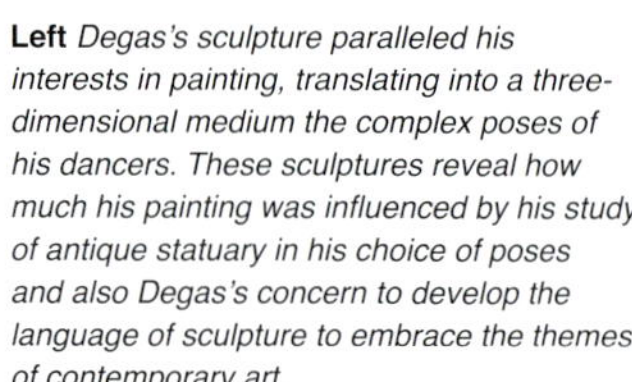

Degas's Sculpture

By the late 1870s Degas was working in a range of different media, from painting to prints and pastel, and also beginning to experiment with sculpture. In each case, Degas combined his knowledge of tradition with an extraordinary flair for innovation. His sculpture reflects his preoccupation with the dominant themes of dancers, nudes and horses found in his painting. Although after the 1881 Impressionist exhibition he never showed his sculptures in public again, they could be seen by visitors to Degas's apartment in the rue Victor Massé and were much admired by contemporaries. In 1886, Felix Fénéon referred to Degas's "living painted waxes" as among his greatest achievements.

Above *Degas was always mindful of tradition, and his* Little Dancer *(1880–1) looked back to a tradition of naturalistic sculpture in tinted wax deriving from the Renaissance and Baroque which in the nineteenth century only survived in a debased form at the Musée Grévin. When it was exhibited, one critic described it as "the first formulation of a new art".*

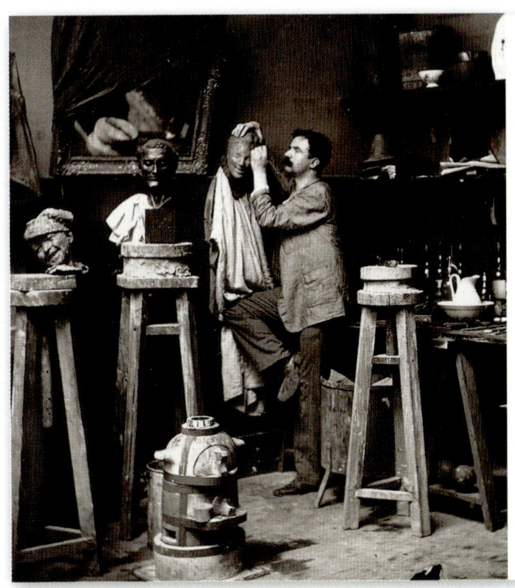

Medardo Rosso
1858–1928

The son of a stationmaster, Medardo Rosso was born in Turin but grew up in Milan where he studied at the Berea Academy. Disenchanted by Academic art, he moved to Rome, where he struggled to make a living. In 1884, he had an exhibition in Paris and also showed at the Salon des Indépendants where he met Degas and Rodin and began working as a studio assistant for the sculptor Jules Dalou. Although he returned to Milan in 1885, he maintained close links to Paris. Degas and Rodin were much impressed by his sculpture and Zola purchased one of his bronzes in 1886.

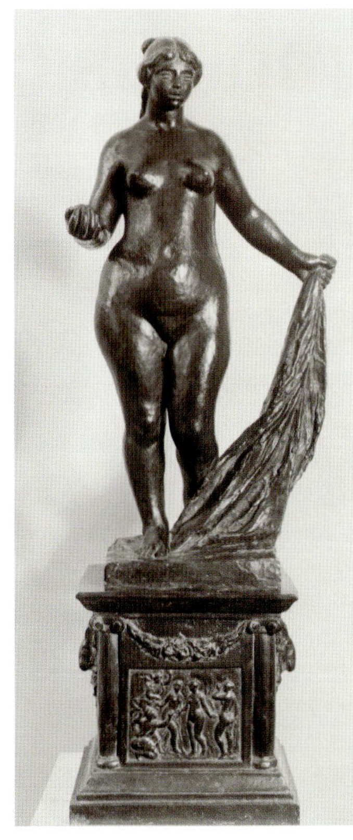

Right *Around 1907 Renoir's association with the sculptor Aristide Maillol encouraged him to try his hand at sculpture, initially making medallions and later, after this dealer Ambroise Vollard found him an assistant, the Spanish sculptor Richard Guino, translating his nudes into sculpture. These works share the ample proportions of his works depicting single bathers from the 1900s onwards.*

Below *Though famous for his monumental sculptures, Rodin often explored more discreet transitory and erotic motifs that he later incorporated into his masterpiece,* The Gates of Hell. *The theme of* Fugitive Love *draws upon Dante's story of the fated lovers, Francesca da Rimini and Paolo Malatesta, murdered for their illicit love and eternally damned. Rodin translates the story into a general theme of longing and desire.*

was draped in. Although Nina de Villiers wrote, "I experienced before this statuette one of the most violent artistic impressions of my life," and predicted rightly it would be seen as one of Degas's great masterpieces, other critics were more ambivalent. Degas's lack of idealization of his model was a constant point of discussion. Elie de Mont called her "a repulsive model, an opera rat… one would be tempted to enclose her in a glass jar of alcohol", while Paul Mantz characterized her as "a precociously depraved flower".

While most ballerinas came from affluent, middle-class backgrounds, Degas's understanding of the ballerina, like that of his peers, was informed by contemporary myths that misrepresented the dancers as from low and questionable origins. Degas's own sonnet "Little Dancer" contains the line: "She remembers her race, her descent from the street". Though, occasionally, Degas chose to depict the glamour and celebrity of the individual dancer, more customarily he depicted the dancer as a social type with little individuality. The *Little Dancer* shares the blunt, coarse features and sallow complexions of many of Degas's ballerinas, some of which are given simian profiles – the stereotypical sign of poverty and low breeding – characteristics that suggested to his audience the ballerina's lowly origins, degraded condition and "easy virtue".

Degas's attraction to modelling in wax was shared by the Italian sculptor Medardo Rosso, whose sculpture exploits the soft malleable form of wax to evoke the transient and fugitive qualities often regarded as beyond sculpture. Much impressed by his reading of Baudelaire, Rosso eschewed classical subjects for realist themes taken from everyday life. His ghostly figures radiate light and suggest movement and transition in ways comparable to the effects of the Impressionist painters. Rosso's sculpture may well have influenced the late style of Rodin, whose work in the 1880s began to embrace the fugitive qualities associated with Rosso. Sculptures such as *Fugitive Love* (c.1881–87) share the same simplification of form and suggestion of movement through light and

viewpoint. Rodin was arguably the greatest sculptor of the nineteenth century, and his concern to renew sculpture in relation to the ideas, experiences and subject matter of his own times paralleled the works of the Impressionists.

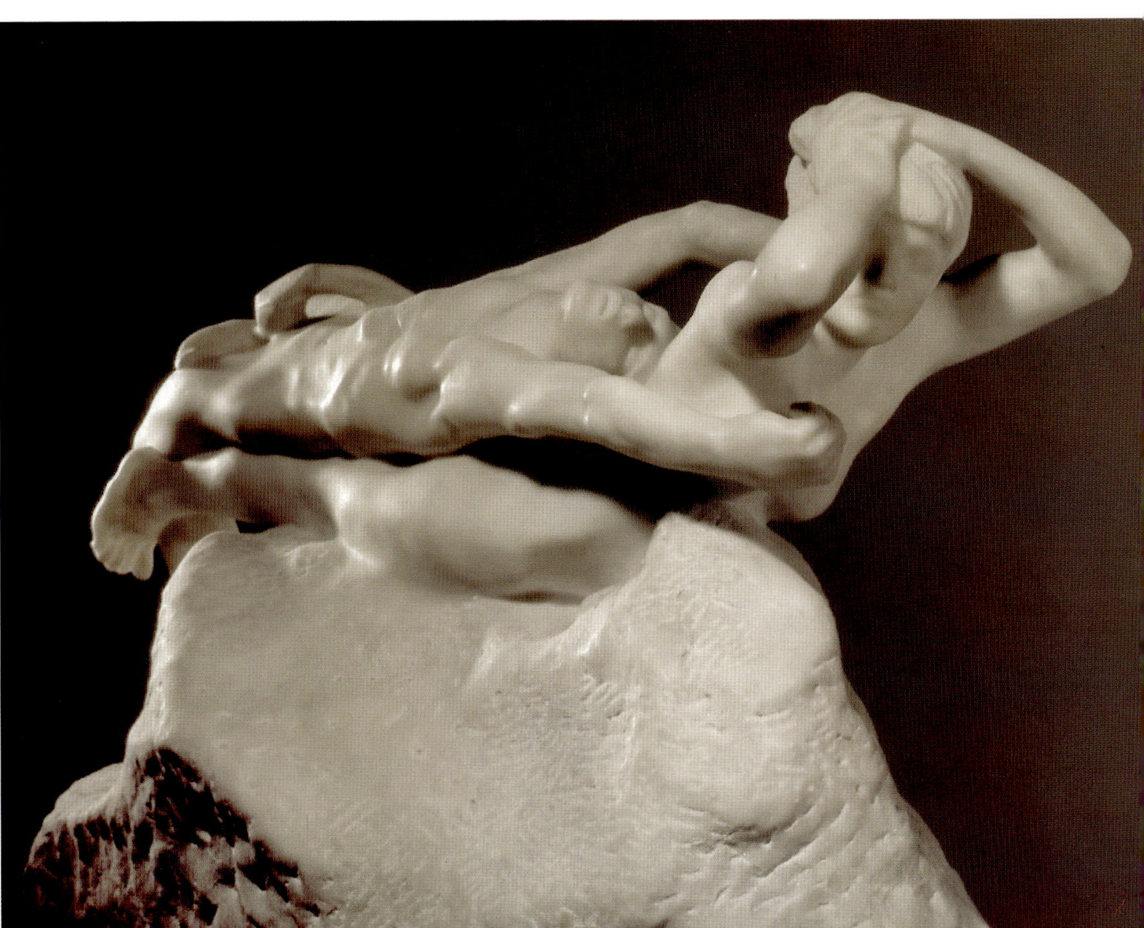

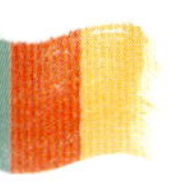

Impressionism, Post-Impressionism and Symbolism

By the 1880s, the younger generation of avant garde artists began to turn away from Impressionism and embrace more theoretical, literary and cerebral art forms. The leading tendency in Paris was Symbolism, a broad based and primarily literary movement that spawned many styles of painting, from the flat, decorative surfaces of Paul Gauguin and van Gogh to the more academic pictures of Puvis de Chavannes and Gustave Moreau. Symbolism sought to reclaim the onus of imagination, fantasy and the unconscious that it associated with Romanticism. For the theorists of Symbolism, Impressionism was excessively attached to appearances to the exclusion of the idea and the ideal. The influential Symbolist writers Albert Aurier and Gustave Kahn argued for an art that abstracted the "essence" and "universal significance" of what it represented. Gauguin famously advised his followers to work from memory alone and Maurice Denis, a painter and one of the main theorists of Symbolism emphasized that a picture before being a representation of anything was first and foremost the decoration of a flat surface.

In a letter to his brother Theo in August 1888, Vincent van Gogh, who like Gauguin had earlier experimented with Impressionism, stated he was now "an arbitrary colourist" who "exaggerated" what he saw in order to express his feelings "forcibly". Landscapes like *Wheat Field with Cypresses, Saint-Rémy* (1889) express the kind of dramatic, visionary attitude to nature that the more outward-looking Impressionists sought to exclude from their art. For Impressionists like Pissarro, who was committed to a materialist painting of nature, Symbolism seemed ostentatious and fettered by literary preoccupations. In January 1892, Pissarro wrote to Octave Mirbeau that the majority of Symbolist artists possessed "no appreciation of the sensations which emanate from a work of art". The elevation of the inner visions and fantasies of the painter over external appearances in Gauguin's Vision *After the Sermon: Jacob Wrestling with the Angel* (1888) with its mysterious combination of

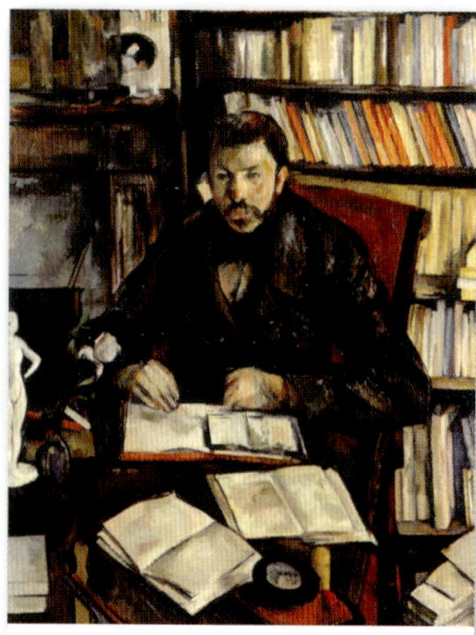

Gustave Geffroy
1855–1926

Cézanne's memorable portrait of Gustave Geffroy, depicts one of the greatest critics of the nineteenth century and a writer who moved freely between the Impressionist circle of painters and the younger generation of Symbolists. Geffroy was a radical socialist who started his journalistic career working for Clemenceau's newspaper *La Justice*, writing about political and social questions. He was also an accomplished novelist, but his criticism is his lasting legacy. His writings on the Impressionists, in particular on the works of Cézanne and Monet, were important in establishing the terms of the critical reception of their work.

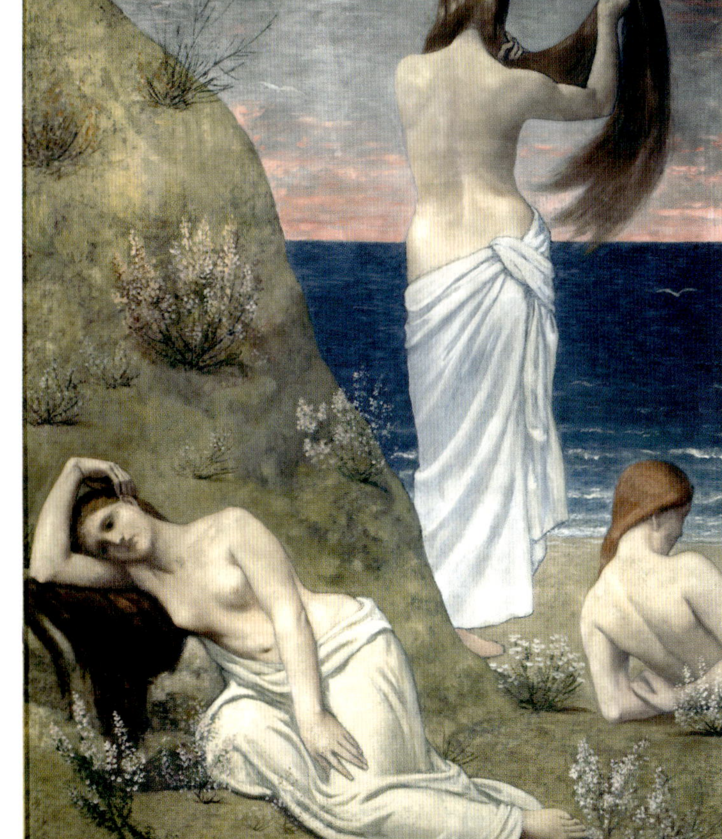

Left *Puvis de Chavannes was one of the leading French painters associated with Symbolism. His Young Women by the Seashore (1879) captures a dream-like mood of deep serenity. Symbolist painters admired his archaic classicism that looked back to the example of early Greek classical sculpture. His monotone colour schemes, often organized around a dominant blue tonality, also proved highly influential.*

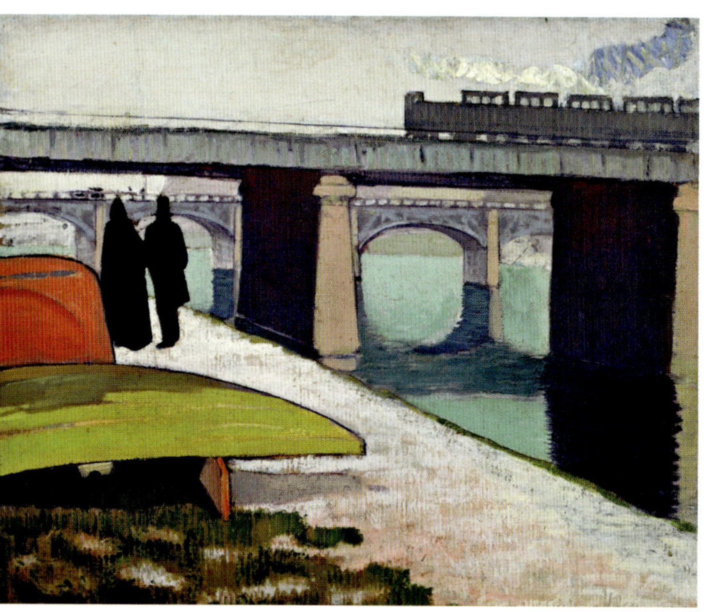

Above *Emile Bernard was closely associated with Paul Gauguin and the Pont-Aven group. While admiring the bold technique and colour use of Impressionism, he sought to dispense with their regard for nature. His flat blocks of colour and thick black contouring sacrificed pictorial detail and incident for a more abstract and purely pictorial effect that owed much to the influence of Paul Gauguin.*

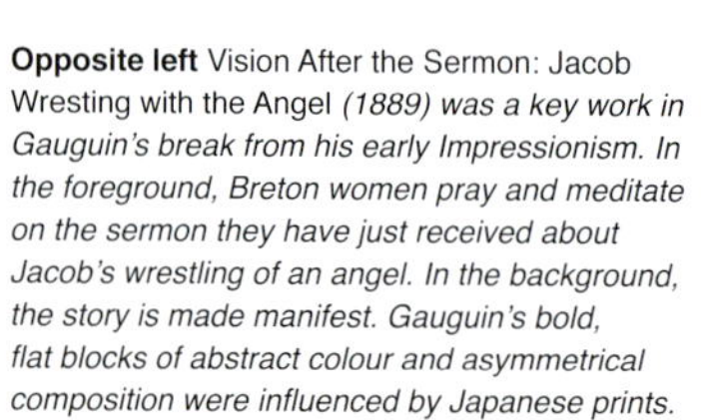

Opposite left *Vision After the Sermon: Jacob Wresting with the Angel (1889) was a key work in Gauguin's break from his early Impressionism. In the foreground, Breton women pray and meditate on the sermon they have just received about Jacob's wrestling of an angel. In the background, the story is made manifest. Gauguin's bold, flat blocks of abstract colour and asymmetrical composition were influenced by Japanese prints.*

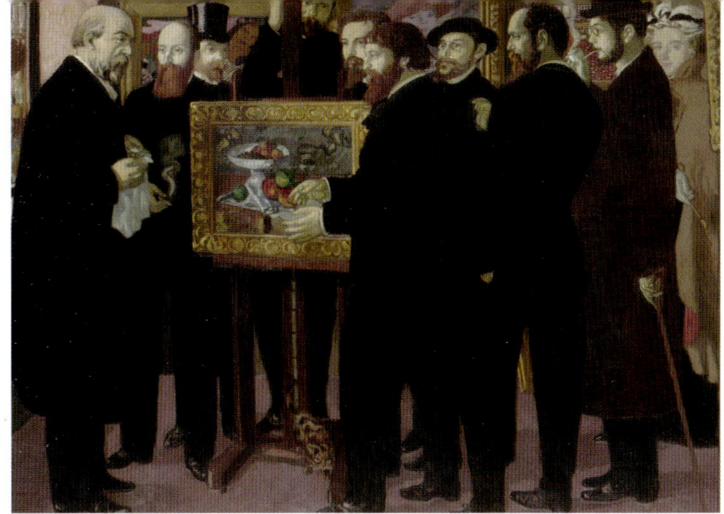

dreams and reality, were an anathema to Pissarro's sensibility. Somewhat sanctimoniously, he regarded Gauguin and his followers as opportunists and their art as dishonest and escapist. Cézanne also had no fondness for Symbolist painting, urging Emile Bernard to "turn your back on the Gauguin and (van) Goghs" and privately criticizing his "overly intellectualized attitude" to art.

Despite the reservations of the Impressionists towards the Symbolists and their critique of Impressionism's reliance on nature, Symbolists acknowledged the key role Impressionism had played in liberating painting from traditional rules and formulae. Their writings on painting often employed similar terms to those used by the Impressionists. In arguing for the objectification of subjective states of mind the Symbolists freely used the same language of sensation that the Impressionists had, but emphasized far more the role of memory, subjective states of mind and personally conceived ideals. Their admiration of Impressionist painting was genuine but they viewed it through the prism of their own attitudes ignoring the painters' statements about their art.

Monet's evocative later landscapes from the 1890s onwards drew particular praise from Symbolist critics, who responded to the expansiveness of their vision of nature, their decorative painterly qualities and their atmosphere of melancholy and mystery. Denis's painting *The Visit to Cézanne* (1906) commemorated the long journey he made in January that year to Provence to visit the painter, paying homage to an artist that he and many other Symbolist painters believed to be a modern master and the primitive of a new art. Denis also published a seminal article on the painter the following year. For Symbolist artists, Cézanne's greater concern with form, his attempt, in his own words, to make something "more durable of impressionism", had led his art beyond the limits of his Impressionist colleagues. Later, the British critic and artist, Roger Fry, indebted to Denis's essay, would refer to the art of Cézanne and his Symbolist admirers as Post-Impressionism and to regard their work as the starting point for the tradition of modern abstraction.

Above left *Maurice Denis produced two paintings in homage to Cézanne indicating the massive interest in him among avant garde painters. Here, Cézanne is represented by his painting* Fruit Bowl, Glass and Apples, *owned by Gauguin. The painting includes many luminaries of the Symbolist art world, including Odilon Redon, Edouard Vuillard, the critic André Mellerio, Paul Ranson, Ker Xavier Roussel, Pierre Bonnard, the dealer Ambroise Vollard and Maurice Denis himself.*

Below *On his arrival in Paris, van Gogh was very influenced by Impressionism, but under Gauguin's influence explored a more subjective type of picture in which nature is invested with deeper symbolic meaning. Attracted to cypresses for their association with death and immortality, van Gogh expressed the force and religious feeling towards nature. The wheat field, as something sown and eventually harvested, conforms to the painting's theme of the cycle of life and death.*

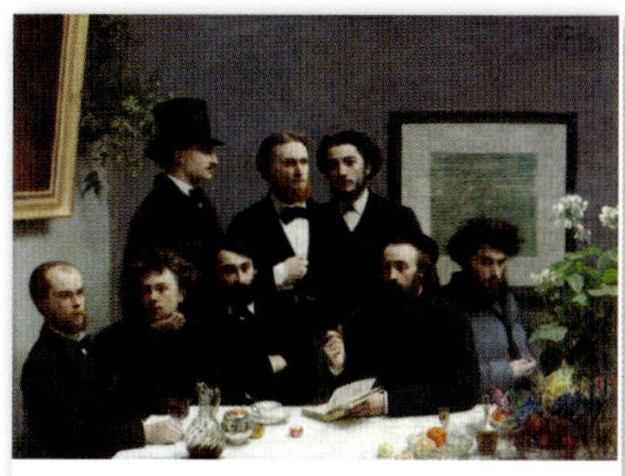

Literary Circles

Fantin-Latour's *A Corner of the Table* shows many of the leading figures associated with the literary wing of the Symbolism in the 1870s and can be seen as a companion piece to his earlier *Homage to Delacroix* (1864) and *A Studio in the Batignolles* (1870). Like these pictures, it is a group portrait and depicts among others the poets Verlaine and Rimbaud, who are seated on the far left, as well as others associated with the Parnassians, including Emile Blémont, Camille Pelletan and Ernest d'Hervilly. Begun as an homage to Baudelaire, whose poetry and criticism deeply influenced the Symbolist movement, the picture evolved into a more general portrait of the intelligentsia whose ideas shaped Symbolism.

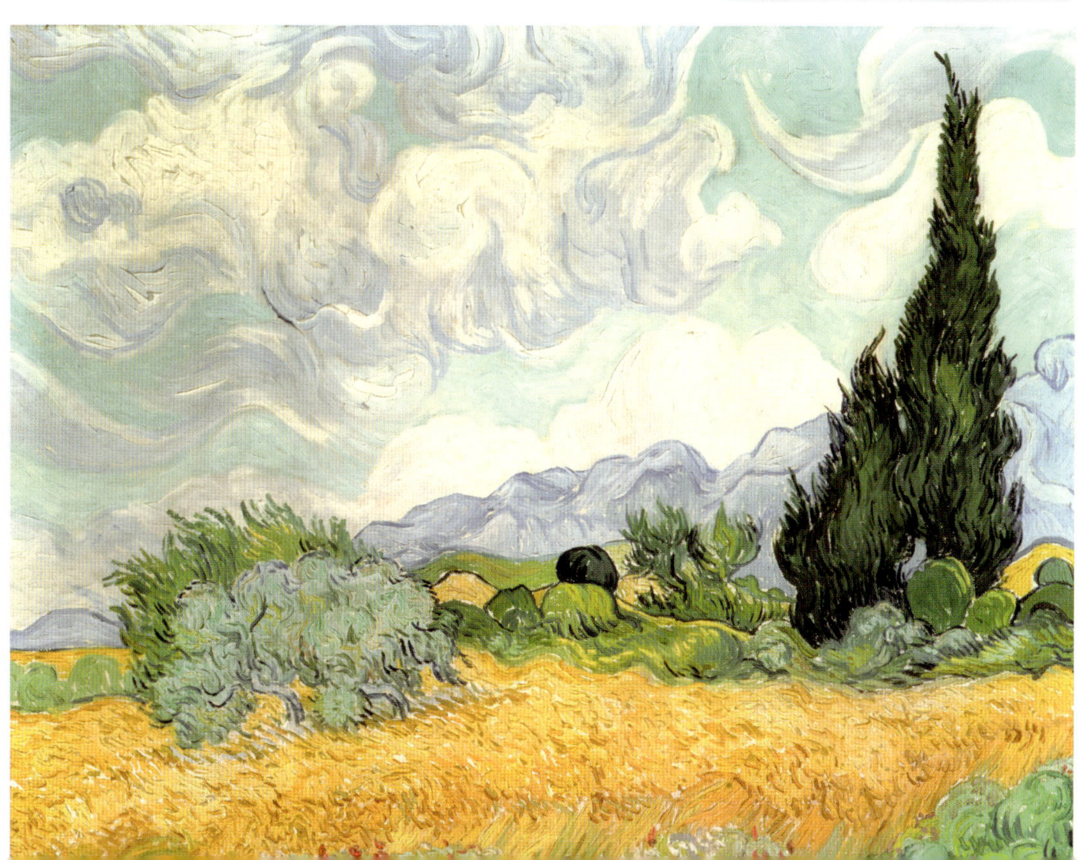

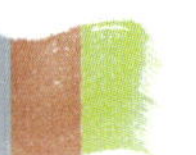

Cézanne's Late Works

In the 1860s and 1870s, Cézanne had divided his time between Paris, Pontoise and his native Provence, but discouraged by his lack of success at the end of the 1870s, he left Paris and re-settled in his native Aix-en-Provence. Inevitably, his relationship to the Impressionist group became remote, despite his lasting friendships with Pissarro and Renoir and his admiration for Monet. In 1882, he withdrew from exhibiting his work in Paris and did not exhibit there again until 1895, when the dealer Ambroise Vollard, aware of the increasing interest that his work was attracting among the younger generation of artists, put on the first of a series of three one-man retrospectives of his work.

In line with other Impressionists, the late 1880s saw broad changes in Cézanne's approach. In the late 1870s, Cézanne had narrowed the range of his brushstrokes to give his pictures a greater sense of form and compositional unity, but in the 1880s, his brushwork became more varied and spontaneous, embracing a wider range of effects. His choice of landscape subjects also changed. During the 1870s, his landscape painting in the north had focused on the agrarian landscape of Pontoise, however, by contrast, in the south he had focused on L'Estaque, near the busy industrial port of Marseille, which had become the heartland of the modernized Provence. During the 1880s, Cézanne began to turn his attention away from this kind of modern Provençal landscape subject in favour of more traditional and rural sites, such as the Montagne Sainte-Victoire, which became his principal motif.

The mountain was a landmark that had strong historical associations and was integral to Provençal regional identity. It was at the foot of the Montagne Sainte-Victoire that Marius defeated the Teutons, 100 years before the birth of Christ. According to legend, the reddish earth of the fields resulted from the blood spilt on the battlefield. The site had an important place in the imagery of Méridional painting; Prosper Grésy, Justinien Gaut, Jean-Antoine Constantin and François Marius Granet among others had all been attracted to it as a motif. From the mid-1880s, Cézanne explored its various "physiognomies" from numerous vantage points. In these pictures, the mountain is presented in bright sunlight or more subdued illumination, ornately framed by other elements or presented more starkly and frontally, from high and low vantage points,

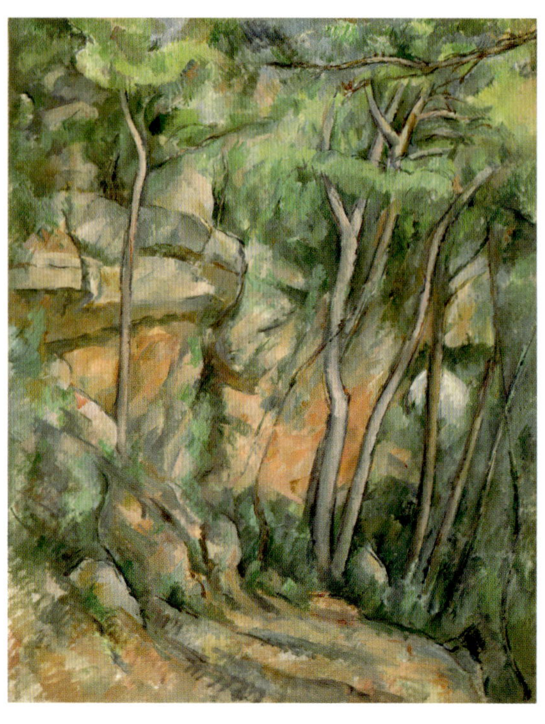

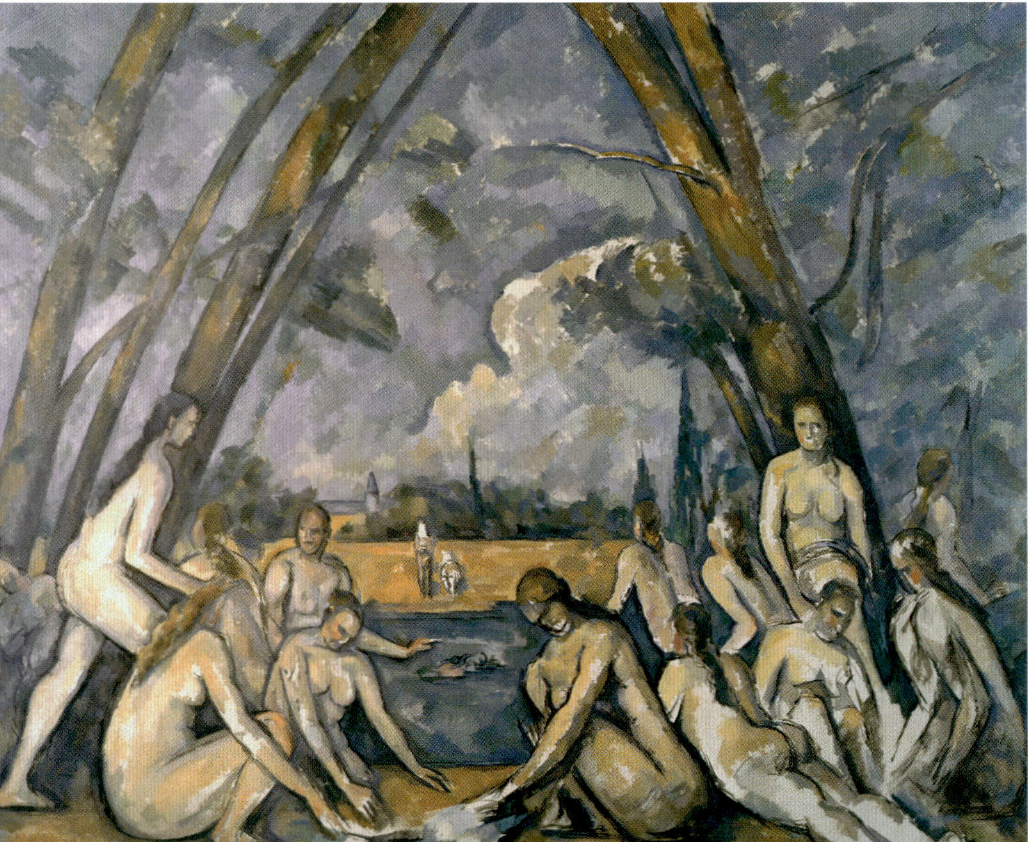

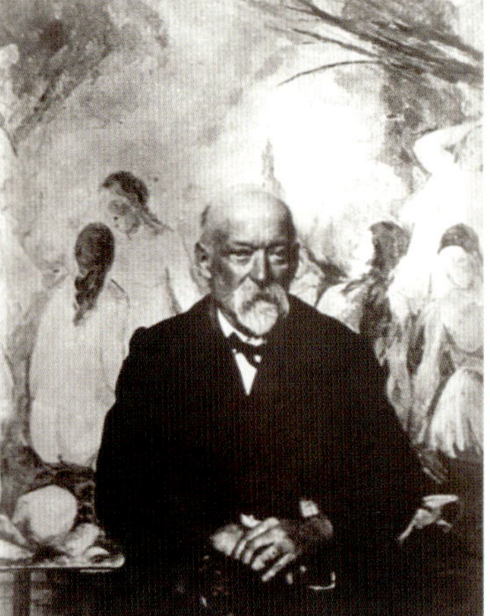

Cézanne at Work

In 1904, the Symbolist artist and critic Emile Bernard visited Cézanne in his studio in Aix-en-Provence. During his stay, he took a number of photographs of him. In the most emblematic of these Cézanne poses in the dim light of his austere studio at Les Lauves, his clasped hands resting on his paint-spattered trousers, before the version of the *Grandes Baigneuses* now in the Barnes collection in Philadelphia. Cézanne worked on these large paintings over the last 13 years of his life, beginning the Barnes version in 1894 on the eve of his return to exhibiting.

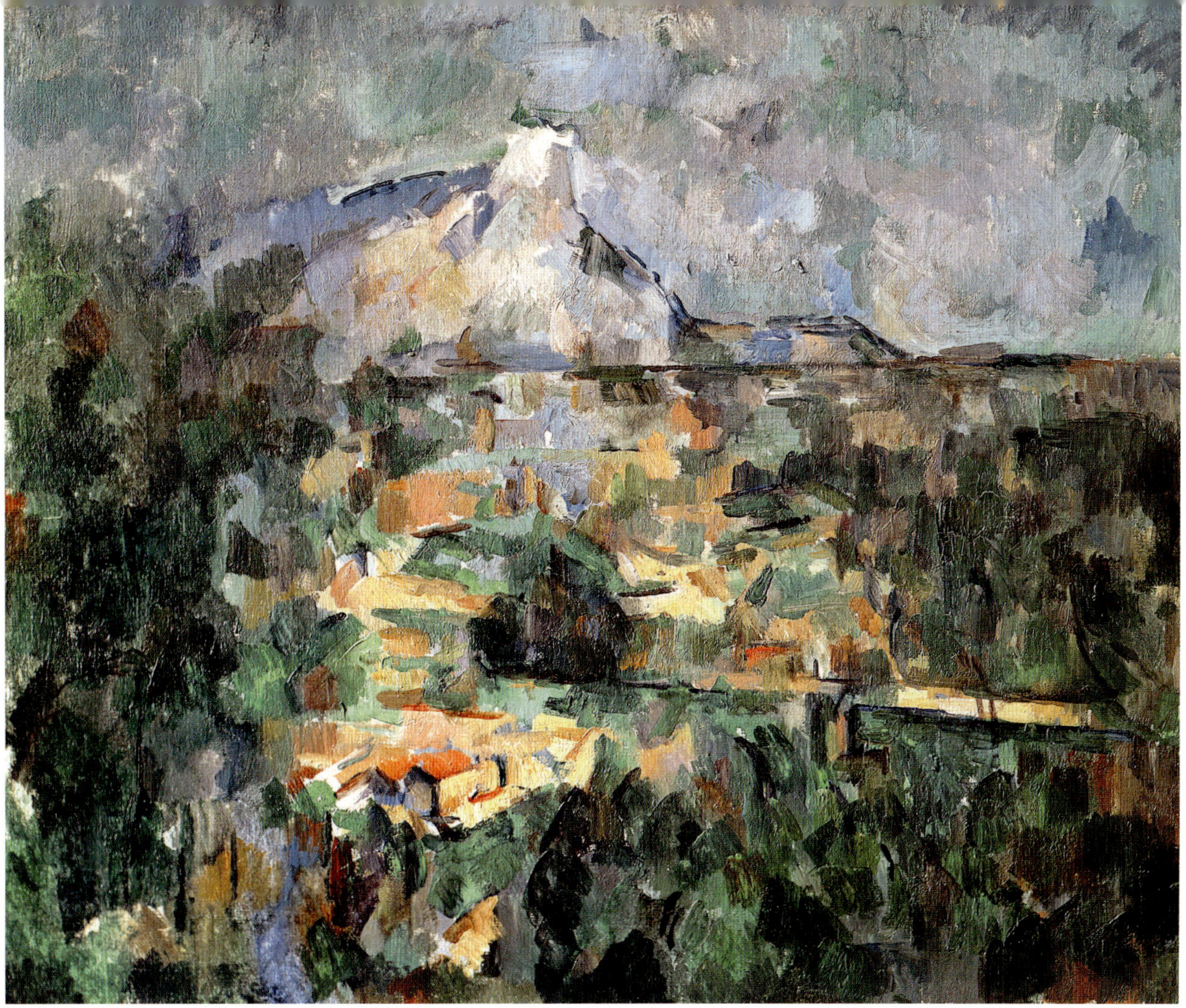

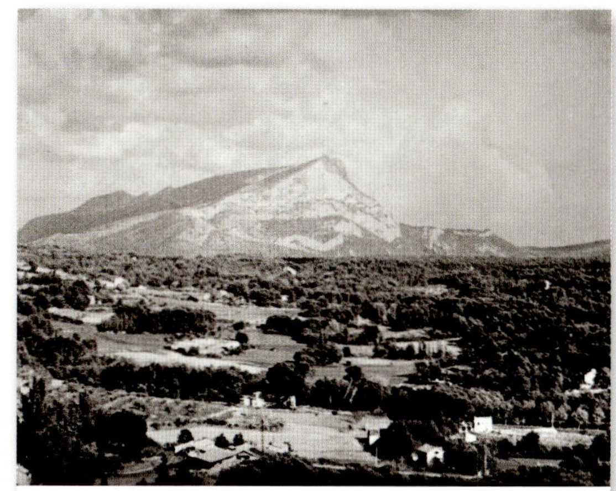

Montagne Sainte-Victoire

No painter is as indelibly associated with a single motif as Cézanne is with the Montagne Sainte-Victoire. Although some of his early pictures feature the mountain in the background of his landscapes, it was only during the late 1880s that it became his favourite motif. The imposing form of the mountain offered Cézanne a strong structure for his landscape compositions but one whose appearance continually shifted according to the changing light. As the poet Joachim Gasquet, who formed a close friendship with the painter, stated, Cézanne's attraction to such motifs reflected his deep love for his native Provence and his later landscape motifs return to the sites he had visited with his friend, the novelist Emile Zola, during their youth.

close and far away, centrally or from the side, Cézanne alternately viewing it from a position deep within the landscape or looking out from the terrace of the Montbriand estate owned by his brother-in-law, situated to the west of Aix.

The majestic views of the Montagne Sainte-Victoire contrast with his more intimate paintings of the abandoned Bibemus quarry and the grounds of Château Noir. These pictures of the woods and caves present densely clustered and almost airless spaces and are among the most complex and intricate of his chosen motifs. They also reflect Cézanne's fascination in his last years with sites of decay and ruin, expressed in the many abandoned buildings in his late landscapes and also in his still lifes with skulls from the late 1890s.

In addition to his landscape paintings, Cézanne continued to explore a wide range of genres, from still life and portraiture to the nude, which became the focus of his artistic ambitions in the mid-1890s. Cézanne began work on three large, mural-scale paintings, known as *Les Grandes Baigneuses* (*The Great Bathers*), of female figures bathing or sunning themselves by the Arc river, which he told Emile Bernard were to be the testing ground of his artistic theories and the culmination of his long fascination with painting the nude. Although on his death in 1906 these works remained unresolved, they exerted a tremendous influence on later generations of avant-garde artists.

Above *Cézanne's preoccupation with the Montagne Sainte-Victoire continued until his death in 1906. The late views of the mountain show a freer, more summary and improvised treatment that was influenced by his experiments with watercolour.*

Right *Cézanne's Still Life with Plaster Cupid (1892–95) is one of his most intricate still-life compositions. The artist made many preparatory sketches for the picture and produced several versions of it. Cézanne believed the plaster cupid was by Pugin, a much revered Provençal sculptor of the baroque period, whom the painter admired and he may have intended the picture as an homage to him.*

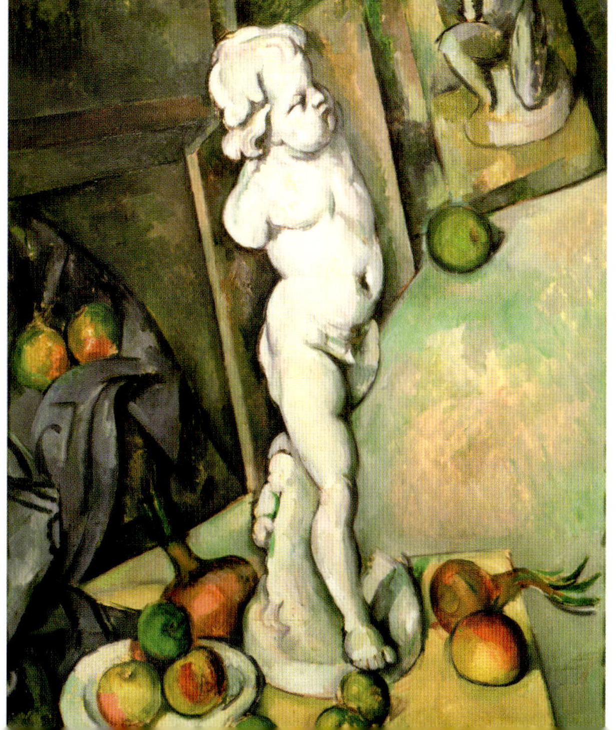

Monet's Water Lilies and *L'Art Décoratif*

In April 1883, Monet moved into a large house in the picturesque village of Giverny, acquiring the property in November 1890 when it came up for sale. Almost immediately, he began work on reconstructing the garden and bought an additional plot of land in 1893 to extend the grounds. The garden was to be one of his greatest works of art, comprising two main complementary parts: a country-house flower garden loosely based on eighteenth-century models and a tranquil, artfully arranged oriental garden. From the turn of the century until his death in 1926 the garden became his principal motif. The many views he made of the oriental garden, with its expansive pond, water lilies and the arched wooden Japanese footbridge that crossed it, are among his most serene and greatest paintings. As had become his practice, Monet produced series of works of the Japanese bridge and the pond, making subtle adjustments in his vantage point and altering the format and the tonality of his palette to suggest different climatic conditions and vary the aesthetic effect. In 1900, he showed 12 Japanese bridge pictures at the Durand-Ruel gallery that displayed the bold treatment and colour of his late style and the influence of Japanese prints on his choice of asymmetrical compositions.

By 1907, Monet's eyesight had begun to decline severely, eventually leaving him blind in his right eye and with distorted colour vision in his left. He was forced to wear special spectacles with a curved green lens to correct the colour imbalance in his left eye and an opaque lens in the right. Nevertheless, with great difficulty, he continued to paint his garden at Giverny and many of his most innovative and influential pictures date from these years. From 1905 onwards, he turned his attention to producing a majestic and ethereal series of pictures of the pond's water lilies in alternately square, circular, vertical and horizontal formats. Monet placed himself at the right-hand side of the pond looking obliquely down and across the foliated shore of the receding river, excluding the horizon in favour of focusing attention resolutely on the lilies themselves and the play of light and reflection on the water, which sometimes mirrors

Left *Monet experimented with different ways of presenting the Japanese bridge in his water-lily paintings. In earlier pictures, it is shown frontally, but here it occupies a slightly asymmetrical position, cloaking it in shadow. Monet's fluid, lush brushwork creates a vibrant surface that balances warm and cool colours. The foreground is dominated by cool blues and greens, but the warmer palette of the background suggests amber sunlight penetrating through the deep shadow.*

Monet's *Grandes Décorations*

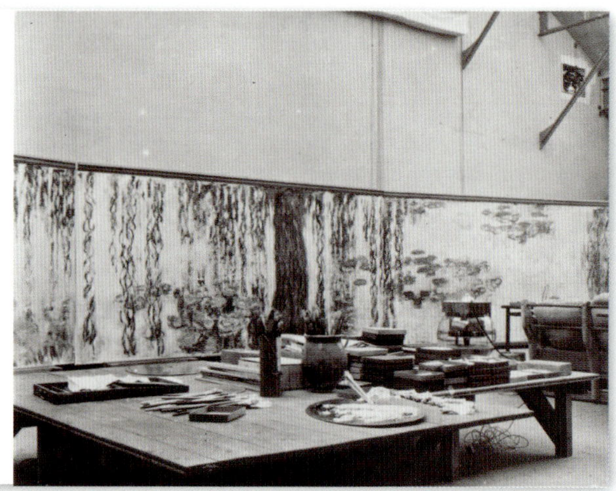

Moved by the carnage of the war and wanting to make a suitable memorial to the soldiers who had lost their lives fighting for France, Monet promised to donate two very large water-lily panels to the French nation. These took many years and much struggle to complete, and in 1922 Monet confided to his friend George Clemenceau, twice prime minister of France, that he feared he would not complete them. Eventually, they were finished and on 17 May 1927, the lyrical cycle of *Les Nymphéas (Water Lilies),* was placed on view at the Musée de l'Orangerie, especially constructed to house them.

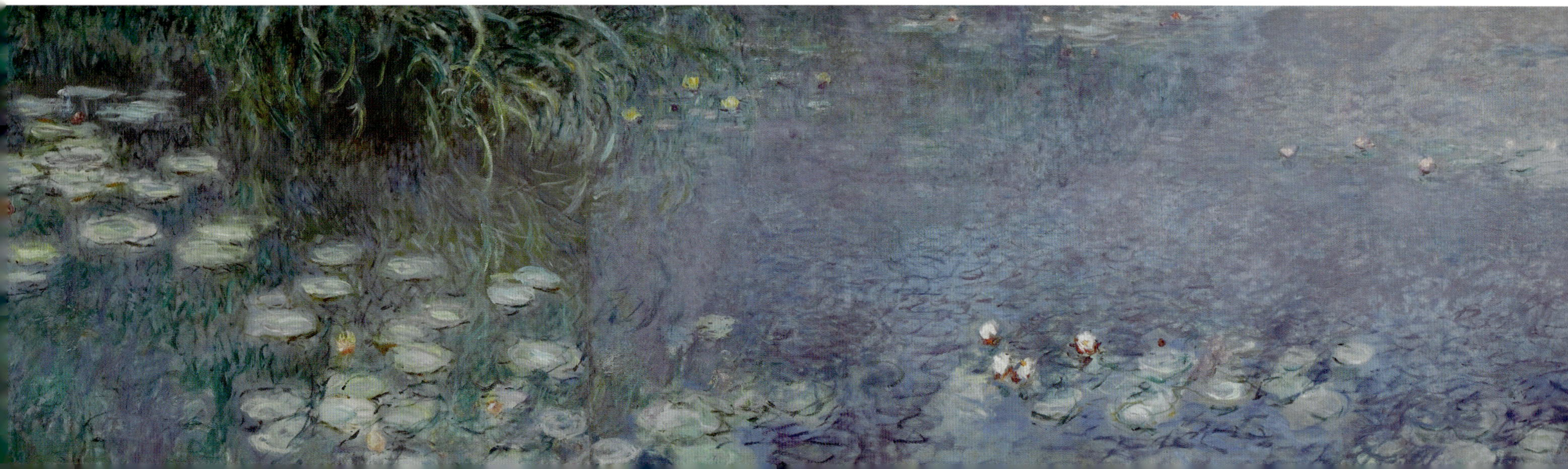

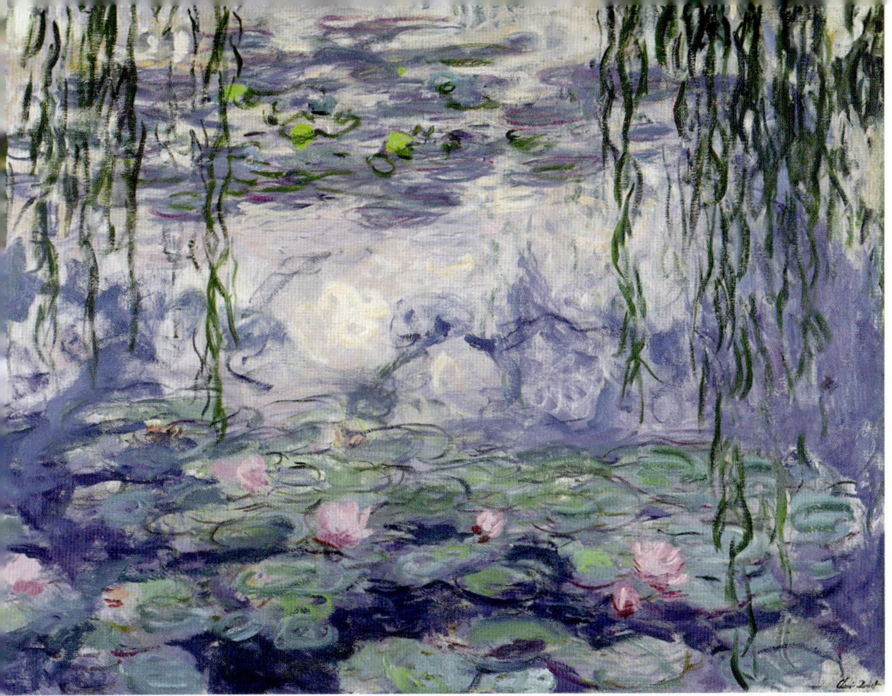

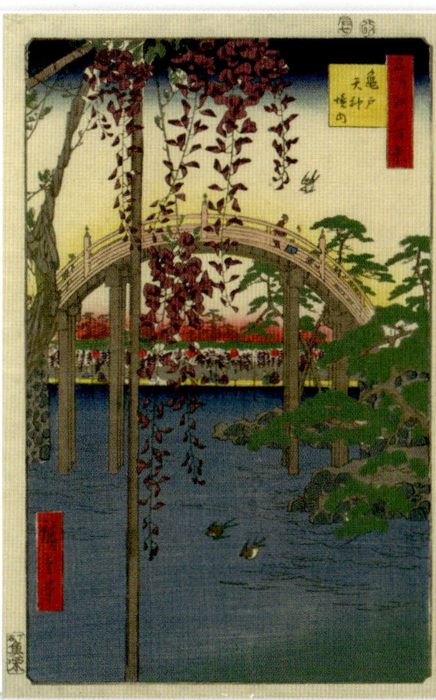

A Japanese Influence

The influence of Japanese prints on Monet was a continuous feature of his career, but Monet's understanding of Japanese art and aesthetics deepened as the years went by. He particularly admired the Japanese feeling for nature and regarded the Japanese as "a profoundly artistic people". In 1891, Monet employed a Japanese gardener to come to Giverny to advise him and his Japanese bridge was a favoured motif in his paintings of the garden. Like many of the Impressionists, Monet was an avid collector of Japanese woodblock engravings and assembled a collection of 231 Ukiyo-E (floating world) prints some of which were displayed in his home and which clearly influenced his own work.

the sky and clouds on its rippling surface. No works more elegantly express Monet's desire, as he put it, "to merge myself more intimately with nature".

When Monet exhibited 48 of these pictures in an exhibition at the Durand-Ruel gallery in 1909, one critic compared them with Michelangelo's Sistine Chapel and Beethoven's last quartets. While another wrote, "Under the pretext of simplicity, there is everything that the eye can perceive and understand; there is the infinity of forms and nuances, [and] the complex life of things."

The culmination of Monet's water-lily paintings was the large panoramic murals, the *Grandes Décorations*, which took him many years to complete. Under the Third Republic mural painting had undergone a substantial revival and decorative art was reappraised. The large scale of some of the later work of the Impressionists reflects the desire to show that Impressionism could provide ambitious decorative paintings. Monet had already tried his hand at decorative painting in the series of interior panels that he produced for Ernest Hoschedé, but his Nymphéas were on a much grander and ambitious scale. The serenity of these pictures, which invite lingering contemplation and visual pleasure, contrasts with the conditions under which some of them were executed. The garden at Giverny was divided by a railway line that separated the pond from the main house and grounds. During the First World War, the line was used to convey armaments and troops to the front-line, which was close enough for Monet to hear the guns firing. Monet probably included the weeping willows gently cascading over the pond in some of the murals as a discreet allusion to the terrible toll the war exacted.

Above left *In this watercolour version of the water-lilies motif, Monet frames the composition with the weeping willows that stood at the north end of the pond, bringing a decidedly Japanese inflection to the painting. Passing clouds are caught in the reflection of the blue water, their patterns echoing the clustered lily pads in the foreground.*

Bottom *Around 1903 Monet began to remove the banks that frame the pond in his earlier Giverny landscapes, allowing his pictures to become entirely devoted to the surface of the water and its reflections. In Water Lilies (1907), the reflections of light and the foliage of the bank-side are reflected in the mirror-like surface of the water, creating an extraordinary impression of lightness, process and movement.*

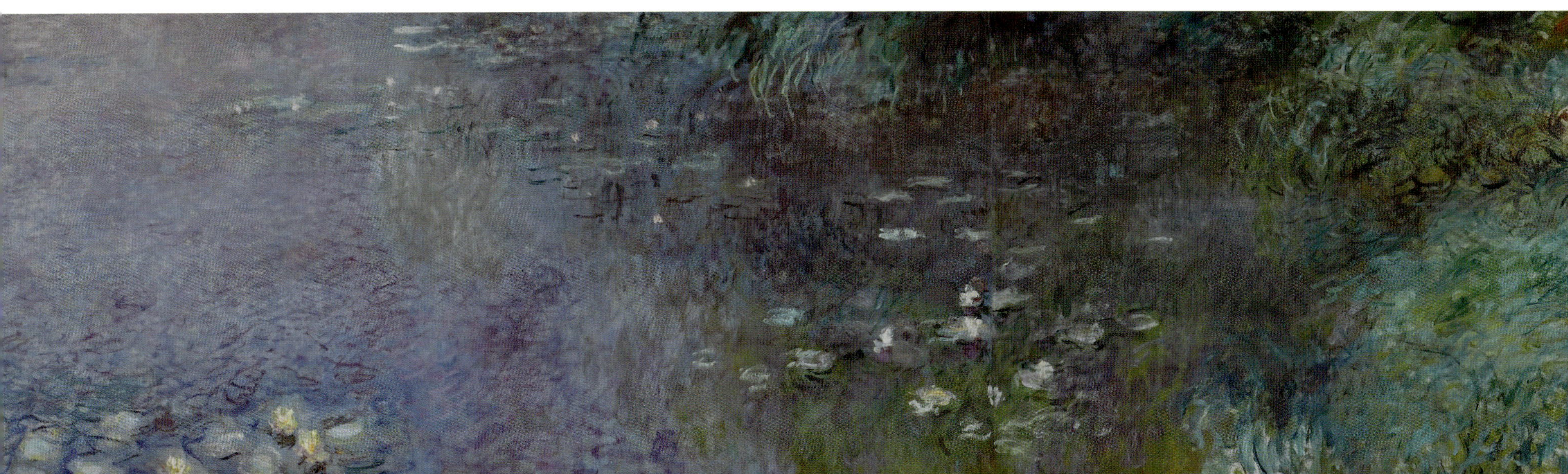

After Impressionism

Although many of the Impressionists would live on into the first decade of the twentieth century, by 1900 Impressionism was seen as a movement that had run its course and become a tradition. Despite the many masterpieces produced in the latter stages of the painters' careers, the absorption of Impressionism into the canon of French art meant that it was no longer seen as being at the cutting edge of modern art. As Impressionist paintings entered into museum collections around the world and Impressionism itself began to be written into the histories of modern art, it now came to be viewed as purely an historical phenomenon. Nevertheless, it remained a vital resource for modern painting and continued to exert a great influence on its development. Many of those who rejected it were nevertheless the beneficiaries of its pioneering innovations. The influence of Impressionist artists spread far and wide, across Europe and beyond. In England, Impressionism was continued in Walter Sickert's Camden Town Group and remained a dominant presence in British art in the 1920s and '30s, while in America it became almost a national movement. By the end of the nineteenth century the influence of Impressionism had also spread to other media and a movement of literary impressionism had emerged with writers like Henry James and Ford Maddox Ford.

The immediate heirs to Impressionism drew heavily on its artistic innovations but often pushed these in a different direction. Vincent van Gogh, Emile Bonnard and Edouard Vuillard all understood their art to be a continuation and development of the Impressionists, but developed the Impressionist tradition into a more subjective and idealized form, much as Castagnary had predicted. The colour schemes of these artists were no longer based on perceptions in nature but purely expressed the subjective emotional response of the painter and led to an expressionist movement, whose most vital exponents were German artists like Wassily Kandinsky, Ernst Kirchner and Der Blaue Reiter group.

In France, the legacy of Impressionism was taken up most influentially by the avant garde group, the Fauves. The name Fauvism (from "wild beasts"), referred to the strident, arbitrary colour schemes and primitive drawing of Henri Matisse, André Derain, Maurice Vlaminck and Georges Braque. The Fauves often revisited sites that the Impressionists had painted, most especially the Provençal motifs of Cézanne, reworking them according to their own highly saturated palette and broad, broken brushwork. Matisse and his group took from Impressionism the values of freedom of artistic means and the subjective point of view, characteristics he developed into an artistic language of abstraction.

Although Cubists rejected Impressionism's concern with visual perception in favour of a more conceptual art, based not on what the artist sees but what he knows, the development of their art initially owed

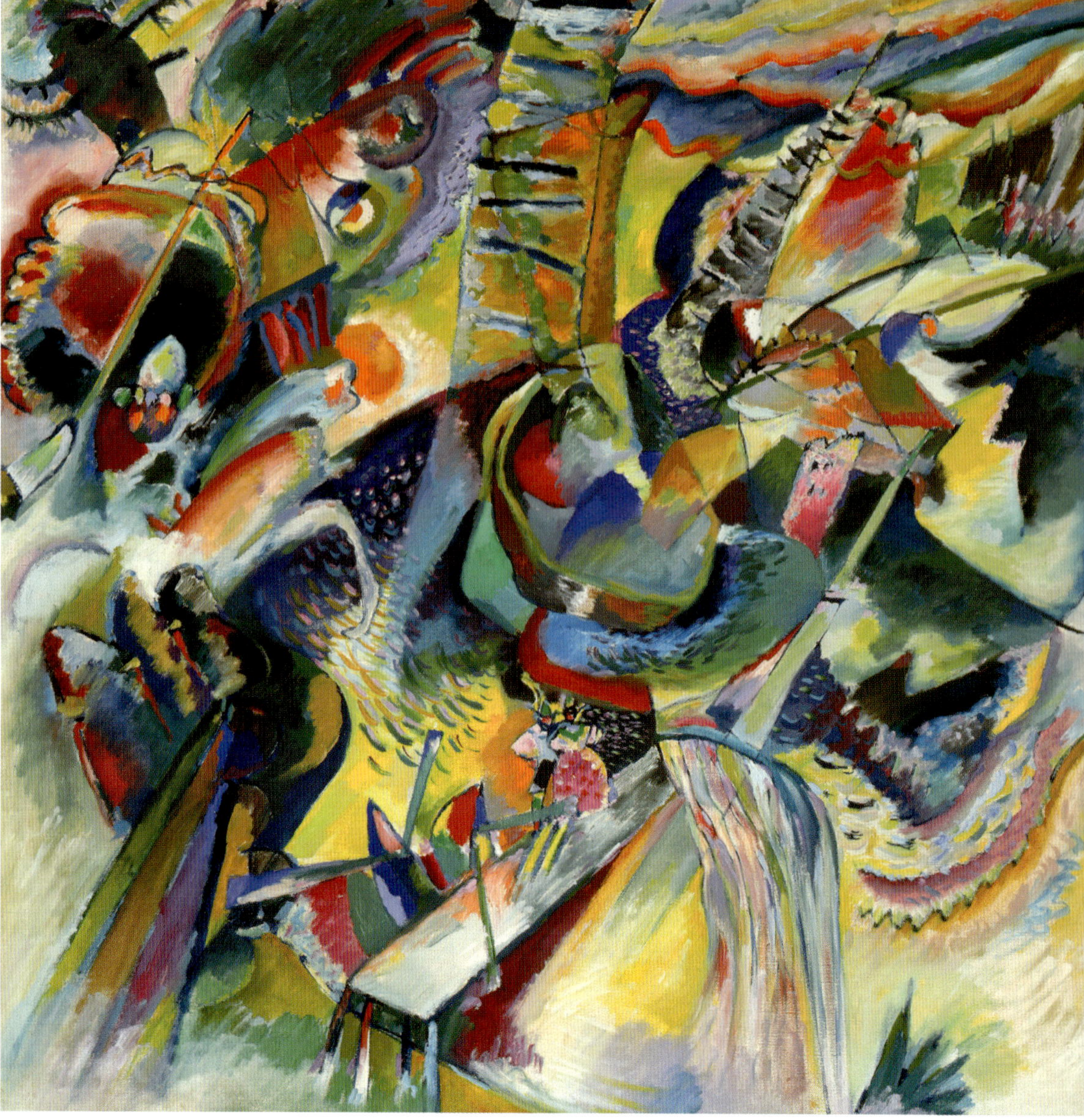

much to the example of Cézanne and the greater form he had given to Impressionism. Like the Fauves, the Cubists' early pictures revisited and reworked Cézanne's landscapes and nudes bringing a greater geometrical inflection and abstraction to them.

The reaction against abstract art in France in the aftermath of the First World War led to a revival of interest in the late nudes of Renoir as part of a turn towards neo-traditionalism, and artists like Picasso and Derain both looked to these for inspiration. Picasso's monumental nudes of the 1920s owe much to Renoir's late works. Likewise, after the Second World War, the tide turned against geometrical abstraction, and Impressionist artists, most especially Monet, enjoyed a significant revival of interest.

The fluid, all over painterly effects of the large mural-scale paintings of Abstract Expressionists, such as Jackson Pollock or painters like Joan Mitchell and Morris Louis, owe much to the brilliant colour, amplitude and painterly-ness of Monet's late *Nymphéas*.

Above *The evolution of Kandinsky's work shows how he developed a highly abstract, artistic vocabulary from his initial concerns with translating sensations of nature, here the experience of walking up a steep gorge, into pure pictorial form. Kandinsky sought to use colour and line to convey, as directly as possible, feeling and mood. In Gorge Improvisation, he suggests the swirling energy and powerful forces of the natural landscape.*

Further Information

BOOKS

Charles Baudelaire, *The Painter of Modern Life and Other Essays*, translated and edited by PE Charvet, Cambridge University Press, Cambridge, 1972.

David Bomberg, *Impressionism in the Making*, Exh. Cat., National Gallery of London, 1990.

Timothy J Clark, *The Painting of Modern Life in the Work of Manet and His Followers,* Alfred A Knopf, New York, 1985.

Bernard Denvir, *The Impressionists at First Hand,* Thames & Hudson, London, 1987.

T J Edelstein, ed., *Perspectives on Morisot*, Hudson Hill Press, New York, 1990.

Robert L Herbert, *Impressionism: Art, Leisure and Society*, Yale University Press, New Haven and London, 1988.

John House, *Impressionism: Painting and Politics*, Yale University Press, New Haven and London, 2003.

Richard Kendall, *Degas: Beyond Impressionism*, Exh. Cat., National Gallery of London, London, 1996.

Charles Moffett ed., *The New Painting, Impressionism 1874–86*, Exh. Cat., Fine Arts Museums of San Francisco and National Gallery of Washington, Burton Publishers, Geneva, Switzerland, 1986.

John Rewald, *The History of Impressionism*, Simon and Schuster, New York, 1946.

John Rewald, *Cézanne*, Thames and Hudson, London and New Haven, 1986.

John Rewald, ed. Irene Gordon and Frances Weitzenhoffer, *Studies in Impressionism*, Thames and Hudson, London, 1985.

James Rubin, *Impressionism*, Phaidon Press, London, 2002.

Meyer Schapiro, *Impressionism: Perceptions and Reflections*, George Brazillier, New York, 1997.

Mary Anne Stevens ed., *Alfred Sisley*, Exh. Cat., Yale University Press, New Haven and London, 1992.

Paul Smith, *Seurat and the Avant Garde*, Yale University Press, New Haven and London, 1997.

Richard Thomson, *Degas: The Nudes*, Thames & Hudson, London, 1988.

Richard Thomson, *Camille Pissarro: Impressionism, Landscape and Rural Labour*, The Herbert Press, London, 1990.

Paul Tucker, *Claude Monet: Life and Art*, Yale University Press, New Haven and London, 1992.

USEFUL WEBSITES

http://www.royalcollection.org.uk/collection-search
http://www.bibliotecaleonardiana.it/bbl/home.shtml
http://www.universalleonardo.org/
http://www.bbk.ac.uk/hosted/leonardo/

COLLECTIONS OF IMPRESSIONISM AROUND THE WORLD

UK

National Gallery, London
Tel: 020 7747 2885
www.nationalgallery.org.uk

Courtauld Institute of Art Gallery, London
http://www.courtauld.ac.uk/gallery/index.shtml

FRANCE

Museé Marmottan Monet, Paris
www.marmottan.com

Museé de l'Orangerie, Paris
www.musee-orangerie.fr

Museé d'Orsay, Paris
www.musee-orsay.fr

Museé A.G.Poulain, Vernon
http://giverny.org/museums/

Monet's House at Giverny, Giverny
www.fondation-monet.com

Studio of Paul Cézanne, Aix-en-Provence
www.atelier-cezanne.com

JAPAN

National Museum of Western Art, Tokyo
www.nmwa.go.jp

SWITZERLAND

Kunsthaus, Zurich
www.kunsthaus.ch

USA

The Museum of Fine Arts, Boston
www.mfa.org

The Art Institute of Chicago, Chicago
www.artic.edu

The Metropolitan Museum of Art, New York
www.metmuseum.org

Museum of Art, Philadelphia
www.philamuseum.org

National Gallery of Art Washington DC.
www.nga.gov

Index

Publishers' Acknowledgements

MEMORABILIA CREDITS

Item 1: Personal Card issued by the Paris Federation of Artists during the Commune of Paris and belonging to Gustave Courbet, 1871 (cardboard), French School, (19th century)/Musée de la Ville de Paris, Musée Carnavalet, Paris, France, Archives Charmet/The Bridgeman Art Library. Item 2: Bibliothèque Nationale de France. Item 3: © Photo RMN – © Thierry Le Mage/Gérard Blot/Michèle Bellot (3). Item 4: © Photo RMN – © Gérard Blot. Item 5: © Photo RMN – ©René-Gabriel Ojéda. Item 6: © Photo RMN – © Thierry Le Mage. Item 7: © Photo RMN – © Jean-Gilles Berizzi. Item 8: © Photo RMN – © Thierry Le Mage. Item 9: © Photo RMN – © Michèle Bellot. Item 10: © Photo RMN – © Gérard Blot. Item 11: © Photo RMN – © Gérard Blot. Item 12: The Three Trees (pencil on paper), Monet, Claude (1840–1926)/Musée Marmottan, Paris, France, Giraudon/The Bridgeman Art Library, 248622 Poplars on the Epte at the Limetz Marsh (pencil on paper), Monet, Claude (1840–1926)/Musée Marmottan, Paris, France, Giraudon/The Bridgeman Art Library. Item 14: © Photo RMN – © Photographe inconnu. Item 15: © Photo RMN – © Droits réservés.

PICTURE CREDITS

The publishers would like to thank the following sources for their kind permission to reproduce the pictures in this book.

Key: t=Top, b=Bottom, c=Centre, l=Left, r=Right

Front Endpaper: ©Photo RMN/Droits Réservés
Back Endpaper: ©Photo RMN/Hervé Lewandowski

1 Corbis/©Christie's Images; 2l The Bridgeman Art Library/Private Collection, Photo ©Lefevre Fine Art Ltd., London, Mery Laurent in a Veil (pastel, gouache and oil), Manet, Edouard (1832-83); 2r The Bridgeman Art Library/Musee de l'Orangerie, Paris, France, Lauros, Giraudon, Flowers and Fruit, c.1886 (oil on canvas), Cezanne, Paul (1839-1906); 3 The Bridgeman Art Library/Louvre, Paris, France, Giraudon, Dancer viewed from the back, Degas, Edgar (1834-1917); 4tr Scala, Florence/The Philadelphia Museum of Art/Art Resource; 5tl The Bridgeman Art Library)/Hamburger Kunsthalle, Hamburg, Germany, Phryne Before the Jury, 1861 (oil on canvas), Gerome, Jean Leon (1824-1904); 5tr ©Photo RMN/Gérard Blot; 5bl ©Photo RMN/Hervé Lewandowski; 5br Bibliothèque nationale de France; 6tr ©Photo RMN/Droits Réservés; 6cl ©Photo RMN/A. Danvers; 6cr The Bridgeman Art Library/Musee de la Ville de Paris, Musee Carnavalet, Paris, France, Archives Charmet Gustave Courbet (1819-77) in front of his self portrait, cover illustration from 'La Lune' magazine, 9th June 1867 (colour litho), Gill, Andre (1840-85); 7tr Toledo Museum of Art, Gift of Arthur J.Secor, 1933.37, Pierre Etienne Théodore Rouseau (French, 1812-1867), Under the Birches, Evening, 1842-43, oil on wood panel, 42.3x64.4cm; 7bl ©Photo RMN/Jean Schormans; 7br ©Photo RMN/Jean-Gilles Berizzi; 8tl&br ©Photo RMN/Hervé Lewandowski; 8bl The Bridgeman Art Library/Private Collection, Archives Charmet, Portrait of Edouard Manet (1832-83), c. 1870-80 (b/w photo), Nadar, (Gaspard Felix Tournachon) (1820-1910); 9t The Bridgeman Art Library Music/ National Gallery, London, UK, in the Tuileries Gardens, 1862 (oil on canvas), Manet, Edouard (1832-83); 9br ©Photo RMN/Hervé Lewandowski; 10bl ©Photo RMN/Bulloz; 10tr The Bridgeman Art Library/Nelson-Atkins Museum of Art, Kansas City, USA Boulevard des Capucines, 1873-4 (oil on canvas), Monet, Claude (1840-1926); 11t ©Rennes, Dist RMN/Adélaide Beaudon; 12t ©Photo RMN/Daniel Arnaudet; 12b ©The Metropolitan Museum of Art, Rogers Fund, 1937 (37.165.98); 13l The Bridgeman Art Library/©Walters Art Museum, Baltimore, USA, At the Cafe - Concert, 1878-79 (oil on canvas), Manet, Edouard (1832-83); 13r The Bridgeman Art Library/National Gallery, London, UK, The Umbrellas, c.1881-6 (oil on canvas), Renoir, Pierre Auguste (1841-1919); 14tl The Bridgeman Art Library/Musee d'Orsay, Paris, France, Lauros /Giraudon The Hotel des Roches Noires at Trouville, 1870 (oil on canvas), Monet, Claude (1840-1926); 14tr The Bridgeman Art Library/Metropolitan Museum of Art, New York, USA, Lauros/Giraudon/ The Terrace at Sainte-Adresse, 1867 (oil on canvas), Monet, Claude (1840-1926); 14br The

Bridgeman Art Library/Private Collection, Photo ©Held Collection Fuji from the Sazai Hall at the Temple of the Five Hundred Rakan (Gohyakurakandera sazaido), from '36 Views of Fuji' ('Fugaku sanjurokkei') 1830-35 (woodblock print), Hokusai, Katsushika (1760-1849); 15tl ©Photo RMN/Hervé Lewandowski; 15br The Bridgeman Art Library/National Gallery, London, The Beach at Trouville, 1870 (oil on canvas), Monet, Claude (1840-1926); 16tr The Bridgeman Art Library/Metropolitan Museum of Art, New York, USA La Grenouillere, 1869 (oil on canvas), Monet, Claude (1840-1926); 16bl The Bridgeman Art Library/©National-museum, Stockholm, Sweden, La Grenouillere, 1869 (oil on canvas), Renoir, Pierre Auguste (1841-1919); 17tr The Bridgeman Art Library/Pushkin Museum, Moscow, Russia, Giraudon, Bathing on the Seine or, La Grenouillere, c.1869 (oil on canvas), Renoir, Pierre Auguste (1841-1919); 17bl Private collection; 17br The Bridgeman Art Library/Kunstmuseum, Winterthur, Switzerland, La Grenouillere, 1869 (oil on canvas), Renoir, Pierre Auguste (1841-1919); 18tl Tate Britain; 18tr ©Photo RMN/Droits Réservés; 18br The Bridgeman Art Library/Pushkin Museum, Moscow, Russia, Le Dejeuner sur l'Herbe, 1866 (oil on canvas), Monet, Claude (1840-1926); 19tl ©/Scala, Florence/The Metropolitan Museum of Art/Art Resource; 19tr The J. Paul Getty Museum, Los Angeles, Pierre-Auguste Renoir, La Promenade, 1870, Oil on Canvas, 81.3x65cm; 19br ©Photo RMN/Droits reserves; 20tr akg-images; 20tl The Bridgeman Art Library/Chateau de Compiegne, Oise, France, Peter Willi, The Ruins of the Tuileries, 1871, Meissonier, Jean-Louis Ernest (1815-91); 20bl ©Photo RMN/Hervé Lewandowski; 21tr & bl akg-images/Erich Lessing; 21br Illustrated London News; 22tl ©Photo RMN/René-Gabriel Ojéda; 22tr ©Photo RMN/Daniel Arnaudet; 22br Museum of Fine Arts, Springfield, Massachusetts, U.S.A, James Philip Gray Collection; 23tr Artothek/Ursula Edelmann; 23bl The Bridgeman Art Library/©Samuel Courtauld Trust, Courtauld Institute of Art Gallery, Autumn Effect at Argenteuil, 1873, Monet, Claude (1840-1926); 23br The Bridgeman Art Library/ Museum of Fine Arts, Houston, Texas, USA, Gift of Audrey Jones Beck, The Seine at Paris, 1871 (oil on canvas), Guillaumin, Jean Baptiste Armand (1841-1927); 24tl The Bridgeman Art Library/Private Collection, Photo ©Christie's Images, Argenteuil, at the End of the Afternoon, 1872 (oil on canvas), Monet, Claude (1840-1926); 24tr The Bridgeman Art Library, Portland Art Museum, Oregon, USA, The Seine at Argenteuil, 1874 (oil on canvas), Renoir, Pierre Auguste (1841-1919); 24br The British Library; 25tr ©Photo RMN/Hervé Lewandowski; 25bl Christie's Images Ltd; 25br The Bridgeman Art Library/Musee des Beaux-Arts, Tournai, Belgium, Argenteuil, 1874 (oil on canvas), Manet, Edouard (1832-83); 26tr ©Photo RMN/René-Gabriel Ojéda; 26bl Artothek/Hans Hinz; 26br ©Photo RMN/Hervé Lewandowski; 27tl National Gallery London; 31tr ©Photo RMN/Hervé Lewandowski; 27tr The Bridgeman Art Library/Private Collection, Roger-Viollet, Paris, Portrait photograph of Camille Pissarro (1830-1903) and Paul Cezanne (1839-1906) (b/w photo); 27br The Bridgeman Art Library/© Samuel Courtauld Trust, Courtauld Institute of Art Gallery, The Etang des Soeurs,

Osny, c.1875 (oil on canvas), Cezanne, Paul (1839-1906); 28tl The Bridgeman Art Library/Musee d'Orsay, Paris, France, Peter Willi, A Meeting of the Judges of the Salon des Artistes Francais, 1885, Gervex, Henri (1852-1929); 28tr The Bridgeman Art Library/Bibliotheque Nationale, Paris, France, Archives Charmet, Caricature of the first Impressionist Exhibition in Paris, 'Revolution in Painting! And a terrorizing beginning!, 1874 (engraving) (b/w photo), Cham (Amedee Charles Henri de Noe) (1818-79); 28bc The Bridgeman Art Library/Musee Marmottan, Paris, France, Giraudon, Impression: Sunrise, Le Havre, 1872 (oil on canvas), Monet, Claude (1840-1926); 29tl The Bridgeman Art Library/Museum of Fine Arts, Boston, Massachusetts, USA, 1931 Purchase Fund, At the Races in the Countryside, 1869 (oil on canvas), Degas, Edgar (1834-1917); 29tr ©Photo RMN/Hervé Lewandowski; 29c akg-images; 29br The Bridgeman Art Library/Musee d'Orsay, Paris, France, Giraudon, The Cradle, 1872 (oil on canvas), Morisot, Berthe (1841-95); 30tr The Samuel Courtauld Trust, Courtauld Institute of Art Gallery, London; 30bl akg-images/Erich Lessing; 30br Bibliothèque nationale de France; 31tr ©Museo Thyssen-Bornemisza. Madrid; 31bl ©Photo RMN/Bulloz; 31br ©Photo RMN/Hervé Lewandowski; 32tl&tr ©Photo RMN/Hervé Lewandowski; 32bl The Bridgeman Art Library/Musee d'Orsay, Paris, France, Giraudon, Ball at the Moulin de la Galette, 1876 (oil on canvas), Renoir, Pierre Auguste (1841-1919); 33tl The Bridgeman Art Library/©The Barnes Foundation, Merion, Pennsylvania, USA, Bathers at Rest, 1875-76 (oil on canvas), Cezanne, Paul (1839-1906); 33bl The Bridgeman Art Library/Fogg Art Museum, Harvard University Art Museums, USA, Gift of Mr. and Mrs. F. Meynier de Salinelles, Summer Scene, 1869 (oil on canvas), Bazille, Jean Frederic (1841-70); 33br Image courtesy of the Board of Trustees, National Gallery of Art, Washington/Collection of Mr & Mrs Paul Mellon, Claude Monet Woman with a Parasol; 34tl Courtesy of the Corcoran Gallery of Art, Washington, DC/William A. Clark Collection, Edgar Degas The Dance Class, 1873, Oil on Canvas, 26.74; 34tr Scala, Florence/The Metropolitan Museum of Art; 34bl ©Photo RMN/Hervé Lewandowski; 35tr ©Photo RMN/Bulioz; 35bl The Bridgeman Art Library/Metropolitan Museum of Art, New York, USA, The Rehearsal of the Ballet on Stage, c.1878-79 (pastel on paper), Degas, Edgar (1834-1917); 35br Philadelphia Museum of Art/Louis E.Stern Collection, Edgar degas, Two Dancers in Repose; 35c Scala, Florence/The Philadelphia Museum of Art/Art Resource; 36bl ©The Art Institute of Chicago/Gift of Mrs Charles Netcher in memory of Charles Netcher II, Berthe Morisot, On the Balcony, 1871/2, Water, 203x173mm, E9193; 36tr The Bridgeman Art Library/Museum of Fine Arts, Boston, Massachusetts, USA, M. Theresa B. Hopkins Fund, The Tea, c.1880 (oil on canvas), Cassatt, Mary Stevenson (1844-1926); 36bc ©Photo RMN/Hervé Lewandowski; 36br The Bridgeman Art Library/National Gallery, London, UK, Portrait of Eva Gonzales (1849-83) 1870 (oil on canvas), Manet, Edouard (1832-83); 37tr The Bridgeman Art Library/Museum of Fine Arts, Boston, Massachusetts, USA, The Hayden Collection - Charles Henry Hayden Fund, In the Loge, 1879 (oil on

canvas), Cassatt, Mary Stevenson (1844-1926); 37bl The Bridgeman Art Library/Musee Marmottan, Paris, France, Giraudon, Berthe Morisot (1841-95) (19th Century); 37bc The Bridgeman Art Library/©Samuel Courtauld Trust, Courtauld Institute of Art Gallery, La Loge, 1874 (oil on canvas), Renoir, Pierre Auguste (1841-1919); 38tl The Bridgeman Art Library/©Samuel Courtauld Trust, Courtauld Institute of Art Gallery, A Bar at the Folies-Bergere, 1881-82 (oil on canvas), Manet, Edouard (1832-83); 38tr The Bridgeman Art Library/Private Collection, The Stapleton Collection, Reproduction of a poster advertising 'La Goulue' at the Moulin Rouge, Paris (colour litho) (see 454, 7015 and 84446), Toulouse-Lautrec, Henri de (1864-1901); 38br The Bridgeman Art Library/National Gallery of Art, Washington DC, USA, Index, Oarsmen at Chatou, 1879 (oil on canvas), Renoir, Pierre Auguste (1841-1919); 39tl The Bridgeman Art Library/Private Collection, Boaters Rowing on the Yerres, 1877 (oil on canvas), Caillebotte, Gustave (1848-94); 39tr The Bridgeman Art Library/Burrell Collection, Glasgow, Scotland, ©Glasgow City Council (Museums) The Chateau de Medan, c.1880 (oil on canvas), Cezanne, Paul (1839-1906); 39bc The Bridgeman Art Library/Musee des Beaux-Arts, Lyon, France, Giraudon, Cafe Concert at Les Ambassadeurs, 1876-77 (pastel on paper), Degas, Edgar (1834-1917); 39br ©Photo RMN/Hervé Lewandowski; 40tl The Art Institute of Chicago/The Stickney Fund, Berthe Morisot, Woman at her Toilet, 1875, oil on canvas, 60.3x80.4c, 1924.127; 40tr ©Archives Durand-Ruel; 40br Scala, Florence/©The Metropolitan Museum of Art/Art Resource; 41l ©Photo RMN/Hervé Lewandowski; 41r ©Photo RMN/René-Gabriel Ojéda; 42tl The Bridgeman Art Library/Ohara Museum of Art, Kurashiki, Japan, Lauros, Giraudon, The Apple Pickers, 1886 (oil on canvas), Pissarro, Camille (1831-1903); 42tr Musées de Pontoise; 42br The Bridgeman Art Library/ National Gallery, London, UK, Bathers at Asnieres, 1884 (oil on canvas), Seurat, Georges Pierre (1859-91); 43tl The Bridgeman Art Library/©Ashmolean Museum, University of Oxford, UK, View Through a Window, Eragny, 1888 (oil on canvas), Pissarro, Camille (1831-1903); 43tr ©Photo RMN/Christian Jean; 43br The Bridgeman Art Library/Art Institute of Chicago, IL, USA, Sunday Afternoon on the Island of La Grande Jatte, 1884-86 (oil on canvas), Seurat, Georges Pierre (1859-91); 44tr ©The Metropolitan Museum of Art, Gift of Mr & Mrs Nate B. Spingold, 1956 (56.231); 44bl Tate Picture Library; 45tl The Bridgeman Art Library/Private Collection, The Stapleton Collection, Illustration from 'La Maison Tellier' by Guy de Maupassant (1850-93) engraved by Maurice Potin, 1933 (engraving), Degas, Edgar (1834-1917); 45tr ©Photo RMN/Gérard Blot; 45br Hill-Stead Museum, Farmington/Alfred Atmore Pope Collection, The Tub, Edgar Degas, 1886; 46cl The Bridgeman Art Library/Museum of Fine Arts, Boston, Massachusetts, USA, Juliana Cheney Edwards Collection, Grainstack (Sunset) 1891 (oil on canvas), Monet, Claude (1840-1926); 46tr Durand-Ruel et Cie; 47tl The Bridgeman Art Library/Museum of Fine Arts, Boston, Massachusetts, USA, Gift of Miss Aimee and Rosamond Lamb in Memory

of, Grainstack (Snow Effect) 1891 (oil on canvas), Monet, Claude (1840-1926); 47br The Art Institute of Chicago/Potter Palmer Collection, Claude Monet, Stacks of Wheat (Sunset, Snow Effect), 1890-91, oil on canvas, 65.3x100.4cm, 1922.431; 48l Philadelphia Museum of Art/Bequest of Anne Thompson in memory of her father, Frank Thompson & her mother, Mary Elizabeth Clarke Thompson, 1954, Monet, Claude, Poplars on the Bank of the Epte River; 48r Alinari Picture Library; 49l ©Photo RMN/Droits Réservés; 49tr Sterling & Francine Clark Art Institute, Williamstown, Massachusetts/ Purchased in memory of Anne Strang Baxter; 49br The Bridgeman Art Library/Musee Marmottan, Paris, France, Giraudon, Rouen Cathedral, Effects of Sunlight, Sunset, 1892 (oil on canvas), Monet, Claude (1840-1926); 50tl The Bridgeman Art Library/Philadelphia Museum of Art, Pennsylvania, PA, USA, The Bathers, 1887 (oil on canvas), Renoir, Pierre Auguste (1841-1919); 50tr Picture Desk/Art Archive/Culver Pictures; 50br The Bridgeman Art Library/Private Collection, Peter Willi, Bather seated on a rock, 1892 (oil on canvas), Renoir, Pierre Auguste (1841-1919); 51tl The Bridgeman Art Library/©The Barnes Foundation, Merion, Pennsylvania, USA, Bathers, c.1918 (oil on canvas), Renoir, Pierre Auguste (1841-1919); 51br ©The Art Institute of Chicago/Mr & Mrs Lewis Larned Coburn Endowment, through prior request of Annie Swan Coburn to the Mr & Mrs Lewis Larned Coburn Memorial Fund; through prior acquisition of the R.A. Waller Fund, Pierre Auguste Renoir, Seated Bather, 1914, Oil on canvas, 81.4x67.5cm, 1945.27; 52t The Bridgeman Art Library/Metropolitan Museum of Art, New York, USA, Madame Georges Charpentier and her Children, 1878, Renoir, Pierre Auguste (1841-1919); 52bl The Bridgeman Art Library/Art Institute of Chicago, IL, USA, Lauros, Giraudon, Bordighera, 1884 (oil on canvas), Monet, Claude (1840-1926); 52br ©PhotoRMN/René-Gabriel Ojéda; 53t The Bridgeman Art Library/©Samuel Courtauld Trust, Courtauld Institute of Art Gallery, Montagne Sainte-Victoire, c.1887 (oil on canvas), Cezanne, Paul (1839-1906); 53bc akg-images/Erich Lessing; 53br Scala, Florence/The Metropolitan Museum of Art/Art Resource; 54tc The Bridgeman Art Library, Place de la Nation, Paris, France, Lauros, Giraudon, The Triumph of the Republic, 1879-99 (bronze), Dalou, Aime Jules (1838-1902); 54tr ©Photo RMN/René-Gabriel Ojéda; 54bl ©The Metropolitan Museum of Art/H.O.Havemeyer Collection/Bequest of Mrs H.O. Havemeyer, 1929 (29.100.377); 54bc ©Photo RMN/Jean Schormans; 55tl Museo Medardo Rosso; 55tr Photograph ©2008 Museum of Fine Arts Boston; 55br Musée Rodin, Paris; 56bl ©Photo RMN/Gérard Blot/Christian Jean; 56tr akg-images/Laurent Lecat; 56br Scala, Florence/The Metropolitan Museum of Modern Art/©ADAGP Paris and DACS London 2008; 57tl ©Photo RMN/Hervé Lewandowski/©ADAGP Paris and DACS London 2008; 57tr ©Photo RMN/Hervé Lewandowski; 57bl The Bridgeman Art Library/©National Gallery of Scotland, Edinburgh Scotland, The Vision after the Sermon (Jacob wrestling with the Angel) 1888 (oil on canvas), Gauguin, Paul (1848-1903); 57br The Bridgeman Art Library/National Gallery, London, UK, Wheatfield with Cypresses, 1889 (oil on

canvas), Gogh, Vincent van (1853-90); 58tr ©Photo RMN/Hervé Lewandowski; 58bl The Bridgeman Art Library/ Philadelphia Museum of Art, Pennsylvania, PA, USA, The Large Bathers, c.1900-05 (oil on canvas), Cezanne, Paul (1839-1906); 58br The Bridgeman Art Library/Private Collection, Archives Charmet , Paul Cezanne (1839-1906) in front of his painting 'The Large Bathers' 1904 (b/w photo) (see also 217621), French Photographer, (20th century)/©ADAGP Paris and DACS London 2008; 59tl The Bridgeman Art Library/Kunstmuseum, Basel, Switzerland, Montagne Sainte-Victoire from Lauves, 1904-06 (oil on canvas), Cezanne, Paul (1839-1906); 59tr National Gallery of Art Library, Washington DC/John Rewald Archive, Department of Image Collections; 59br The Bridgeman Art Library/©Samuel Courtauld Trust, Courtauld Institute of Art Gallery, Still life with plaster cast, c.1894 (oil on paper), Cezanne, Paul (1839-1906); 60tl The Art Institute of Chicago/Mr & Mrs Lewis Larned Coburn Memorial Collection, Claude Monet, Water Lily Pond, 1900, Oil on Canvas, 89.8x101cm, 1933.441; 60cr Durand-Ruel et Cie; 60-61b ©Photo RMN/Hervé Lewandowski; 61tl & tr ©2008 Museum of Fine Arts, Boston; 62 ©Artothek/©ADAGP Paris and DACS London 2008

Every effort has been made to acknowledge correctly and contact the source and/or copyright holder of each picture and Carlton Books Limited apologises for any unintentional errors or omissions, which will be corrected in future editions of this book.

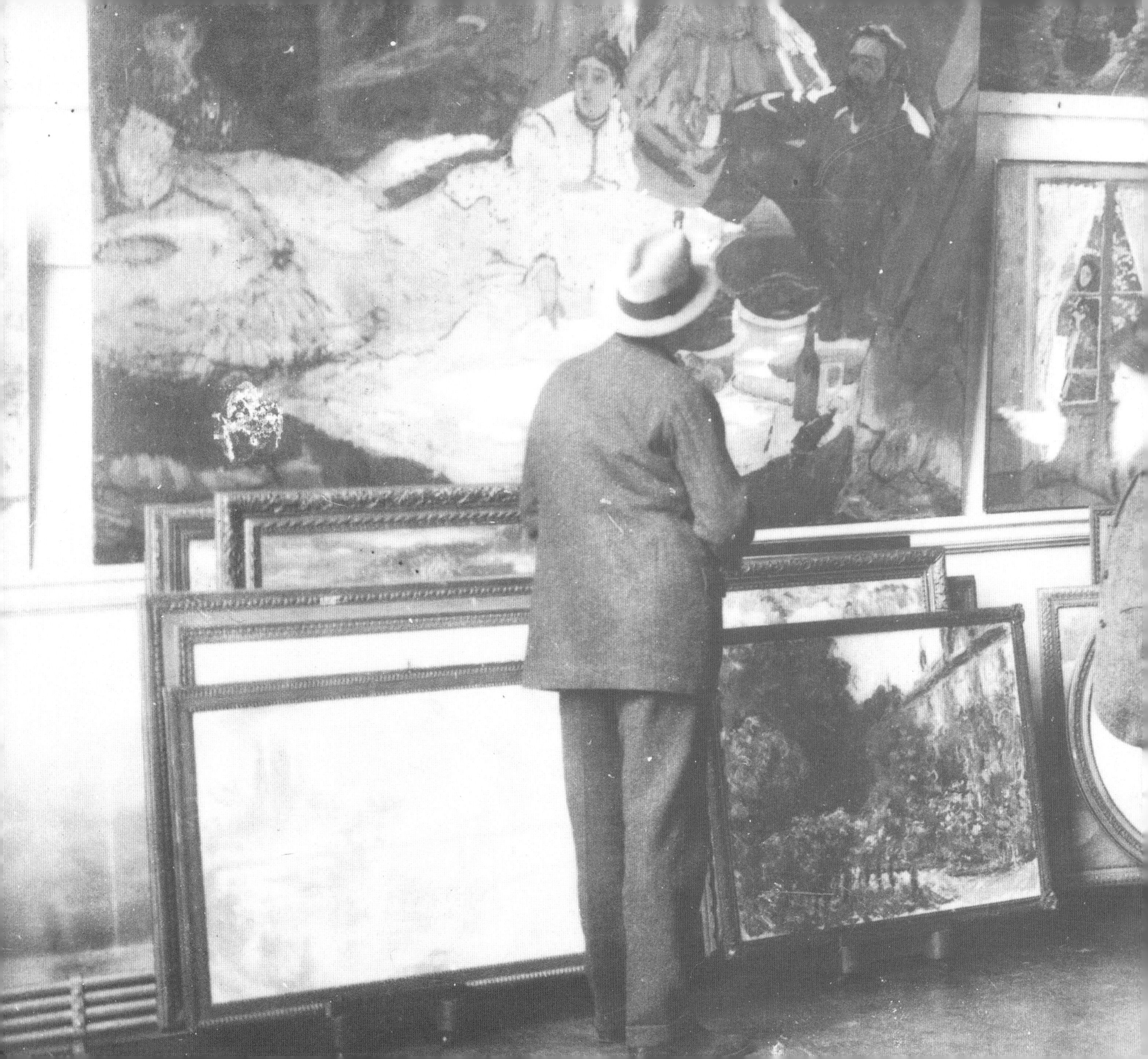